GRACE
And
GRATITUDE

GRACE
And
GRATITUDE

Developing Personal Prayer

Magdalena Edmonson

XULON PRESS

Xulon Press
2301 Lucien Way #415
Maitland, FL 32751
407.339.4217
www.xulonpress.com

© 2022 by Magdalena Edmonson

All rights reserved solely by the author. The author guarantees all contents are original and do not infringe upon the legal rights of any other person or work. No part of this book may be reproduced in any form without the permission of the author.

Due to the changing nature of the Internet, if there are any web addresses, links, or URLs included in this manuscript, these may have been altered and may no longer be accessible. The views and opinions shared in this book belong solely to the author and do not necessarily reflect those of the publisher. The publisher therefore disclaims responsibility for the views or opinions expressed within the work.

Unless otherwise indicated, Scripture quotations taken from the Revised Standard Version (RSV). Copyright © 1946, 1952, and 1971 the Division of Christian Education of the National Council of the Churches of Christ in the United States of America. Used by permission. All rights reserved.

Paperback ISBN-13: 978-1-66286-534-3
Ebook ISBN-13: 978-1-66286-535-0

TABLE OF CONTENTS

Introduction vii
Chapter 1 – Choose to Believe 1
Chapter 2 – Hearing God 9
Chapter 3 – Trusting God 23
Chapter 4 – Obeying God 43
Chapter 5 – Gaining Wisdom 57
Chapter 6 – Pleasing God 81
Chapter 7 – Credit to God's Name 104
Chapter 8 – Walk, Talk and Abide 117
Chapter 9 – Continually Filled 190
Chapter 10 – Do the Things 203
Chapter 11 – Know, Love, and Serve 226
Chapter 12 – Live 284

INTRODUCTION

*I*t is with great gratitude that I present this book. It has taken over 33 years for it to emerge. It had many transformations, and hopefully it will be helpful to many readers. Though it is primarily about my experiences and prayers and conversations with God, it can be adapted to almost anyone. Just replace my name with yours as necessary. A note about my name: It is Magdalena, but most people know me as Maggie, and in my conversations with the Lord, that is the mane mostly used.

I am also grateful for the people who have struggled through the editing process with me. Mrs. Patricia Keimig worked countless hours for well over a year, maybe even two years, to perfect my 1,502 pages of my writings on the first edit. But then I realized that it was not wise to try to publish so much, and it took a couple of years more before I was inspired to bring it to this form. It is a conglomeration of excerpts from my prayer journals. I also thank Mrs. Marion Rathbun who kindly accepted my request to proofread my final attempt.

I have had quite a life and hopefully am not yet at its end. Perhaps it might be helpful to know some of the timeline, as sometimes the excerpts jump around in the different phases of my life. My first nine years were in Communist Hungary, and then we escaped and were welcomed into the United States. At age 11, I realized that God went through a lot of trouble to get us here, and I felt I owed Him for His kindness. It was then that I decided to give my life to Him as a nun at age 19. Still planning to become a nun, I unexpectedly fell in love with Rae Edmonson, Jr. and we were married after I spent a year in college at Virginia Tech. I returned to college and became a math teacher because I did not like to read or write too much.

I left my faith within a year of marriage, and did not come back until after out first son Rae III was born. I taught math off and on but really devoted myself to family life and had two more sons, Karl and Steven. My first formal retreat at Loyola Retreat House was in 1988, and I have been under spiritual direction off and on ever since.

In 1995 I started teaching at Bishop Ireton High School in Alexandria VA. That same year, in November, my husband died of a heart attack. In 1997 I visited Hungary for the first time since my early childhood, with my mother-in-law, my nephew, and the two younger sons. The following year, I "kidnapped" my mother-in-law as she could no longer live alone due to Alzheimer's. I took care of her for the next 5½ years until she died in 2004. During that time, in 2001, I developed what we believe was rheumatic fever, and I needed to give up teaching in order to recover. This was a long and difficult illness. All my sons left, Steven starting college in 1999; in 2000 Karl married Megyn; and Rae III moved out in 2002. My father died in 2003, my mother-in-law in the beginning of 2004, Rae III, married in June of the same year, and at the end of that same month, I entered the convent of the Little Sisters of Jesus and Mary.

I loved being a nun, but after two years, the order felt I should go home and be a grandmother, as Rae and his wife, Michelle, had already had Makenzi, their first daughter, and were expecting their second child. The Sisters also thought that since my health was deteriorating, they might not be able to care for me as my eyesight diminished and my arthritis was causing many problems. Eventually, Rae, to whom I often refer as Raeme, and Michelle, had a son, Rae Adam IV, whom we call Adam, and another daughter, Addi.

It seems that though it was difficult to be sent home, I was needed there. My own mother developed diabetes, and I started by having dinner with her each night and giving her the insulin shot she did not want to give to herself. When her kidneys failed a year and a half later, she came to live with me and I cared for her until she died in 2011, two weeks before Steven's wedding to Devon.

Through all these years, I sometimes taught school, and continually tutored math. Even now, though I am now legally blind, I continue to tutor, and am delighted to do so. The Lord often gives me mathematical inspirations and I hope others will also understand these.

Introduction

As I explain in Chapter 2, I developed a conversational prayer life with God through writing. It started rather simply, but soon I found that I could ask Him questions and would get an answer in my thoughts as I wrote. So I started writing in the conversational style with my own words in regular print, and what I believed were His words in **bold** print. So the first two chapters are simply foundational as to how I arrived at this method, and the rest of the book is some of the conversations I had with the Lord.

My great hope is that this book will be helpful to those who read it, and God will be glorified through all the kindnesses He has shown me.

Chapter 1

CHOOSE TO BELIEVE

We are told that Faith is a gift. This is true. I was given this gift early in life. I was born to Roman Catholic parents, and baptized twelve days later. My father taught me the basic prayers early in my childhood, and we went to Mass regularly on Sundays. Actually, as a small child, I was only allowed to go to church if I had behaved well the previous Sunday. Thus, going to church became a privilege for me. *So, I was given the gift of faith in the form of a seed.*

Since we lived in a Communist country at the time, my parents had to sneak in a priest wearing street clothes to prepare me for First Communion and my sister for Confirmation. I learned readily, and even asked my mother if there was such a thing as people who taught others in far off lands about Jesus. I did not know a word for missionaries. *Thus, the seed was planted and nurtured.*

When we escaped from Communist Hungary in 1956, we ended up in Washington D.C. and Catholic Charities helped us in many ways. My sister and I were enrolled in Assumption School, run by Holy Cross Sisters. That was the first time I had ever seen a nun wearing the religious habit. We actually knew a former nun in Hungary who home taught my sister, but I did not know she had been a nun. When the Communists took over the country, all convents were closed and the nuns could not wear their religious garb any more. As we struggled to learn English and the Sisters cared for our education, I fell in love with the whole idea of religious life. I was a good student, and I excelled in learning all about my Catholic faith. I even won an award for knowing the Catechism. *The little seedling grew by leaps and bounds and became somewhat of a bush.*

In fifth grade, I was assigned to write a book report, and I chose to read the account of my family's escape from Hungary. John Hersey, a relatively famous author had interviewed my father in the refugee camp where we had been placed in Austria. He happened to be there with a film crew from the United Nations doing a documentary about the Hungarian refugees. Originally the article was printed in the New Yorker magazine, but compiled with other articles of Mr. Hersey's in a book called *Here to Stay.*

When I read his account, and also knew the marvelous things that happened subsequent to his account, I was amazed. It was as if God put everything in place to pave our way to come to the United States. Step by step, almost miraculously, we were brought to the very place He wanted us. Tremendous gratefulness filled my eleven-year-old heart. I felt God had a special purpose for my life, and out of gratitude, I thought I needed to repay Him by giving my life to Him. The best way I could think of doing so was to become a nun. I wanted to be a missionary perhaps to Africa. So, for the next eight years, I studied and watched and read books about nuns and saints and tried the best I knew to become good and holy. I started going to daily Mass, did good deeds in secret whenever I could, made sacrifices, and became as helpful as I could to all the Holy Cross Sisters. I knew all the rules, tried my best to keep them, though obeying my parents was not my greatest strength. My parents did not want me to be a nun, but finally my father promised me that if I still wanted to do so when I was two years past high school, then he would not object. I took him at his word, and prepared for religious life. *The bush of faith grew stronger.*

Since I was not planning to go to college, I took a Civil Service test for the government and secured a job after graduation as a physical science aide in a chemical laboratory. When I started working there, I discovered a whole new world I had not been aware of in my restricted focus of preparing for religious life. In the age of mini-skirts, my hemline was still halfway between my knees and ankles. I worked with several young men, and often they were telling off-color jokes, and I would blush and leave the room. But before a year was over, I went through a transformation, fell in love with one of the chemists in the lab, and my life turned completely around. I found I needed college, as the job bored me after I learned everything I needed. I was accepted to Virginia Tech from where my new boyfriend, Rae, had graduated. I needed a college with a good math program, as I wanted to major in Mathematics. *The storms were brewing to test the faith.*

While at college, Rae and I wrote letters to each other, and he visited me for Homecoming. We started looking at engagement rings on that trip, and during Christmas break, he presented me with a diamond. Thus, we were engaged and planned to marry in June. The following September was when I would have been able to enter the convent. But I took the detour, and we were married on June 29th.

Rae was raised Methodist, went to a Lutheran grade school, but was not a churchgoer. I kept going to Mass for a while, but one Sunday I did not like the sermon and walked out of church and did not return for several years. In my quest for unity in our marriage, I threw away my faith for his lack thereof.

I got another government job, but this one only took me two weeks before it became boring. I needed to finish college, and convinced my husband that he could afford to send me to the University of Maryland as a commuting student and three years later I graduated with a degree in Mathematics Education. By this time my faith was practically gone. *It seemed the storm became a hurricane and leveled the bush of my faith*

I taught for about a year and a half, and then became pregnant with our first son. When he was born, I dutifully had him baptized, as my family was expecting that I should. Soon I started thinking that this child needed to be taught some morals, and the only place I knew that was done was in church. Since I could not expect the baby to go there by himself, I started returning to Sunday Mass at the nearest Catholic church. I was surprised that I could not honestly say the creed, as I no longer believed what it claimed. But I listened, and watched the little kids playing in the pews. One Sunday I heard a sermon that caught my attention. It was about a couple who had lost their faith. I identified with that concept. I wondered whether there was a group where such people could discuss faith matters. I belonged to a parent-discussion-group for new parents, and I thought a faith discussion group would be a good idea. I asked the Deacon who had given that sermon if there was such a thing, and he did not seem to understand me. He referred me to the Pastor. Fr. Lawrence Wempe was an elderly priest who was willing to talk to me. I asked him the same question, and he also did not understand. But as I explained that the idea of a faith discussion group came from hearing about people who had lost their faith, he asked, "Have you lost your faith?" I responded as if I was proud of myself, "I certainly have!" We continued the conversation as he asked me what I believed. I said that I only believed that there had to be something or someone that is eternal, but whether it was a god or an atom, I did not know. He then said, "Well, it is not completely gone, but it is a dim flicker of a flame. But keep on coming and let's see what happens." I did. *The soil around what used to be my faith was beginning to be softened.*

Every week thereafter, Fr. Wempe made sure to notice me when I went to Mass. We did not speak much except for a brief greeting, but he encouraged me. I still could not say the Creed, but I kept listening. One day during the week, I was taking my son for a stroller excursion, and remember thinking "I'm not getting much out of this church business." And immediately a voice from the past came to me. It was of a mother who helped on the playground in grade-school, "If you are not getting much out of something, maybe you are not putting enough into it." My response within my thoughts was, "OK, I'll read a book."

The very next Sunday, I noticed that someone had just installed a book rack in the back of the church. People had brought in religious books from home, and anyone who wished, could take them home and bring them back when they were finished. Not quite a library, but it was similar. I looked at all the titles, and brought home one slightly bigger than a pamphlet, *The Power in Penance* by Fr. Michael Scanlan.

There were two things that brought my attention to this book. One was that my husband could not accept the Catholic teaching on Confession, and I could never explain it to him. The other was that right on the front it said, "A Charismatic Renewal Book." One of our neighbors, also a new mother, had recently asked me if I knew anything about the Charismatic Renewal. I knew nothing about it, but this was a way to find out.

As I read the book, it seemed to say that things I was experiencing – anxiety, fear, insecurity, doubt – were sins that could be confessed and gotten rid of. Well, in all my earlier experiences of Confession, I never expected to be rid of my sins, only forgiven until the next time I fell into them. But this book seemed to say that I did not need to live with these things, but that I could be healed of them completely. I exclaimed, "If I ever find such a place where this could happen, I will certainly go." *The softer soil was ready to take some nutrients to grow the faith once again.*

Many years later I bought the book, re-read it, and did not find any part of the book that said this. I later learned that the Holy Spirit can illuminate things and give us understanding we would not have otherwise. But the whole book rack thing was another case of God paving a way for me. The next week I picked up several more books, some explaining what the Charismatic Renewal was all about.

After reading more, I started asking questions at church. I got quite a run-around, but eventually was given the Deacon's phone number. This was the same Deacon who gave the sermon about the people who had lost their faith. After many tries, I finally reached him. It turned out he was the main leader in a Charismatic prayer group that met at Georgetown University on Friday nights. He talked to me for over an hour all about Jesus Christ. It was a bit uncomfortable, as I had not pronounced that name since many years ago after I stopped going to church. I still had the commandment within me not to use His name in vain, but I simply stopped using His name at all. But I was polite and listened. We agreed that in two weeks, I would go to this prayer meeting with him and his wife.

By this time, I had read a bit more about the Charismatic Renewal, and though I was not sure what some things like "praying in tongues" was about, I did know that I was about to experience something entirely new to me.

It was indeed very new. I had never seen over 500 people praying with their hands raised upward, I was not used to so much singing, and when they sang "in tongues," I found it very beautiful. I was also amazed at how they all seemed to stop all at once without anyone directing the singing. The whole prayer meeting lasted about two and a half hours, and there was a teaching given by a Protestant minister.

At the end of the meeting, people were encouraged to go to one or more other rooms. One was for people who had come for the first time, like me. There, I learned about the Charismatic Renewal, and that it was approved by the Church and it was even endorsed by a Cardinal.

I learned more about the Holy Spirit than I had ever heard and was excited to learn that miracles were still happening in this modern era. *New shoots of faith were beginning to spring up.*

When the meeting ended, several people remained there, talking. Many introduced themselves to me, and it seemed like they were each sent specifically to help me with my internal struggles. Several were around my own age and had small children and seemed to identify with anything I said about my own life.

Since my Deacon had the keys to lock up after everything was finished, we did not leave until close to midnight. A priest named Fr. John Lubey rode home with us, he and I in the back seat talking all the way home. I told him of my insecurity, fear, worry, and frustrations with family life, and to each problem he replied, "You can be healed of that." My thoughts ran back to what I had read in *The Power in Penance*, and I said, "I sure hope so." It turned out that Fr. Lubey had a tremendous healing ministry and held healing services all over the area.

It was the beginning of my conversion and many marvelous friendships. Every week I learned new and wonderful truths. The teachings we received were uplifting and useful. It usually took me a whole week to digest them. I often felt like a little dog with its head cocked, trying to understand. *The new shoots of faith grew from being watered and fed.*

The second week I went to the prayer room and asked for prayer about my relationship with my parents. By this time, I could not be in the same room with my parents for two minutes without an argument. I was told that God did not make a mistake in who He gave me for parents. My immediate thought, though I did not voice it, was, "Do you mean He did this to me on purpose?" Then I was told that I needed to go home and thank God for my parents. Well, I wasn't even sure I believed in God any more, and I was supposed to thank Him for the disastrous situation with my parents? But eventually I did exactly that. With the most negative feelings and in a cynical voice late at night, I very quietly said, "Thank You, God, for my parents."

A wondrous miracle happened. I no longer felt the need to express my opinions when I disagreed with Mom or Dad. I could let them have their own opinions and keep mine to myself. Over the following year, my relationship with my parents completely reversed. And they never changed a bit. Soon it was a delight to be with them, and all arguments ceased. They even began to respect me and were no longer so critical. But with my sister, they were just as difficult as they had been with me. It seemed that God accepted my little half-hearted prayer and totally transformed this relationship. *The roots of my faith were strengthened.*

A few weeks into my attendance at these prayer meetings, I was given a pamphlet which stated that nothing negative should come out of our mouths. I thought, "OH NO! If I accept this teaching, I may never speak again at all!" But soon I started trying to speak more positively. I had hated all the criticism I received growing up, but I had become just as critical as my parents had been. I started trying to change. I was also told that it was not always necessary to voice my opinions. This was totally new to me. I thought it was my civic duty to tell people that they were wrong if I disagreed with them. As I stopped arguing, the arguments also stopped. Wonder of wonders, most of my relationships improved. *Growth and strengthening of what was beginning to be a tree.*

I did not know how it happened, but within a few weeks all the faith I had lost returned, this time with depth. All the time I had wanted to become a nun, my faith had been only on the surface. I knew all the external aspects about church – the meaning of all the colors of vestments at Mass, memorized prayers, good deeds, and such things, but I did not have a real personal relationship with God. The Charismatic Renewal centered around a personal relationship with Jesus. It was He who sent the Holy Spirit to help us live the Christian life and would also take us to our Heavenly Father and show us His great love for us. That a personal relationship with God was even possible was totally new to me. I knew all the rules but could not imagine a relationship with Him. I still did not know how to love Him, but somehow, I once again believed in Him.

In the years that followed, I continued to go to Friday night prayer meetings, developed wonderful counselors who helped me with all the new things I learned about the Christian life, went to seminars to learn more about the Bible, and grew in my faith.

One of the most important lessons I learned is that one can **choose** to believe. At first I was still very full of doubt. But I was taught that God responds to our choice to believe what He tells us and only afterwards will he demonstrate the particular truth He wants to show us. Often in Scripture He says, "Your faith has saved you." And then, the person he was speaking to receives a healing.

I found that when doubts came into my mind I could, with an act of my will, choose to believe that God is faithful to His word, and is exactly who He says He is, and then the doubts cease and He shows me that what I chose to believe is indeed true. Apparently, this is what happened when I said my half-hearted prayer thanking Him for my parents. I had made a choice to do what I had been told to do. St. Peter also found this out when he was told to cast his net on the other side of the boat. He did not believe, but chose to do as if he did. And he caught a lot of fish.

Now, after many, many years, the doubts do not even come. I fully accept and try to live my Christian faith. I believe that God is love, that he loves even me, and cares about everything that happens to me. I believe He sent Jesus to redeem me through His life, death, and resurrection, and that I can live with Him eternally. I believe He sent His Holy Spirit to help me along the way, and He continues to prepare the way He wants me to go, just as He brought me to this marvelous country, and brought me back to my faith. *The tree has matured and is strong and tall.*

This reminds me of another wonderful thought that I believe the Holy Spirit gave me. In John's Gospel, Jesus says He is going to prepare a place for us. We usually think He means in heaven for after we die. But through my experience, He continually prepares places for us right here on earth. He did this to my family when we came to America. He did this by getting a book rack in the back of the church when I was ready to read a book. He prepared places for me to teach throughout my career. He even prepares places in line at a grocery store when He wants us to encourage someone. I am often in awe of how many places He has already prepared for me. When I wonder if that is the case, I choose to believe He has a purpose for the circumstance I find myself in, and also choose to believe that He will bring something good out of it. He has never failed me.

*****

Chapter 2

HEARING GOD

When I was in elementary school, one of my teachers kept telling us that we needed to listen to God. Well, I tried. And I tried. And I kept trying without any success. I talked to Him. I prayed formal prayers, I even snuck into the church when I was troubled and poured my heart out to Him and somehow felt better, but I could never "hear" Him. No booming voice from heaven, not even a still small voice. Eventually I gave up and figured I simply was not holy enough or there was something terribly wrong with me, but it just was not happening. I felt really bad when I heard "My sheep hear My voice and follow Me." I longed to follow Him but could not hear His voice. I even wanted to give my whole life to Him as a nun. I felt I owed Him for bringing me so magnificently into this country. But no matter how much I wanted or tried to hear Him, I could not.

It was not until I had almost totally lost my faith and returned to it through the Charismatic renewal, that I discovered that it was not impossible for even plain, unholy, and insignificant people to hear God. It simply was not through the **ears** that we hear God, at least most of the time. We can hear Him through what we read, what we hear others tell us, even a good program we watch. In fact, I am still learning that He can speak to me in any way He chooses.

But the greatest discovery I found was that God can, and often does, speak to me through my thoughts. This was quite a revelation, but it had to be taught to me. I learned that if a thought comes into my mind that seems both good and unusual, it may well be God speaking to me.

Thoughts such as, "Maggie, I love you." I do not usually tell myself that. So I started experimenting. In my thoughts I started asking God some simple questions, praying silently. To my surprise, I had the answers in my own thoughts, but they were not the way I usually thought. They were always positive, encouraging, and loving. I was not.

In this way, I received many wonderful revelations, which I call parables. The Lord often answered my questions with a simple analogy or situation I was familiar with. Some of them I wrote down and have used in my interaction with others. Eventually, I started writing down what I wanted to say to God (my personal prayers) and then also wrote down what I thought He might be saying back to me. What He said to me usually did not sound like me at all and was often surprising. I discovered a two-way communication with God.

I found that it was easier for me to concentrate while I was writing. It slowed my mind down enough and focused my thoughts so the usual distractions of life did not bother me as much. At first, I usually prayed like this in the middle of the night, as that was the only time in my busy life as wife, mother, and teacher I could find quiet enough. But eventually, I kept my notebook handy whenever I needed to converse with God. I wish I could say that I did it faithfully every day, but there were times that I did not write anything for weeks or months. Other times I was writing pretty regularly.

I thought some of the inspirations or conversations, and especially my personal parables should be shared with others. That is how this book originally began. I hope it helps others to also develop their own conversations with God, perhaps not in the same way I did, but in their own way. I was taught early in my spiritual awakening that anything we think we are hearing from God needs to be tested. It must not contradict Scripture, it needs to be uplifting, and it is good to have wise counselors who can advise us on whether it is really God who is speaking to us. I was blessed to have such people in my life. I can get too big a head thinking that God Almighty is actually speaking to me. But having to check with others as to the authenticity of any revelation can be humbling as well as encouraging.

By now, I have filled many spiral notebooks with my prayers and conversations, sometimes soliloquies. I transferred them to the computer when my eyesight was beginning to fail, and even began to type faster than I ever could in my high school typing classes. But I digress. In these typed notes, I write my own words, questions, musings, complaints, and often thanksgivings in regular print, and what I thought God spoke to me in **bold** print. In later chapters, I also *italicize* comments that were not part of the prayer.

I have had a grace-filled life. I have experienced many great, wonderful, and some tragic situations. But through good teaching, I have learned to see the graces God has given me and be thoroughly grateful for them. That is why I name this book Grace and Gratitude.

Here are some of the parables I have received:

General Parables and Lessons Learned

The Automatic Transmission – or How Come I Can Sometimes Hear God

One day, while driving, I started praying:

Lord, how come there are times I can clearly know that You are talking to me, but at other times I am not at all aware of You?

What kind of transmission does your car have?

Automatic.

With an automatic transmission, how does the car switch gears? Can you hear it when it does?

If I am listening for it, I can hear it happen. But usually I am not aware of it.

But it works whether you are listening or not, and if you listen, you can hear.

I see. You speak to me, but I have to be listening to be able to hear You.

*****

Virtues and Long Division

When we see the need to build a virtue into our lives, like patience, first we ask the Lord to give it to us. Like a good teacher, He teaches us all about patience. He shows us examples in His own life, He shows us examples in the lives of Scriptural characters, and He even shows us examples in the lives of other people around us. He might even point out the mistakes we or others have made and how to keep from making those mistakes. But then He gives us "practice problems." We find all sorts of situations in which we have the opportunity to practice patience. It is very much like long division. We don't like doing the homework, but unless we get the practice, we won't ever get good at it.

*****

The Parable of the Kiss

It is so much easier for me to call You "Lord" than "Father." I guess "Lord" covers all three Persons while "Father" seems to speak only to one. Then I feel like I should also give equal time to Jesus and Holy Spirit.

You do not understand unconditional love. There is no competition within God for your affection. You do not offend one Person of the Trinity when you speak exclusively to another. Father, Son, and Spirit together rejoice at your prayer. There are times when you feel your Father's love, care, and action. There are other times when it is your Lord, Redeemer, Savior, Brother that is working in your life. Still other times it is Teacher, Counselor, Comforter, or Friend that you need. I Am Who Am. All your needs and prayers are responded to without problem. If you do something for your husband with your hands and he thanks you by kissing you on the lips, do your hands get offended? Of course not. They are as completely joined to your body as your lips. All are pleased. So it is with your God. Be at peace.

*****

Sometimes we lose awareness of God: and think we have lost intimacy with Him:

Lord, would You come and speak to me?

Of course I would. I want the intimacy more than you do. You think it is so hard yet it is so simple. I do not stop loving you just because you lose your awareness of My love. You have not lost your relationship with Me because you have stopped doing some things you consider important. You have not spoken to some of your friends much lately. Do you love them less? When you have a chance to speak will you have to start your friendship over from the beginning? Of course not. You pick up where you left off and grow closer still. So it is with Me. Though these times when you give Me your undivided attention are precious, that is not the only way for our relationship to grow. Take the stiffness and formality out of it and relax. There are times for formality, but they are rare. Start living with the King – instead of seeking an audience with Him. When you stop writing or praying, I do not vanish and reappear only the next time you call on Me. I stick around. You can't get rid of Me. I don't get in your way, I don't bother you, but I stay, and I keep loving you and helping you and the relationship grows. Your activities need not compete with your prayer life; they are a part of it. Do your work, your play, your rest and everything while you are in My presence. Your lack of awareness of Me does not make Me go away. If you lose the awareness, I will gently remind you occasionally. But I do not remind you in order to embarrass or condemn you. I touch you only out of love. I am not hurt by your concentrating on other things. My touch is never a rebuke; it's more of a hug. So when you suddenly become aware that I'm with you, that's a sign that I want a hug.

*****

The parable of the milk pitcher:

Lord, I get excited and pleased when You use me to help other people's lives, but then I find myself in sin and wonder if I have rendered myself unfit and untrustworthy for Your service.

Maggie, I will call you my little pitcher. I have used you to pour milk this week. You have nourished, refreshed, and soothed your family with the milk I have poured into you. They needed it, and you were able to supply it. But when it was finished, you didn't return to Me afterwards to be washed out. The leftovers soured in you. And now, you are upset that you are dirty and smelly. A useful pitcher must be washed after every use and sometimes before use. You are like fine silver in My hand. I have to polish you before I can display or use you. And when I do use you, I have to wash you quickly and well. So now, it is time for washing. A pot does not wash itself. It cannot make itself clean. See, I make all things new. Though your sins be as scarlet, I shall make you white as snow. I do the work. You receive the benefits of it. It is good and right. I have ordained it so. So, my little pitcher, relax and enjoy your Master's care as He washes and polishes you and makes you ready for His use again. I don't love you less because you got dirty. I shall take more care to cleanse you. Be patient. Come for washing often. Part of your cleansing is forgiveness. Not just the forgiveness I offer you but also the forgiveness you must extend to those you see in need of it. It is easier for you to forgive some than others. But you must show no partiality. I forgive long before I am asked. So must you. Especially in cases where you are not the victim, you must forgive quickly. When others come to you for help, use the wisdom I give you, and then return to Me immediately so you are either refilled or emptied and washed. Otherwise, the leftovers will sour. Child, I do love you. I am delighted in your readiness and willingness for service. I am also delighted to cleanse you after use. I will use you again and again. You have learned an important lesson. Don't be discouraged if it happens again. In time, you will find yourself coming for washing very quickly. Enjoy My pleasure in you. I approve of you.

Once I found myself wonderfully used by God in some people's lives, but then I lost my peace and joy when some harsh words came out of my mouth. The Lord reminded me of the parable of the milk pitcher and inspired me to write a prayer for whenever I found myself needing His care. I've entitled my prayer "Prayer to regain peace and joy after service." ((Perhaps a better title would be "A servant's prayer."))

Dear Lord, You know that I delight in serving You and being used by You in the lives of others. You have also shown me that when You use me in such a way, I am like a milk pitcher that You have filled me with exactly what is needed by those I serve. But when I have been emptied, I must return to You for cleansing and washing lest I remain a dirty vessel and fall into sin and be unfit for further use.

So, Lord, I now present myself to You. I thank You for the joy of having been useful to You. I ask You to cleanse me, wash me, and even scrub me if necessary. I seek to be fit for Your use again and again. I place myself in Your loving hands and trust You to do to and for me whatever You see fit. You, Lord, know all things and do whatever is best for me. Whether I feel anything or not, I believe You have heard and answered me. Thank You, Lord Jesus. Amen.

*****

BUCKETS, KETTLES AND TEACUPS

As I was growing up, I often held in my negative emotions and then burst into tears at the slightest provocation. I felt like I had a bucket of tears inside of me, and when it was full, the next difficulty would knock it over and all would spill out. After my husband's death, I was again feeling this way, but I thought the bucket was full of evil within me.

One morning I had an incredible time of peace and joy and love and the lifting of the burdens of duty and sorrow. But by midafternoon I was in tears and ready to verbally attack a fellow teacher. How fragile is that container within us that holds peace and joy and love – yet how strong the one that keeps hate and revenge and strife.

Maggie, you are getting the point. This is another parable. Remember the bucket of tears? There is room within you for more than one bucket. The bucket that holds the evil is like a cast-iron kettle – heavy, indestructible, sturdy, not easily tipped over. The one that holds the good is like a delicate teacup – breakable, easily tipped over, can't hold too much at a time, needs to be filled often. The kettle can hold much more – it won't spill easily – but it can boil over if heated. Both can be emptied and washed and cleaned – both can hold good things – a soup in the kettle tastes good and is good

if the right amounts of ingredients are put in. It does not have to contain evil. Just because it is a pot, it cannot be judged by how it looks on the outside. The same is true of the teacup – what fills it is more important.

*****

The ring of Keys

When I was a full-time teacher and also working on my Master's Degree, I had this conversation:

Dear Jesus, it's been a long and hard week. I've talked to many parents, tutored lots of kids, and the last couple of days I have really been running on "empty."

Maggie, I have been with you through it all and I know your fears. You see the next couple of weeks as a list of "have to do" things. And you are tired of being tired and you see no relief in sight. Your nerves are frayed, you are trying not to fail, and you have pressures and deadlines and demands on you at every turn.

I've forgotten love again, haven't I?

That's the key. Now you need to unlock something with it.

I'm afraid – I don't know what will be on the other side. I don't know if I am about to open a closet into which all sorts of things have been stuffed – and if the door is opened, all sorts of things will tumble out and then I have a mess to deal with.

You, alone?

That too is a key, isn't it?

You have a whole ring of keys. Do you use them all at the same time?

No, only one at a time. But some doors have more than one lock.

Exactly. So your fear needs the key of My love and the key of My Presence and even the key of My power. Some things require the key of diligence or perseverance. Some keys operate things, not just

open things. Some keys open big things, some very small things. You just bought a key that will turn on lights. You have so many keys. And you know what every one of them can do. You do know what is behind every door – or at least you have a pretty good idea of it.

*****

The Sower and the Seed (or the Soil)

Lord Jesus, You and I are having breakfast together.

I don't get invited to breakfast often. Thank you.

You are more than welcome. In fact, I invite You to my whole day. But You will have to nudge me occasionally if I forget You are there. That invisibility aspect of Your nature makes it difficult.

I know, but for now it is necessary. You need the blessing that comes with believing though not seeing. It strengthens you. As you practice My Presence, your faith will become stronger. Why is the faith the size of a mustard seed so great? Not its size, but its potential. It has strength within to become great. If it stays a seed, it will never move mountains – but if it is allowed to grow, then the mountains must move. You have seen grass grow through concrete. Roots break through pavement and pipes. There is great strength in slow, imperceptible growth. My way may not seem to be powerful or dynamic, but it works. You have noticed before that destruction is sudden and quick. But healing, building, and growing take time and often go unnoticed. When I died, there was much noise. But when I rose, it was almost unnoticed. Your holiness must grow slowly, imperceptibly. Otherwise pride takes root and destroys it. My Father is a good gardener. He will not allow the weeds to choke out the good seed. He knows the difference. He knows what He planted in you.

Remember the parable of the sower and the seed? The sower is My Father. The seed is Me – the living Word. The soil is you. My Father has dug up the path you once were, softened the ground, broken up the clumps – softened your heart. He has removed the rocks – stumbling blocks – sifted you. He continually removes the weeds – Confession – and plants Me in you – Communion. He waters

and warms – provision – gives you all you need; fertilizes – troubles, pains, disappointments; even prunes – bigger pains. But afterwards, does anyone see the soil in a field that has produced much fruit? Before the harvest, does anyone think of the soil? The soil then becomes invisible, just as the seed once was. This is My plan for you. As My word – My very self – is planted in you, I am invisible – just as the seed in the ground is invisible to anyone looking at the field. But as the seed germinates and begins to grow, it soon covers the entire ground with growth, and deep underneath there is also growth in the roots. In a field of corn, all you see is the plants and the corn. No longer is the ground visible. It is still there – without it there would be no growth – but it has been transformed into a cornfield. Now aren't you glad you invited Me to breakfast?

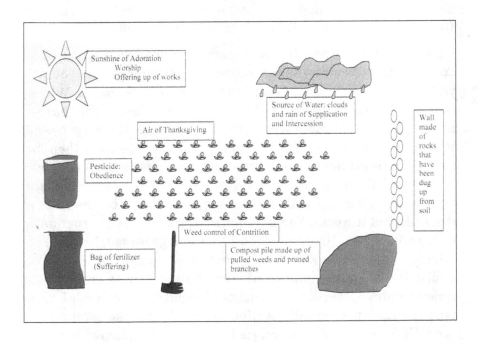

*****

DANCING AND FLOWERS

In prayer one day, somehow, I imagined myself dancing with You – a regal, graceful waltz – and I realized how I would love to be held and guided gracefully and beautifully by You. Somehow the grace and beauty of ballroom dancing and the thought of You holding and leading me that way became more real – almost like a dim image in the distance becoming clearer and what was more of a mist taking form and color with music. Gentleness, goodness, grace, and beauty all materializing from a thought, an imagination. Perhaps this is Your Transfiguration personalized just for me? Somehow loving You became a possibility – it too was taking form and shape and color and music. Lord, in Heaven would You take me dancing? I know that here and now I'm as graceful and lovely as a grizzly bear, but in Heaven I can be like Cinderella at the ball.

And then as I read a meditation about love not being selfish, I was surprised that I did not feel my inadequacies or lament how far from the ideal I really am. I was simply struck by how I have tried to do all the right things most of my life without the benefit of the motivating force that makes all those things possible. I have loved and served and cared for people (and animals and things) all my life. I have often done it quite unselfishly. I have cared for the unlovely and the strays and the rejects. But I did not do it out of love for You – I did it for a variety of other reasons. I did not know how to love You, but I thought I did know how to love them. I was attentive to their needs and filled those needs the best I could, and I found I could fill the needs of others pretty well. It became a pleasure in itself to serve others. But loving You still seemed so difficult – so unreal, so invisible, so unattainable – a lofty ideal. But all my good works seemed hollow – as dirty rags – because they were missing the core; the motivating force was all wrong. It was the difference of individual flowers – they are pretty in themselves, but when combined by a skillful florist into an arrangement, they become glorious. They are set in the foundation of the container and the grounding – be it clay or Styrofoam or moss or even mud – but held together, and full of grace and beauty. A flower by itself cannot stand. It has to be supported by the bush or plant or vase or pot or dish. So also our good works must be supported by the core of love for You. But love for You without good works is like an empty vase or pot – the good works are the flowers.

*****

Shoelaces

I often found myself slipping from the good things I had tried to commit myself to such as prayer, a diet, exercise, and housework. The Lord showed me that when my shoelaces came loose, I needed to tighten or re-tie them. In other words, come back to Him, rely on His strength, and renew my commitment.

*****

The Squirrel and the Bear

I have often noticed how some people can pray so much easier than I can. They seem to reach the heights of intimacy with the Lord, while I struggle at times to even spend five minutes with Him.

Lord, You are so good to me! This morning You drew me to prayer and settled the matter that disturbed me yesterday. You showed me the grace and agility and beauty of a squirrel running with joy through the tops of trees. It does not have to work at climbing a tree, for that comes naturally to it. Then there is a lumbering bear that can also climb the tree, but there is much effort and much less grace and agility. There are differences between the two animals – one cannot be the other – yet You created and love both. And You provide for both and You have a plan for both – neither can be happy trying to be the other. Each can admire the qualities and strengths and abilities of the other without needing to become like the other. I am a bear while those whose prayer life seems so much better than mine are squirrels.

Lord, You created nothing hating it. You created me a bear, and You love my lumbering ways. I have to work hard to climb the heights, but You approve and appreciate my efforts. If You did not create me a squirrel, You do not expect me to run and leap through the tops of trees, though I might climb one occasionally and find the sweetness of honey inside. But You fulfill the bearlike desires of my heart and meet all my bearlike needs.

*****

God's Gloves

The Lord showed me that we can be like His gloves. He is on the inside, in full contact with us and we are blessed. But we are the gloves that touch others with His purpose and strength and often gentleness. Sometimes we are mittens, when someone needs to be warmed and encouraged and restored after a cold and difficult situation. Sometimes we are surgical gloves, required to heal or remove a difficulty. Sometimes we are work gloves, getting into dirt and ready to do heavy lifting. The people we minister to see and feel us, but it is God supplying all they need.

*****

The Garden Hose

Lord, this morning I think You gave me a parable again. Your love is like the water that comes through a garden hose. And we are the nozzles that intensify the stream or make it into a gentle mist. Thank You for allowing us to dispense Your marvelous love.

*****

trifocal Glasses

Maggie, I do love you. I love you through all those who love you. I am teaching you once again about love and joy and surrender. Look for My love and joy through these. It is like looking through your glasses. If you focus on the glasses or the lines or spots on them, you cannot see what you are supposed to see. But the glasses are meant to correct your vision so you can see things better and more clearly. That is what patience, obedience, and surrender do – they are your tri-focals that you look through to see the love, joy, beauty, and truth that I have right before you.

Lord, thank You for Your parable.

Maggie's Prayer

Lord, let me or make me and help me:
Trust You completely,
Be obedient to You in all things,
Be wise in Your ways,
Be a pleasure in Your sight,
Be a credit to Your name,
Walk with You, talk with You, and abide in Your love,
Be continually filled with Your Holy Spirit,
Do the things You do and want me to do,
Know You, love You, and serve You more each day,
Live with You eternally.
Amen

This prayer (or some form of it) is on the cover of my journal notebooks, my Bible, and I hope will be on the holy cards at my funeral.

It started as what I felt was my ultimate goal in life. I remember being on a retreat and finding myself shaking my fist at heaven saying to God: "I will not be satisfied until I have total union with You!" I did not usually talk to God that way, but I meant it.

This prayer seems to cover what I mean by "total union" with Him.

The remainder of this book will focus on each part of my prayer.

*****

Chapter 3

TRUSTING GOD

*I*t would seem that trusting God should be instinctive. After all, He is all-good, all-knowing, all-loving, and only wants the best for us. But I had to be taught to trust Him despite all the ways He had proven to me over the years that He is trustworthy. At times, He still encourages me to trust Him when I seem to falter.

Once I recommitted my life to God, I found I often needed to trust Him much more than I knew how to do. Even after He had proven His trustworthiness to me many times, I still lacked the trust I felt I should have had.

Lord, is my attitude wrong? It seems that I'm still trying to test You. That seems wrong.

Until you trust Me completely, every request will seem that you are testing Me. But the trust will grow, and the time will come that you will not hesitate to ask Me anything. Keep asking. The motives will be purified in time.

Lord, somehow, I have not kept up with my prayer life, yet I have come to You here and there and You have been faithful and loving and kind. I am in a difficult situation right now. Lord, forgive me for not coming to You more. Help me to be totally committed to hearing You and praying. How much I have missed! By not asking for Your guidance and directions I have wasted so much time and energy.

It's that fear of coming close.

That's it, Lord, I don't want to be far away, yet I am so reluctant to come close. I don't want to love You only from a distance; I want to love You intimately, to know Your presence and love so well that it would not occur to me to run away any more – but instead to run TO Your arms every chance I get.

Lord, I've waited all day– *and immediately the thought came to me,*

How many times have I waited all day, all week, or all month to hear from you, and didn't?

Catching myself, I said I choose to believe that You will give me what I need. I choose to believe that I am not deprived but exceptionally blessed. And Your presence came upon me and calmed me and I got through the rest of the day. So now, "Speak, Lord, Your servant is listening."

Maggie, you are having quite a lesson in trusting Me. Everything is in My hands. You are having to trust Me because you can't control situations.

But Lord, I still make feeble efforts to control even though I know I can't or shouldn't. I know Your ways are better than my ways, but I'm still fighting for my way.

Today you have had one victory. You chose to believe in My goodness and provision. I will guide you and help you along the way. I have longed for your company. I am not ready to share you with anyone else yet. Wait and be patient.

Some hours later I prayed: Lord, You are wonderfully incredible. I spent an hour walking and talking to You this evening and rejoicing in Your desire to keep me to Yourself. My will was as completely submitted to Yours as I can ever remember. I want only to please You.

Soon after that little prayer, I received the very answer I desired in the first place.

On another occasion:

I find that recently things don't bother me like they used to. I am not overly upset by family problems. The preparations for Christmas were not as much of a problem this year. I trusted that everything important would get done – and it did.

So now I need a cleansing and getting closer to You. I was expecting a time of repentance and perhaps some wonderful revelation, but You took me by surprise. I was encouraged to look for God's love – for it is His love that cleanses us. I was amazed at the constant gentleness and encouragement and love You have shown me ever since I've been journaling. I began to see some progress in my prayer life where I had thought there hadn't been any.

I came expecting the scolding of a servant girl and what I got was a proposal for marriage. Instead of being in trouble, I got an engagement ring. I expected to wait on tables at the Marriage Supper of the Lamb (and would have felt honored to do so) but instead I was asked to be the bride. I realized I had somehow mysteriously grown up. I felt like the ugly duckling suddenly realizing it was a beautiful swan.

The amazement brought me to weeping. Are You sure, Lord? How can this be? I didn't do anything right. I don't deserve this. I'm not worthy.

I know. It's not what you have or haven't done. It's what I am doing. This has always been My plan for you, but I didn't show it to you until you could trust Me to take you the rest of the way.

*****

You are preparing me to be a queen to the King of Kings. Psalm 45 applies to *me*. Where does this leave my earthly husband? Better off than ever. An earthly marriage is to have three persons – man, wife, and God. As I grow in Your love, I am better able to show love to my husband. *One of my questions was a personalization of Mary's question at the Annunciation. She asked, "How can this be since I know not man?" My question was, "How can this be since I do know a man?" But the answer is the same – the power from on High!*

The next day was taken up with a resounding YES! I accept! You lead, I'll follow. You have brought me this far, You are able to teach me whatever else I need to know. You don't make mistakes so if this is what You want, then it shall be. I don't have to try because You are doing it all. You got me this far without my even knowing where You were taking me. Now that You have shown me the destination, You can certainly finish the job. I don't know how long it will take. It really does not matter. You are in charge. You are with me. You are both the journey and the destination; either way I am with You. I am Yours, and You are mine. Everything else will work out. You showed me that You want me to love You with my whole heart, mind, soul, and strength. My love is like a drop of water – Yours is like the ocean. When mine falls in Yours, they are one – all Yours – the ocean.

So now do I feel cleansed? Yes! Do I feel closer to You? Definitely! What happens next? I don't know, but I don't have to know. You will lead me through it in Your own time and in Your own way. Will I ever sin again? I'm sure I will, but You are faithful and merciful and forgiving. Do I ever want to sin again? No! Your love is so wonderful, I want only to please You. Somehow, I trust You enough that I am at peace even about my shortcomings and sinfulness. You can handle it! You have handled it this far, haven't You? You know me. I do not have to hide anything, pretend anything, or put on any performance. You know me, love me, accept me, and even desire me. To You I am beautiful. You have created me. I do not need to conform to anyone else's norm or ideal, only to Yours, and You are the one conforming me. Does this mean I can't be corrected anymore? No. You can and do constantly correct me and You can and do use others to do that. I will not always be right, but I do not need to fear being wrong. Even Your rebuke is wonderful. There is nothing to fear.

*****

Near the end of the same year:

I read many books about prayer. They made me wonder where I really am in prayer. What the author said to beginners I have already done. I believe my goals in prayer are fine. My method may be undisciplined, but seems to be working for me. I find You speaking to me in many ways. Yet I don't understand the desert or the "dark night" experience very well. Whenever I have found that I couldn't reach You, I always assumed that it was some deficiency on my part that was the cause. Then I would not pray for so long that when I finally returned, I was so starved for Your company that I would find You in anything. Am I really still just a beginner, or more advanced? And does it really matter, anyway? I guess I'm still looking for a report card. Do I get an A? Have I been promoted to the next level?

Lord, You showed me the goal. I am headed for a spiritual marriage. You are leading me and I choose to follow.

You bring scripture to my mind often and show me the application to my life. Does this mean that I am advanced beyond this book, or that I am undisciplined, lazy, and not willing to work at it? Lord, do I treat You with less respect than I should, or are You satisfied? Do I really need to come to You prepared better, or can I just continue to plop in Your lap or by Your side and start talking? Lord, I'm willing to listen, but I'm afraid that I will only hear what I want to hear.

Fear not. For I have redeemed you, I have called you by name, you are Mine. I have continually encouraged you to come to Me. I have not put any conditions on you as to how you should come or when you should come. I have always met you when you came. When you sought Me you have found Me. I have been faithful to My Word. I have proven My love to you so you no longer doubt My Love. You are trusting Me much more. But now you want an even closer relationship with Me. You could not desire it without My prompting. You did not choose Me, I have chosen you. I want this closeness more than you do. Continue to seek Me. I do not change. I will continue to draw you closer and I will continue to reveal Myself to you. You also find Me when you are not seeking Me. I delight in surprising you. Yes, I AM the Creator of the universe. Yes, I AM the Lord of all. But I love you and am committed to completing the work I have begun in you. Fear not. Trust Me with all of your life. Even your mistakes can be transformed into good if you bring them to Me. I am not the slave driver or taskmaster of Egypt. I am your Savior, your Redeemer, the One who loves you, your Father, your Spouse, your Friend. Keep doing what you are doing. I will continue to lead you. FEAR NOT.

*****

Over the years, I struggled greatly with my weight.

Lord, If I stop trying to focus on what I want, and comply with working on what You consider important, it sounds like the song we sing: "Seek ye first the Kingdom of God and His righteousness, and all these things shall be added unto you." You let me know the other day that I could get into Heaven with a fat body but not with a proud heart. That is why You are working on my pride while I want to work on my weight. But my pride is keeping me from victory over all my weaknesses – and unless the pride goes, the fat will increase. So, Lord, I surrender. I believe You are calling me to change in the area of pride and I have no clue as to how to change this.

Maggie, it is good that you don't know how. It means you will need to be very attentive to Me to make any progress. In fact, you won't even know if you are progressing. I have the plan, and I keep the records. You follow or don't follow, and I adjust the plans accordingly. You must trust Me. Just as you saw in your student last night the joy and great hope of her ability to learn math, if taught well, so I see that I can teach you humility and get rid of pride in your life if you cooperate with Me and don't try to take over the controls. I know the direction I want to take you and it is not a direction you will want. If you could see the road, you would certainly run away. That is why I only allow you to see a little at a time. But the benefits are well worth the process.

*****

On November 1, 1995, my husband of over 27 years suddenly died of a heart attack.

Lord, You showed me things I could not see before or begin to comprehend without the power of the Holy Spirit. You owe me no explanation for Rae's death, yet You gave me some very healing explanations last night using Luke 6:27-38 (love your enemies). Rae had learned this very thing and was putting it into practice before he died. And now his sons must be taught the same. Then we sang the song, "I will change your name," and Lord, that is when my tears started to flow. You showed me that Rae will no longer be called "wounded, outcast, lonely or afraid," and how ever since his death You have allowed me to think of him only by the new names of "confidence, overcoming one, faithfulness, friend of God, one who seeks My face."

A few days later

Lord, I'm still flitting around. I can't seem to settle down. Here I am. I tried to go for a walk, but it is too cold. I tried praying but I could not concentrate. I'm determined to stay here today until I can spend an hour in Your Presence without running away. I simply need to come before You and face You. You keep loving me and speaking comfort and encouragement to me, and I run from You. I go through the motions of prayer, but cannot keep it up for more than a sentence or two. Mass has been the only time I sit still enough to allow You to touch me. And then I cry. I must be getting close to being serious, for I am now terribly sleepy. I have so many ways of avoiding You, Lord.

Maggie, don't worry. I am still with you and you are in My arms even when you think you are running from Me.

Lord, I've had a nap, I have a cup of hot tea here, and I think I'm ready to get down to business. I thought that I am not even asking You any questions yet. That may not be completely true. I do have questions – but I'm not settled enough to hear Your answers.

Lord, now I wonder if every question I have has the same answer: "Trust Me." So there is no point in asking. Lord, I do need You and though I may run from You, I do seek Your face.

Right now the pain is with me. Lord, I miss Rae! And I cry more easily. I suppose that is good. It doesn't feel all that good, but I suppose it is.

*****

When I was teaching, and very busy with what I considered serving the Lord. He said:

Maggie, you have been a faithful servant, but I want more than your service. You have turned to Me this week. That, too, is good. But I still want more. I want your prayer time with Me to be more personal.

How do I do that?

You don't – I do. You simply keep coming and let Me lead you. When you go to spend time alone with Me, be prepared for Me to lead you.

It sounds easy enough, and I'll gladly do that, but what if I don't see or feel anything different happening?

This is a time for you to trust Me. You have been learning to trust Me and have often been surprised. I am with you.

*****

I had been taught that it is good to give our rights to God, and if He chooses, He will return them to us as privileges. This took me a long time to learn, but the results were good. As I was beginning a new teaching job, I felt very unprepared.

Maggie, I accept your gifts. Your rights – imagined or legitimate – are not easy to give up. Trust Me – I will be with you. Remember to FEAR NOT. You have been disappointed with your own shortcomings this past week. Look to Me and not to yourself. Take the joys and strength I give you. Remember how much I love you, and be radiant. This work you are about to begin is Mine – I will do it through you. It is not you doing a work for Me or with My help or in any other way your work – it is Mine. You are also Mine. And I will use you in My work. Do come to Me daily. You need to be continually cleansed and strengthened and built up. Come to Me in the mornings and in the evenings, or late at night. I will always welcome you. Tell Me whatever is on your heart so I can love your problems away. It is good. It will be good. Trust Me.

Jesus, I trust You. Please keep reminding me that it is indeed Your work – not mine. Let me listen and follow well. Help me to not get in Your way, but to be an open channel for Your work. Thank You for allowing me to participate in Your work. Transform me into whatever You desire. Just don't let me lose sight of You.

Maggie, your sight of Me will improve, but do not expect even that you will be aware of Me. Just come to Me often – your awareness will grow. I do not want you discouraged if you think you have lost your focus. It will come and go – but in time you will learn to keep

it on Me. This is a process, a journey – do not be so anxious to be at the destination that you miss all the beauty and joy along the way. I am the Way, not just the End. So come, begin this day – see, the light is beginning to come. There is much to be done.**

*****

As I taught summer school math classes

Lord Jesus, I'm kind-of restless tonight. I could do a lot of stuff, but don't want to do much of anything. Too often I do something useless in this condition, but tonight I want to try to pray instead. Tomorrow I teach summer-school classes – in fact, all week I teach morning and afternoon. Geometry is going well, but I really need help with Algebra II.

Lord, You have been with me even though I really haven't given You much time. Thank You, and I'm sorry. I need another new beginning. I haven't much energy and I hurt a lot. Yet I know I need to start somewhere, somehow. If You give me the grace, I will start in the morning.

Maggie, I have not left you nor will I leave You. I know your struggles, your fears, and your frustrations. I will give you the grace to begin again. Trust Me for your success. Do not be afraid. My love and My grace will be enough for you.

Lord, my prayer life needs a boost also.

I know. Be patient – you can pray. Pray any way you can. I will accept it. Give Me your prayers as a gift. Spontaneous, memorized, in the Spirit, anything. I will take it and perfect it. But you must begin to do it. Give Me something to work with. I will show you what I can do with the small beginnings.

I know – You have done it before in my life. Would it be OK to offer it all for my kids and family? Lord, I want so much – I feel really greedy.

I can handle it. But you must leave the means to Me. Start to pray. Let Me take care of the rest. Remember My great love and that there is nothing too hard for Me.

Lord, make me content with where You have me in my life.

Your contentment requires sacrifice. You must sacrifice your desires for My will. This is not a one-time decision, but a moment-by-moment series of decisions. You must again choose to believe that this is My perfect will for you at this time. I will lead You and train you. Your docility will grow as you continually look for My will.

*****

Another time when I felt I was failing

You are painfully aware of how terribly fragile you are. It takes so little to wound or destroy you. Yet I come only to encourage, to build up, to restore. A bruised reed I will not break, a smoldering wick I will not quench. Others see you as strong but you feel so weak. I provide the strength you need. I fill in when you can no longer go on. It is My power and strength that others see. Do not be dismayed; your weakness is also My gift to you so you are able to rely on Me, trust Me, and yield to Me. I am doing a great work in you. It is not yet finished but it is going well. Continue to bring to Me all the problems that are too big for you. Also bring Me the little, seemingly insignificant things. Let Me surprise you with My love and care.

*****

As a widow, my desire to become a nun resurfaced. When I saw an opportunity to possibly pursue religious life I wondered if I should go and visit the small group of nuns I hoped to join. I still had responsibilities at home, but an opportunity to get away for a couple of days emerged.

So, You approve of what I am doing?

Wholeheartedly.

I'm not just being pushy and willing to settle for Your permissive will?

Is it so hard for you to believe that I am on your side? That I want your total happiness? That I am the One who put these desires in your heart and nurtured them for so many years? Trust Me.

OK, Lord, I trust You to work out the glitches and I will deal with what I can before I leave and then choose not to worry once I do leave. Thank You, Lord. Now I am at peace, at least for now.

Good. Let My peace guide you.

*****

In March of 2004, the way had opened for me to enter the convent. I had already had one shoulder surgery and I was afraid I needed a second one as well. I did not know if that would cancel my plans.

Lord Jesus, today I'm to see my orthopedic doctor with right-shoulder MRI in hand. Stay with me, Lord, please help. I seem to be presuming so much on the future. Lord, I want only Your will to be done in my life, but that is a goal, not a reality. It's more like I want to want Your will. Right now I am still so full of my own wants that I can't even see Your will.

Scared again?

Yes, very much so.

Can you trust Me?

I have to. Otherwise I'll drive myself nuts.

So trust Me until you get to the doctor. Then trust Me with the plans. Then trust Me after that.

A little at a time? That makes sense. This is all part of the romance, isn't it? There is joy trickling in as trust wins over fear. Suddenly I want to dance.

So, dance your way to Mass and then to the doctor.

Thank You. I'm on my way.

*****

In 2005, while in the convent I still had questions and needs and was glad to hear His reassurance.

Lord, please direct me clearly that I may be truly helpful in whatever I do. I offer You my service. Thank You that my arthritis is not as painful. It has been such a delight to be able to get around better.

Maggie, here I am. My love surrounds your and My help is ever-present. Keep listening to and seeking My voice of guidance. Replace fear with trust whenever it rears its head. Right now there is apprehension – that is the beginning of fear. Choose to trust Me – before you even feel the fear or the trust. Just as you can choose to believe, you can also choose to trust. Speak this trust throughout the day. Say "I trust You in this matter" – whatever it is. Your being needs to hear and see the trust you choose. My perfect love casts out all fear. Avail yourself of this power – remember My love as you choose to trust Me. And don't forget to come back to Me for cleansing and refreshing after you have been used to help people. I do love you – yes, even when you fail or fall, I am there.

*****

During a retreat in May of 2006, still as a nun:

Lord, You have proven Your love to me over and over throughout my life. I have felt Your Presence – I have heard Your voice – I have received Your power, Your healing, Your strength in my weakness, your consolation in my sorrow, Your wisdom, Your guidance, Your correction, Your forgiveness. My longing for You is so strong, but the realization that I already have You does not seem to penetrate. I am Yours and You are mine – I seem to need that etched in my being.

Maggie, I am yours and you are Mine. You have been Mine since before your birth. I *have* chosen you – it was not you who chose Me. But now you have the opportunity to choose Me daily. Choose to believe that you are Mine. Choose to accept My love daily. Choose to return to Me whenever you realize that you have strayed. Choose to call to Me in your pain, your frustrations, your uncertainties. Choose to trust Me when you find yourself gripped by worry. Choose to *FEAR NOT!!*

Lord, I cannot thank You enough. Please hold me tightly in Your arms through the night. Let me come to You again either during the night or in the morning.

*****

In October of 2006, I was sent home from the convent due to health issues. The Sisters also thought I should concentrate on being a grandmother. I also started caring for my mother. By March of 2007, her health was beginning to deteriorate.

Lord, I am distressed about Mom's health. Her breathing seems difficult. I know she is 84 years old, but please bring her heart, breathing, blood pressure, and blood sugar under control. The doctors and the medicines don't seem to be able to do it, but You are God, and can. I know I have not reacted as well as I should to having to come home from the convent, but I do thank You for giving me the time with Mom. We certainly have enjoyed each other's company. Thank You so much also for all the time I get to spend with my son Rae, his wife Michelle, and my little granddaughter Makenzi. Please forgive my complaining. Help me start again to do more things around the house, and guide me into whatever work You would have me do. My spiritual director, Fr. Sanders, said that I have been given much love and I need to share that love. He is so right. Please show me how, when, and where.

Now are you ready to listen to Me?

I think so, Lord. But I see how reluctant I am.

I see it as well. But you have not left or run away. That is progress.

Thank You, Lord, both for Your patience and Your encouragement.

Maggie, I have shown you that I am with you and continue to be in your life no matter what you do or don't do. I will *not* leave you. Do not be afraid to seek out avenues for service. I will help you discern what to accept and what to leave for others. A schedule is also a good idea. Planning for prayer is necessary. It is good various prayers have become priorities in your life. Adding some you were accustomed to in the convent with personal prayer will definitely help. But keep it simple. Do not overwhelm yourself. Do all things in moderation.

Make room in your schedule for changes and rest. Don't forget to include exercise. I see your fears that you are becoming an invalid. I do not want that to happen! I will be with you through it all. Avoid discouragement. Remember that I am with you and on your side. I am a God of joy and order and fulfillment, not of sadness and frustration and emptiness. It is possible. Trust Me, consult Me often, listen to Me, and watch Me fill your emptiness.

*****

By December of 2008, even though I was sure I was doing God's will in caring for my mother, I was again having trouble with my prayer life.

Lord, I am avoiding prayer because my prayers of late have not been personal enough. I don't feel engaged in the prayers most of the time. So the questions came to me, "Is it because I am failing to make them personal?" Am I doing it just so I can check off a list of things I have to do? Or are You calling me to a different form of prayer?" Lord, I need Your guidance.

Maggie, I am guiding you. Just to ask these questions is a part of My guidance. You are glad that you know you are doing My will in caring for your mother. You are not wondering what My will for your life might be. But the constant threat of this phase coming to an end is frightening, so you don't want to think or talk about it. There is still a lot of uncertainty in your life. You still need to trust Me. Yes, you do know I love you, and that I can be trusted, but knowing and doing are different.

What should I do? Keep repeating "Jesus, I trust in You?" until it becomes a reality?

You would get tired of that pretty quickly. But you can recognize the uncertainties in your life as opportunities to choose to trust Me.

OK. Lord, right now I choose to trust You with my mother's health and care. Please help us make good decisions.

*****

In November of 2010, I was no longer able to drive due to my failing eyesight. My mother was doing OK with dialysis, and others transported us wherever we went.

Lord Jesus, I have been taught that the spiritual life is not about us but about finding and fulfilling Your will. You send us to do Your work as soon as we have our encounter with You and You fix the brokenness of our lives. Lord, I thought the convent was to be where You sent me, but here I am – back home and without transportation.

I did send you there for over two years, but then I had a ministry here for you. Remember one of your first teaching jobs many years ago? You heard My call to leave the job and stay home – "Other people's children have many teachers, but your children have only one mother, and that is a more important job." You never regretted leaving the school because you saw the benefits in your relationship with your own children. Then when you stopped teaching in order to help your husband, you again saw the benefits. Now it is the care of your mother. You again see the benefits, but occasionally you wonder if there is more you could be doing. When the time comes to send you elsewhere, trust Me to let you know where I want you.

Thank You, Lord. I worried that I am getting too self-absorbed. It seems that my prayer life consists of relating the events of the day to You.

The intercessions, devotions and church services, the thanksgiving, the service to others – you think they don't count? Trust Me, they do. I am not the One who is dissatisfied.

Lord, I see. I repent. Please forgive me for my discontent.

You are forgiven. You need to learn to cherish when I give you rest. Lately when you come to Me at night so tired that you can barely move, I send you back for sleep – and you feel somewhat like you failed at prayer because you did not spend a whole hour. I do not count the minutes. I look at your needs. Once again, I am no slave driver. My love for you is complete. I don't love just your service. I do love your service, but there is more to you than service. You need to lighten up again.

Lord Jesus, You seem to be calling me.

You are having trouble.

I sure am. I feel like I've lost my way.

Here I am.

So I have found my Way?

Yes, if you will follow.

I haven't been – have I?

You start out doing so, but then the wind and waves distract you.

So how can that be fixed?

You need to be bound closer to Me and, like your shoelaces, when they loosen up you bend down and tighten them. You must recommit yourself to My will often.

This is the "parable of the shoelaces"?

If you wish! But you see My point. Once a week – or even once a day – is not enough anymore. Now you need to ask, seek, and knock often.

Lord, I don't even have daily prayer down yet – what chance have I of several times a day?

With Me all things are possible. Do you refuse your students algebra just because they have not really mastered arithmetic? No; you teach the algebra and reinforce and improve their arithmetic along the way. It will come.

Lord, it seems I'm caught between gratitude and fear. That seems an odd combination, but I am very grateful for the opportunities You have given me for service, yet I'm afraid to start anything.

It's the old fire-bell – it could go off at any time. You are expecting things to go wrong.

That's it.

Don't worry about it until it actually happens.

So worry has crept in?

It has. And when coupled with fear, it can wreck your life.

I have noticed the fear. It has been growing.

What is the opposite or antidote to fear?

Trust in You?

That also works for worry.

Choosing to believe?

That, too. You see, you already have the answers.

I just have to use them?

It's like that garden of yours. You have everything you need, but you have to use the tools and plant the plants and put the water on them.

Knowledge is not enough, is it?

No. Practice is also required.

Lord, I feel so weak.

I have plenty of strength you can use. Fighting temptation is one of My specialties.

That it is. So, it's tightening the shoelaces again?

Try it.

I will.

And now just rest in My Presence.

I think I can do that – thank You.

*****

Maggie, I will show you the way. I am the way, the truth, and the life. You are losing sight of Me, and are thus under much attack. Resist these attacks. Loneliness, sadness, fear, lethargy, and depression are not from Me. I have come that you might have life, and have it more abundantly. Breathe in My life. Breathe out your weaknesses. I strengthen you and provide all you need – including joy and confidence and much, much love. Fear not. You are indeed Mine. I am quite capable of meeting all your needs. And yes, I know *all* your needs. I also know all your desires and dreams, and do not find them trivial or wrong. I know what makes you happy and I

desire your happiness even more than you do. It is coming. It will not be late. Trust Me.

*****

Lord, this morning I thought I heard You begin to talk to me about trust.

It is another tightrope. You need to be confident – not wavering – in following Me, but also you have to watch out for pride and presumption. It is a bit like the songs you sing at prayers. When you are confident you know the song, you give it more voice. At other times you only mouth the words in order not to make mistakes – but if you think you know it and find you are wrong; it is more difficult.

So how do I learn to do it confidently?

By practice. By asking for help. By keeping at it until you get it right. But also, by keeping alert for My guidance as you go along. And by being willing to make mistakes as well as admitting them and learning from them.

Lord, I see, but some mistakes have serious consequences.

Trust Me to guide you through the serious situations. You do hear My voice. You have had plenty of practice at it. Fear not.

*****

When I was sent home from the convent, I was disappointed that I had not been consecrated to the Lord, but two years later, I was indeed accepted as a consecrated widow in the Society of our Lady of the Most Holy Trinity community.

I often started my prayers with recounting the previous day, but then, once in a while, I asked the Lord about His day.

So that was my day. How was Yours?

My days are never boring. I delight in being invited into the lives of those who love Me.

Lord, I do indeed invite You into mine.

And I have accepted your invitation. That is why you are Mine and I am yours. Yesterday as you were typing about your exit from the convent, you were amazed that I promised you that you shall indeed be consecrated to Me. It happened less than two years later on the feast of Corpus Christi. I have indeed called you and chosen you for My bride. I have been delighted that you responded and accepted. My love for you is very great. Your love for Me has truly grown. I promised you that you shall never again doubt that you love Me. That has also come to pass. I also told you that your prayer life shall blossom, and that is also happening. Do you see a pattern here?

Yes, Lord, You do keep Your promises. Thank You so much. I did not even remember that You said those things to me. I would not have known how marvelously You have acted in my life if I were not typing up these notes. Thank You for Your promises and for fulfilling them. Once again, I am at a loss as to how I can sufficiently thank You for all the wonderful ways You treat me, care for me, love me, and participate in my life. Even my life is Your gift. *Everything* is Your gift! Thank You.

Maggie, you are welcome. You now see even more than before that you can place your trust in Me. I have brought you through devastating losses, and blessed you abundantly. I have made you My very own. I am filling your loneliness and now I can promise you that you will not be lonely any more. And I keep My promises.

Lord, that is a big hole You are filling in my life.

What is hard for you to realize is that you are filling such a hole in My life as well. You have a God-sized hole in your heart – I have a Maggie-sized hole in Mine. And My heart is not just Mine – it is Trinitarian. Your Father's heart, the Spirit's heart, and even the human heart of My Mother all are joined to My heart in desiring and accepting your love. And is delighting to lavish love upon you.

Lord, once again I don't know how to thank You sufficiently. But please keep reminding me of all this until my gratefulness and love for You have grown enough that I will find better ways to respond. I guess that is why we need eternity.

It is, indeed. And it is a heavenly prospect.

*****

After so many years, I still have not arrived at trusting God completely, but I have grown in trust and with His faithfulness will continue to do so. Things are a bit calmer, and I don't seem to worry as much, and when I do, I am quicker to remember to bring my fears and worries to Him. I am grateful for the progress.

*****

Chapter 4

OBEYING GOD

Throughout my life, obedience never seemed easy for me. I suppose I am not alone in our current society. Even as a child, it was hardest for me to obey my parents. I could obey those I did not live with much easier. Thus, I could be a good student, a good helper to others, even a good citizen. But obey those God put in charge of me? That was a challenge.

When I recommitted my life to the Lord, I learned that I needed to be obedient to Him. This added a more extreme challenge and I often complained to Him about it. He is invisible. I cannot see Him. It is much easier to ignore Him. So, I had to learn how to be obedient to Him.

As I studied Scripture, I found that there were commandments I needed to obey. I had been taught these early enough in life, but now they became more important. So, I did the best I could. And whenever I failed, I repented.

But the closer I came to the Lord, and started to listen to Him, I found it surprising that obeying Him was neither difficult nor distasteful. Somehow, we have given obedience a bad name. We dread it. It took the Lord a long time to convince me that He is on my side and anything He asks me to do, He also provides me with the means and strength to do it. I always expected Him to be much more exacting, unreasonable, and severe. He has not been that way to me. Many times, He reminded me that He was not like a slave driver in Egypt that the Israelites were escaping from, but one who loves me and only wants the best for me.

I often saw that my own attitude was the problem. I asked the Lord for an attitude transplant in those cases. Just talking to Him often provided just that.

Help!!! Lord, everything seems to be falling apart. I'm too busy. I don't want to go to work today. But I don't want to stay home, either. I need an attitude transplant really fast. It's almost time to leave already. I need to get the younger kids up, make lunches – without lunchmeats; I never got to the store yesterday.

Maggie, stop for a moment. Has My love for you diminished? Has My power disappeared? Am I not able to redeem? You are in a mess. But I am the Lord your God and I shall walk with you and talk with you, and together we will get through as we have done countless other times. Be calm. Do what you need to do now, and the rest will wait for you.

*****

On Easter vacation in 1997, I had worked really hard to get my housekeeping done, and I had lots of work left to do, and no-one in the family seemed to appreciate all my work. I was complaining to the Lord:

Maggie, I can take your problems and complaints. This has been building up in you for some time, but the responsibilities and fatigue of teaching, as well as its joys and fulfillment, did not allow you time to let any of this come out. But a whole week at home, and all the old frustrations are coming out.

Maggie, there is something else. Just for a little while you have been doing things *you* want done. You want a clean and neat house. Most of your life is wrapped up in what others want or need, and you are uncomfortable with your own wants and needs, especially when those you love and serve seem not to care at all about these things.

Lord, You hit on it. So how can it be fixed?

Slowly and gently. First try to get the mountain of paperwork done. You don't want to return to school with excuses, but I don't want you to bury your needs and wants under a frenzy of activity

again. The balance here is tricky. It is good for you to serve others and not be concerned with yourself, but on the other hand, it is not good for you to neglect the things you need – sleep, proper food, exercise – and, yes, prayer.

Lord, I've never been good at this balancing act. I either fall on one side or the other.

I know. But here is where I am calling you to change. This is the work I am calling you to. This is My work of cleansing you. You are not free to love Me when you are filled with resentment. You are not free to love Me when you are running away from yourself. My love sets you free. I am not interested in a worn-out shell of a person. I want you whole and strong and pure.

Lord, I'll do everything in my power to cooperate with You, and I thank You with all my heart. I have felt You telling me that You are not a tyrant or slave driver that insists that I be busy all the time, but I could not sort things out.

I know. It is so hard for you to comprehend My love. But don't give up. There is progress.

Lord, I am totally undone, yet I am so happy to be so. I have felt so misunderstood and neglected and insignificant recently. It was all coming from within me, but I wanted to blame others. Tonight You have understood me, paid attention to me, and made me feel important, not in a false or pretentious way, but in complete truth. Lord, I feel loved. How marvelous this is!

So, you have your work ahead of you. Attack it with fervor.

OK, Lord, thank You so much.

*****

During a long and difficult illness and still trying to teach, I was struggling with making time for prayer.

Here I am, Lord, ready to spend an hour with You. I will need You to guide me as I am tired tonight and not quite sure how to begin.

Maggie, I felt the longing in your heart as you read to your classes about the joys of prayer. It is time you began to enjoy it. Many times I have reminded you that I am not the slave driver of Egypt. I have shown and proven My love and care and provision and protection for you. Yet you still come to Me out of obligation rather than joy.

Lord, the awful truth is that I still run from You rather than to You.

Yet you keep coming back. You still hope that it will get better.

Will it? Will I ever open up enough for You to touch me so I will permanently change? Is my dream of being a nun or total union with You unattainable? Or is it worth pursuing?

Maggie, your hope is well-founded. Who do you think gave you those dreams? Have I not been teaching you to trust Me? Am I not helping and preparing you? Can you not feel My embrace? You are closer than you think. Remember how difficult it was for the Israelites to keep the Sabbath? Yet it was My intention that it should be their delight. Instead it became a bunch of rules and don'ts. Prayer has been like that for you. Learn to play again as you pray. It is so hard for you to laugh because you think it has to be so serious. That is why I gave you a husband with such a sense of humor. Remember the fun and joy of being in love. It can be like that again.

Lord, I believe – yet I still just want to cry.

I know. But laughter and fun will return. Right now, you are not yet well. You are preoccupied with doctors and pain and death. But the resurrection will come. Don't give up. Rest, relax, work when you can, and remember that I am with you and on your side. You will again dance for joy. And I will be right there dancing with you.

Thank You, Lord. Even when You show me my faults, You encourage me. Hold me tight.

*****

Several years later, after I crashed two cars within a year, I had to rely on my family to care for me.

Obeying God

Lord, I have had a hard time being faithful to my prayers. I long for some intimate time with You, yet I have been avoiding coming to You. Lord, I do thank You that my body is mostly healed from the car accident. I also thank you for all the help that my son Rae, my niece Julie and her husband, Paul, and my sister Clara have given me. But it was difficult to be so dependent. I am ready to do almost anything to regain some independence – yet I am fearful of it!

Lord, Fr. Sanders' prayer puts it best: "I can't, You can, I'm Yours!" Here I am again at Your feet – somewhat surrendering – knowing that only You can comfort, soothe, fill, encourage, empower, restore, heal, calm, focus, guide, lead, and re-direct my troubled spirit, soul, body, mind, will, and emotions. In other words, Lord, I'm a mess.

Maggie, I know and recognize this mess. I have been waiting for you to fully turn to Me. I know you have been making feeble attempts, but even that longing you have felt has been My gently pulling you closer to Me. It is not just you longing for Me, but also that I am longing for you. Is that so hard to believe?

Lord, I'm stunned! I don't know why hearing of Your great love for me takes me by surprise each time, but it does. So how do I proceed? I long for You, You long for me, yet I run from You again and again.

Are you ready to stop running?

Lord, what I really want to do is run into Your arms and cry until I can't cry any more.

What is stopping you?

First of all, it's Your invisibility.

Your faith can overcome that.

I also feel that, as good as You have been to me, I have no right to cry – it would be ungrateful. And besides, crying just stops up my nose and gives me a headache.

And most of the important people in your life cannot handle your crying.

Lord, You are so right! That is why for a long time I felt emotionally dead – or at least crippled. My true emotions were suppressed for so long that they erupted like a volcano at the wrong times.

Maggie, *I* can handle your emotions.

Thank You, Lord. I feel Your Presence and it is wonderful. I need You so much.

I'm glad. And I'm here. And invisible though I be, I can hold you and love you and take care of you – all of you. Mind, will, emotions, spirit, soul, body – everything. Yes, even your driving. And a car for you to drive. And your mother and all your cares and all the people you pray for. *Be not afraid!* And when you are afraid, don't fear to come to Me and tell Me about it. I will build up your faith. I can do that. I had to do it with My apostles – why wouldn't I do it for you?

Wow, Lord, what a great perspective! So how can I serve You better?

Right now, it is not your service I desire. I desire only and exactly what you desire – that you run into My arms and stay there as long as you can. All through the night cry if you want, or laugh or sleep, but feel My love until you are filled up to the brim with My love and care and all those other things you have been longing for.

*****

Shortly thereafter, I had to stop driving altogether. My eyesight had deteriorated to where that was no longer safe. It was quite difficult at first, and the frustration often surfaced in my eating wrong. As I complained to the Lord again, He questioned me:

What is really eating away at you?

Lord, I think it is my deteriorating eyesight. I feel more and more dependent and isolated. I try to stay positive and grateful, but sometimes it gets me down. I think that is what happened yesterday. I need one of those attitude transplants – do You have one around that You can give me?

I'm sure there is one lying around here somewhere. I'll find it for you by morning.

Thank You, Lord, for not scolding me.

Maggie, I do not need to scold you. You are doing a fine job of that yourself. You do need a big dose of My love. If you lose sight

of that, it is worse than losing your sight. **Some things are indeed difficult. Losing the mobility of driving is not as traumatic as losing your husband, having to give up your job, or being sent home from the convent. Each of those were difficult, but with My help you made it through. You will get through this as well.**

Lord, that is indeed comforting. Fears are trying to come, but I don't want to cry. I want to hug and hold on to one of my sons, but I don't want to try to explain any of this to them. And besides, it makes no sense to fall apart now.

Oh yes, it does. This is a year since that second car accident.

Lord, it is You I need to hold on to. But Your invisibility is very frustrating again.

I know. When in the flesh, one wants flesh to hug. Why do you think I spent so many nights in out-of-the-way places? I also needed the touch of My Father – but ran into the same invisibility thing.

See, crying is so useless. Now my nose is all stopped up.

I know. At least you have tissues.

I won't even ask how people handled it in Your time on earth.

Yes, let's not go there. But know that I love you and that I do understand, and I will hold you together.

*****

The very next night, Scripture tickled me:

The best part of the day was just before 11:00 PM when I started reading Evening prayer. It was as if You directly answered my complaint of the previous night. The little verse before the Psalm was: "Although you have never seen Him, you love Him. Though you do not see Him now, you believe in Him." This was as if You were telling me that Your invisibility thing is really not a problem. I laughed so hard that had to call my friend Anne to tell her how great You are. She loved it.

*****

Another day, I was again having trouble:

Maggie, caring for a sick loved one does wear you down, as does the inability to go places. But I am with you and continue to supply your needs. Rejoice and be glad. This is now My command.

Aye, aye, Sir.

You see, it is possible. Your smile shows how quickly you obey.

Sure, I obey when Your command is such a pleasant one.

Oh, you think My commands should always be difficult and unpleasant? Even burdensome?

Now that You put it that way, I suppose I (and most people) consider commands to be obeyed as that. Obedience has never sounded easy.

So, you asked for an attitude transplant. Here it is. Begin to think of My commandments as delightful. As lifting burdens off of you rather than putting them on you. Think of yourself as obedient.

Lord, that is a totally new concept for me. I have tried to be obedient, but never felt successful at that.

Your desire for direction is in itself a willingness and desire to obey. You only see your failures – I see your heart. You love to serve Me and others – is that not obedience? You delight in anticipating and fulfilling the desires of others. You want to please your God and you please those around you. In other words, you love. That is My greatest command. You obey. You are obedient. You even obeyed in choosing to be joyful when you felt completely the opposite. Have you not heard that love covers a multitude of sins? Not just My love but also yours.

Lord, You always encourage me.

I love you. That is not just My job, but Who I am. Now come to the Father.

*****

After another busy day, I was again dismayed.

I guess the day was a success.

Maggie, if it was a success, why are you dissatisfied?

Good question, Lord. I really don't have an answer. I feel like I am wasting time.

Yes, you are. And not even enjoying it.

It seems I need an attitude transplant again. Lord, I just need more of You. Not that You haven't given me all of You, but I seem to need more of a capacity to enjoy Your gifts, blessings, Presence, and friendship. I need to be overwhelmed with gratitude that You give me all these things. I need to fight the feelings of discontent and self-pity that are attacking me.

Lord, now that I see them, I do fight them. I choose to be grateful for all Your gifts, graces, and blessings. I am grateful for Your Presence and Your friendship. Hold me close, Lord, and allow me to feel Your love and goodness.

Yes, that is better. You had to identify the demons attacking you. Now you will be able to experience the joy I have for you. Sleep well in My arms.

*****

Early in my journals, I was talking to the Lord about obedience, and the topic of keeping the Sabbath came up:

In the Old Testament book of Jeremiah, the problem of the Sabbath day seems to stick out. We as a nation have not kept the Sabbath. The Old Testament is full of stories that show Your anger with Your people for forgetting the Sabbath. Yet it is balanced in the New Testament, where the Pharisees overdid this and were rebuked.

This all proves that nothing should be done to excess, not even religion. My people forget Me. The Sabbath is created to help them remember. It is meant to be a joy and a pleasure and an aid – but men have made it a rule and law and burden. Holiness is not supposed to be tedious or burdensome. When you come into My presence, I do not weigh you down with more problems, I lift you up out of your

problems. I created man for fellowship with Me. When he does not get it, he is miserable. Just like I created man to need food physically, he must also have spiritual food. But he can only get this spiritual food if he stops all his business and activity to listen to My still small voice. I didn't get angry with My people because they disobeyed a law of mine. I was angry because they forgot Me and they and their children were spiritually starving. Famines only showed physically what was already a fact spiritually in their lives.

So where does this leave me and those I teach? I admire those who take a stand on not working on Sunday, yet I do not take that stand.

If you keep seeking Me, you will come to see the balance. A mindless stand on a principle is useless. But without principles, the people forget completely. Instead of a rule or law, let the Sabbath day become once again a joy and pleasure in spending time loving Me and one another. Don't fill it with "shoulds" and "oughts." Fill it instead with seeking and finding and loving and serving Me and those I call you to love. Throw off the limits that rules and regulations have put on you. If you say only, "I must keep the Sabbath holy by not working," then you are focused on a very insignificant part of what the Sabbath is for. I want to have a wonderful time with you, but if you are busy with your work, you'll miss Me. Do you turn on the shower and do noisy things when you are expecting an important phone call? Of course not. You listen and wait. That is what a Sabbath is – a listening, a waiting, and a wonderful time of loving between you and Me.

Thank You, Lord. I know I've heard You today.

I've wanted to say this to My people, "Thank you for listening. See the earnestness of My heart." Tell My people My frustration when they take a gift and make it a burden. I love you.

*****

Over a year later, I was lagging in my commitment to prayer.

Lord God, it's been a long time since I've written my prayers down. My thoughts flow much faster than my pen and perhaps I've grown better at concentrating on You and don't need the physical help of pen and paper to keep me focused. Yet my lack of discipline is still a problem; weeks go by between times of prayer. I wonder how much more I could serve You if I spent time with You daily in prayer, adoration, worship, and listening to Your instructions for the day. If I spent more time in Your presence doing that, would I be able to hear Your voice better or quicker and would I obey immediately? I'm pretty sure it would be better than it is now. Then the where, when, and how become problems. (I can make a problem out of anything, can't I, Lord?) But the fact remains, I need to spend more time with You, and You want me to do it, so the one thing that is left is to actually obey. Well, we know I can't do that without major help, so I'm asking for major help. I will leave the when, where, and how up to You. I know all my pledges, promises, and good intentions in the past have eventually failed.

Lord, I'm desperate for Your companionship. I find that I have grown in the past years, and I am much more willing and able to trust You. I am much more willing and able to put aside my strong will and want Your will instead. I am willing and more able to let You guide me. But I am not satisfied. I want much more.

My child, now I give you more. I come guiding and strengthening you. But you need to submit your will to Mine. I allow troubles, persecutions, sicknesses, irritations, and even pests into your life in order to build you up, strengthen you, and help you to grow. If I allowed you to choose your problems, how would you choose? Without physical exercise, the muscles grow weak and useless. With too much or the wrong kind of exercise, they can be damaged, painful, and useless. With the proper kind and amount of exercise the muscles become strong, useful, and even beautiful. That is what I want for you physically, emotionally, and spiritually. I know your needs, abilities, limits, and endurance. I allow into your life only what I know you can endure and what will help you if you allow Me to teach you through it. You have grown attentive to My teaching over the years but there is much more yet to learn. I have repeatedly called you to daily communication and communion with Me. That is a need you have if you are to gain the strength you and I want for you. You can begin now. You do not need to wait. I am here ready, willing, and able. You are no longer afraid; I have proven My love and trustworthiness

to you. Your daily chores and duties need not keep you away from the communication and communion with Me; they can become a part of it. You have felt My presence more and more recently in everyday things. You were right – it was I! I have not left you; I continue to remain with you. I want you to notice Me more. You know I have used you powerfully as well as ordinarily in the past. I am not finished with you yet. I am very pleased with the thrill in your heart at the thought of My using you. You are My friend as well as My servant, and your willingness to serve is a delight to Me. You know I am able to use anyone who is willing. Perfection is not a prerequisite but a final result. Be patient with yourself and others in the process.

*****

As the Lord taught me more and more how His commandments were not to be burdensome, but a joy, I realized how poorly we have interpreted His Ten Commandments. I rewrote them for my students from a perspective of obeying out of love.

Is it hard to keep the Ten Commandments?

What if we tried to keep the Commandments not because we have to, or that we should, or because we would get into trouble if we didn't, but simply because we are grateful for God's love?

So out of a response to the love of God, could we look at the Ten Commandments this way?

1. Because God loves me so much, I will not let anything be more important to me than my relationship with Him. (You shall have no other gods before me.)
2. As my response to His love, I will show my love for Him by speaking of Him only with respect and reverence. (You shall not take the name of the Lord in vain.)
3. Since He loves me so much as to give me seven days every week, I will spend the day He wants: with Him, enjoying His goodness, and learning more about Him. (Keep holy the Lord's day.)
4. He gave me my earthly parents to care for me and teach me about His great love so I will thank God for all the good I received

through my parents by honoring them, obeying them, being respectful to them, loving them, caring for them when needed, and appreciating them. (Honor your father and your mother.)
5. God's greatest gift to me is life itself, and since He considers life so important as to send His Son to experience our humanity, I will show my love for God by doing all I can to preserve and value life as His gift. (You shall not kill.)
6. God, who IS love, has designed me to love and be loved. He has given me the ability to express that love through vows in marriage, or He has given me the grace to forego marriage to reserve my love for Him and His people through service. Therefore, I will honor His gift when I am able to make such vows and honor the vows of others as well. (You shall not commit adultery.)
7. Because God has given me so much out of His great love for me, I will not take anything He has not given me, especially anything He has chosen to give to someone else. (You shall not steal.)
8. God is ultimate truth, and because He loves me, and I desire in my love for Him to imitate Him, I will commit myself to truthfulness. (You shall not bear false witness against your neighbor.)
9. Because He knows me better than I know myself, and He loves me better than I can love myself, I will trust Him and be satisfied with His choice for my life partner and desire no one else. (You shall not covet your neighbor's wife.)
10. As He has been faithful and kind to me in providing all that I truly need, I will be satisfied with His provision and not desire anything more than what He chooses to give me. (You shall not covet your neighbor's goods.)

(The Ten Commandments are taken from the Catholic Bible.)

Maggie, it is all about balance. You are right, there is a great need for obedience – but it is not a forced obedience I desire – it is a willed laying down of your own desires in order to take up Mine. Not because of consequences, not out of fear, but out of love. Love makes it possible; it gives the needed energy. It is a choice. But it is a continual stream of choices.

Lord, how do mine stack up?

You are here, are you not? You seek My voice so you may obey. Keep listening. I will speak. Be patient with yourself. I am patient with you.

Lord Jesus, I just received a neat little nugget. Holy Spirit, You get Your wisdom into me in the neatest ways. I just remembered that I wanted to copy the papers on the Ten Commandments that my grad-school class was given last weekend. That thought led me to the difference between the Protestant and Catholic ways of presenting them. The Protestants count as two what is the first for the Catholics. The Catholics count as two what is the last for the Protestants. Then I realized that the Catholic way would have been more instructive to King David, who coveted his neighbor's wife, while the Protestant way would have been more instructive to King Solomon, who set up idols.

*****

The Ten Commandments from the Protestant Bible

1. You shall have no other gods before me.
2. You shall not make or worship any idols.
3. You shall not take the name of the Lord in vain.
4. Remember to keep holy the Lord's Day.
5. Honor your father and mother.
6. You shall not kill.
7. You shall not commit adultery
8. You shall not steal
9. You shall not bear false witness against your neighbor.
10. You shall not covet your neighbor's wife or goods.

*****

Chapter 5

GAINING WISDOM

Grace, according to Webster's dictionary, is "unmerited divine assistance given to humans for their regeneration or sanctification." In other words, a gift from God. That is how I see my entire life. Not just a gift, but a continual stream of gifts and assistance from God. They are unmerited, as they started before I was born and continue regardless of my own devices.

Wisdom, on the other hand, is defined as "ability to discern inner qualities and relationships; insight." This, to me, is also a great gift or grace. It says in the book of James, "If any of you lacks wisdom, let him ask God, who gives to all men generously and without reproaching, and it will be given him." (Jas 1:5) It seems I have been seeking God's wisdom for most of my life, and He has been faithful to His word and has given it to me often.

One of the first Scriptures I committed to memory was (Prov 3:5-6), "Trust in the LORD with all your heart, and do not rely on your own insight. In all your ways acknowledge him, and he will make straight your paths." I found through much trial and error that my own wisdom, insight, or understanding did not usually work well, but when I turned to God, and asked for His wisdom or insight, things worked much better. Eventually I learned that His ways and wisdom are so often the complete opposite of what comes naturally to us. This, too, has been a great gift or grace.

When I first came back to the Lord, I had so much to learn. The first seminar I attended took place after a prayer meeting and was called the "Life in the Spirit Seminar". It was led by a team of people from the prayer meeting. There I learned that the Holy Spirit, the Spirit of

Wisdom, who came upon the disciples on Pentecost, the third Person of the Holy Trinity, was still working and active today. I learned about His gifts and was encouraged to desire not only the ones we learned about before Confirmation, wisdom, understanding, counsel, fortitude, knowledge, piety, and fear of the Lord; but the Charismatic gifts found in I Corinthians 12 as well. I was prayed with and received the Baptism of the Holy Spirit.

Being prayed with or over was a relatively new experience for me. It meant people gathered around the chair where I was sitting, gently put their hands on my head, shoulders, or back, and started praying. They would pray in tongues or in English, and if someone felt the Lord wanted to specifically tell me something, they would speak as if God was Himself speaking. I learned this was called prophecy. I loved it. Even now, when I feel the Presence of the Lord, it is as if gentle hands were on my head.

One of the results of being baptized in the Holy Spirit is a thirst to learn more about God. I studied Scripture every chance I could and went to seminars whenever my busy life as wife and mother allowed me. I discussed matters I did not understand with people smarter and more experienced than I, usually from the prayer group. I listened to tapes of Teaching from the Bible, watched programs on TV that taught about Scripture, and slowly things started to make sense. I was amazed that Scripture was not as hard to understand as I had thought.

The Mass also became so much more meaningful to me. Almost every reading and prayer would speak directly to me and I marveled at this in prayer one time:

Lord, Mass was wonderful. How is it that now every word of the Mass is wonderful and meaningful and touches me right where I need Your touch? That same Mass that used to be an empty ritual is now an intimate communication between You and me.

*****

I discovered that there is a wealth of Scripture about wisdom. In fact, there is a whole book of Wisdom in the Catholic Bible, or in the Apocrypha of some protestant Bibles. One of the seminars I attended, encouraged us to learn wisdom from the book of Proverbs. It was amazing! Over and over

I saw how God's wisdom was so contrary to the world's wisdom. And yet, the world's wisdom did not usually have good results. But as I started following what God said, the results were awesome.

One day, I was driving my car with a friend, and someone cursed at me and my reaction was calm, and I was not at all upset by it. My friend commented that I just showed her Proverbs 15:1 how a soft answer turns away wrath.

My marriage improved as I learned to be less critical and value my husband's care for the family. My relationship with my parents miraculously grew better. I became much happier. God had answers to most of life's problems, and they were all right there in the Bible. Of course, I had good teachers, but early on, I was taught to "eat the meat and spit out the bones." This meant that if I did not understand something or found it too difficult at the moment, I could just set it aside and accept and use what did make sense and could be applied to my life.

I found that I had been taught a lot of God's wisdom in my upbringing, but I was not given the reasons behind the teachings. That is the way it was done back then. We were taught what to do and not to do, but explanations were few. Now I began to see the explanations and found that the old morals I tried to ditch still applied, but now I could understand why.

I had heard that it is good to have a spiritual director. Shortly after my first prayer meeting in 1975, I started looking for one. But the Lord did not allow it at the time. Every time I mustered up enough courage to ask someone, usually a priest, the Lord would have them reassigned far away. One even left for Poland. I finally realized that the Lord wanted me to develop that personal relationship with Him before looking for someone else.

It was not until 1988, when I first was free to go on a three-day retreat at a Jesuit retreat house, that I was introduced to spiritual direction. It was not what I expected at all. I thought I would have a new authority in my life telling me what to do, and I simply had to obey. Fr. John Brady, S.J., was definitely not such a person. In fact, none of my spiritual directors since have been.

Spiritual directors may ask questions to see where you are spiritually, and then give you scriptures or writings that help you figure out what God wants to teach you. Then they simply accompany you on the journey as

God Himself guides you. They take on the role of encouraging and helping you keep listening to God. I have found that getting away from everyday life and spending a few days away in beautiful surroundings and calm and quiet have been very beneficial to me. At first, I had a new director every time I went on a retreat. Each one taught me very valuable lessons. But it was really God who took me by the hand and opened my eyes to see what I needed. I always came home with a renewed strength and sense of how to proceed in my life. After several years, I settled on a particular director, and he helped me for over nine years until he was reassigned in another state. Eventually I was reacquainted with a priest I had met when I was 13, at the girls' summer camp I attended, where he had been the chaplain. Fr. Edwin Sanders S.J. has been my spiritual director for many years now.

Whenever I had the opportunity to have a retreat, I always learned volumes. I usually journaled so I could look back and be reminded of what the Lord taught me when things got hectic at home, as they usually did.

But the Lord used other occasions to teach me His wisdom as well. One day I was walking through the woods in a nearby park and noticed a dogwood tree in full bloom. It was mostly tall and straight, but one large branch had been broken though not completely severed. The break must have happened a year or so previously, as it was healed over, and had new leaves and flowers on this branch. I saw that the flowers on the broken branch were more beautiful than the ones I could hardly see way up at the top. The Lord showed me how sometimes we experience great breakings in our lives, but He allows us to continue through the break, heal only a part of the hurt, but then bring even more beauty in our lives.

I experienced this through the death of my husband. Though it was painful and difficult at the time, He brought me through and healed the hurt, and now I can help others in similar situations. His love was even more evident to me having been through the sorrow. I also learned another lesson about timing.

Lord, You are awesome. Here I am just sitting and pondering a topic I haven't understood for a long time, and You explain it so clearly and easily. I remember how, just a few days before Rae died, You and I had made plans as to how I could be a better wife and what to do around the house. I often wondered why You let me go on like that when You knew Rae was about to die. Suddenly I understood. You live in the present. I have often marveled at how in Your earthly life You never seemed to dwell on either the past or the future – yes, You knew it, but You always dealt with the present moment. That freed You from fear as well as second-guessing. You enter our lives in the same way. You deal with us in the present. That is why prophecy does not usually tell us the future, only what You want so we would *have* a future. Of course, this is the way You usually work. Since You are God, You can do the supernatural – but usually You operate in and with the natural, for You created all nature. Somehow it makes sense now. Thank You.

*****

Such lessons in His wisdom can come through Scripture, through interaction with others, or just out of the blue during a walk through the woods. But God's timing is different from ours. I often got frustrated with Him because He was moving too slow for me. I wanted to follow Him, but I kept running ahead of Him and then wondering why I could not find Him. I had to learn that following meant according to His timing and desires.

Yet I also learned that He uses our own talents and desires to accomplish His will in our lives. Following Him is not always contrary to what we would desire to do. The first time I learned this I caught myself asking God for more closeness to Him. He showed me how often He puts a desire in our hearts that is also His desire. Sort-of like a parent buying a new shiny red bicycle for his son several months before Christmas. He then points out to his son how great riding a bicycle would be. Then, every time a red one is spotted, he points out to his son how nice and shiny that red bike is. Before Christmas, the son can almost taste wanting a red bike. Then there is joy for both father and son on Christmas day, when the gift is given.

God worked like that with me and my desire to be a nun. When I took a detour, and got married instead, I thought that desire was never attainable. But after my husband died, the desire returned, and I told the Lord, "I don't know if this is Your will for me, but I know You are kind enough to at least let me try it." And he did. I spent a bit over two years being a nun, and I loved it. I was able to do much good and felt I was following Him. But then He called me elsewhere. After a year of wondering what He wanted of me, I found to my amazement that I was exactly doing His will and loving it, taking care of my mother. After all, I had spent most of my life caring for others and became pretty good at it.

One of the questions I asked of the Lord, was about giving Him our pains and discomforts. When I was a child in Catholic school, we were often told that if we did not like something, we should "offer it up." So, I finally asked the Lord what good did my offering Him these things do for Him. He explained that it was not what good it would do for Him, but that He accepted such things from us and used them as raw materials to fashion a blessing either for us or someone else. Since then, I have had many opportunities to give Him the gifts of my pains, frustrations, uncertainties, and distresses. He has always gratefully accepted them and often I have seen the blessings He fashioned out of them.

Another great gift or grace of wisdom He gave me is to take things as they come, and not anticipate pain or discomfort before it arrives. This has been very valuable in simple things like going to the dentist, or in greater events such as hospitalizations and surgeries. I have had much pain in my life, but I need not live in fear of it before it comes. This required the practice of telling myself, "right now, it does not hurt." Jesus told us this when He said: (Mt 6:25-34) and (Lk 12:22-31), that we should not worry about anything, for God knows what we need and will give it to us. I have found this to be so in my life. I have been both in poverty and disability, yet the Lord always provided what I needed.

One day, as I was thinking about all His gifts and provisions, I realized that so many of His gifts are so often abused by humanity:

I see how little I know You. Hard as I try, I can't seem to get rid of all those misconceptions. You are not the stiff, formal, prim and proper God I imagined You to be. I suppose today You would be quite comfortable in blue jeans. You are far more reachable than I ever knew. And yet, what You showed me yesterday showed me how I (we) can only see such a limited little particle of Your whole idea on any subject and we distort it so. Lord, every good gift You have given us; we have distorted and made into a curse, or at least treated like a curse.

Food – we get fat.

Drink – we get drunk.

Sex – we get disease.

Shelter – greed.

Children – trouble.

Nature – pollution.

Church – irrelevant.

Lord, how do we turn it around?

Maggie, you know the answer. The only way is the Way. The only truth is the Truth, and the only life is the Life. Everything in your life must proceed from My Son. That is the only way to avoid all those perversions of this generation.

Lord, I lose sight of this so easily.

I know. That is why I am training you and begging you to keep coming to Me. I know how much you need My teaching. Remember that My love is unconditional and for <u>your</u> benefit.

*****

At another time, I was struck by the contrasts of what we know about God.

I had been struck by the fact that certain things about You mean more to me than others. Your beauty, Your glory, Your holiness, Your majesty do not have much meaning to me. The beauty of Your creation, I can appreciate and understand. Your goodness, gentleness, patience, understanding, faithfulness, love all touch me more. Your peace and joy I see more as Your gifts to us than as Your own attributes. You want us to have these because You already have them. I am awed by the contrasts in Your nature – Creator of the whole universe, yet caring about the smallest details (sparrows, hairs, and atoms), King of Kings yet Lord of my own life, holy and just yet merciful and kind, all-powerful yet so gentle. Perhaps You have chosen to reveal Yourself to me differently than to others. Perhaps differences in personalities and experiences make some of Your attributes more meaningful to other people. I have tried to concentrate on the ones that are meaningful to me, and not pay too much attention to the ones that aren't. Is this the best approach?

Maggie, it will do for now. But I want you to know My love for you. The intellectual musings will not help you or change your life. I don't want to only reside in your mind, but in your heart, your life, your actions, words, thoughts, motives, and attitudes. If the thoughts of Me do not stir anything more than thoughts or even emotions, then it is not enough. Come completely into My presence. Let Me love you to wholeness, to holiness, to forgiveness, to My plan for your life.

Lord, I have a question: When I read some prayers, it does not seem like I'm really praying until I get to the intercessions. I suppose that is why I often stop reading devotionals and feel I have not prayed.

It is a different form of prayer. There are many forms. Some are more personal than others, some you will find more comfortable than others. Writing would be very difficult for lots of people, but it works well for you. Praying out loud is best for some, but you find it difficult. Some forms of prayer are worth practicing until they become meaningful and comfortable. Others you leave behind if they do not seem to be effective. This is one of the reasons for much disunity, and it is so unnecessary. People fight about things that they should marvel at. Differences can either enrich or divide people. It takes serious work to understand and be enriched by the differences, and much humility to not try to force others to your ways. My ways are not your ways and My thoughts are not your thoughts, but I became Man and I experienced your ways and thoughts. This is a way you can learn from Me. When confronted with differences in culture or ways of prayer, look for the good in the other. Find and admire the admirable in the other. Share the good of your own perspective or experience if asked. Do not think one is good and the other bad, find the good in both. Do not abandon your own ways without serious reasons. Do not give up your faith or practices without knowing what you are giving up and what you plan to replace it with.

You have seen this and found it lacking in your own life. When you married Rae, you gave up your faith for his lack of faith. It took several years, but you found that you were missing what you had given up. Look for truth and beauty and the good and admirable in all things. There you will find Me as well.

Lord, I am so glad I asked that question.

Me, too. Keep asking, keep seeking, and keep knocking.

Wow! I never thought that "ask and you will receive" meant questions, too.

Another jewel – a new meaning to an old phrase. These are some of the treasures I give you.

Thank You so much, Lord. What can I give You in return?

You have given Me your attention and your awe. That is My jewel which I treasure. And your time with Me. I also treasure that.

Lord, I offer You the rest of this day.

I accept.

Lord, I think what I have is a pretty high form of prayer. Thank You. I was hoping it was, but I was not sure.

Before pride comes in, remember that you are to leave all assessments to Me. Remember that humility is a prerequisite for true prayer.

So as long as I focus on You and not on me I should be OK?

Something like that. We do have a personal relationship and have had it for a long time – that it had times of relative inactivity is a fact, but not a fatal flaw. So rather than analyze it, let's simply live it and enjoy it.

Thank You, Lord. That sounds great. So where would You like to take me today?

Do you have any requests?

Lord, as long as I am in Your arms, You can take me anywhere.

You are still in need of your Father's affection.

Lord, it says in Scripture that no one can come to You unless the Father draws him, and that no one can come to the Father except through You. It seems a bit circular.

Yes, that it is. But the love of God is eternal – also circular: no beginning, no end. It is very good. Come with that smile and let's see the Father.

Lord, it is so good to be loved. I said to the Father that there may be times when I will be afraid to approach Him because of my sins. He replied that I need not worry about that – the Holy Spirit convicts me of sin and You, Jesus, forgive my sin. So as long as I come in Spirit and Truth, the sin is already gone. I can come and be happy in the arms of my Father – how marvelous!

*****

What is the most difficult part of being a parent/adult? The answer is: Keeping a balance. It seems so difficult to maintain that balance between what has to be dealt with vs. what can be overlooked; between trust and guidance (the need for each); between work and home; between giving too much or too little; between work and play.

Maggie, there is a Scripture that addresses this need in Ecclesiastes. The one about "there is a time for …" Wise people through the ages were the ones who were able to discern the proper times and amounts of each. Wisdom is keeping a balance and wisdom is knowing what it is time for. This is the staying in the center of the stream of the movement of God. This is the straight and narrow path – this is the high road of holiness. This is why you need both Spirit and Truth. One to keep you off one side and the other to keep you off the other. This is why excess of any kind is harmful. Child, I keep you in balance. I guide you along the road. Follow Me, and you will be covered on three sides. Father in front, drawing and directing; Son on one side, the Way, the Truth, and the Life; Spirit on the other, Wisdom, Power, Counsel. You will have the devil at your back, but as long as you keep moving, he can't catch you. This is why the armor of God only protects you on the front and sides. The armor of God is I, Myself, in My Trinity and My Unity that you have centered yourself in. So even your rear is covered unless you break out of the triangle. This is how you can be in Me and I in you. This is true worship in Spirit and in Truth – to be in the center of My will – in thoughts, words, deeds, motives, and attitudes.

*****

Spiritual maturity takes a painfully long time. Yet it is not that different from any other maturity.

Children spend much of their time doing what they want to do, occasionally interrupted by what they have to do – put away toys, eat meals, go to the bathroom, etc. As they get older, there are more "have-to's" – homework, church, chores, etc. Adulthood is where the "have-to's" are the major part of the day and the "want-to's" become occasional periods of relaxation or regeneration. Happiness is achieved in different ways. Some grow to enjoy enough of the "have-to's" that their lives intertwine them with the "want-to's" so they are often indistinguishable. Others fill their lives with enough "want-to's" that it is balanced and healthy.

There are temptations to excess on both sides. The irresponsibility of not taking care of enough of the "have-to's" because one is too wrapped up in the "want-to's" on the one side and the workaholic who is so preoccupied with the "have-to's" that he has no time or energy or even the ability to unwind and relax.

I have been on both sides of this at various times in my life. Lord, I believe You want me in balance, not falling into either pit. You have given me a marvelous gift of truly enjoying my profession of teaching, and truly enjoying caring for the people in my life. But recently I have lost touch with my "want-to's" and have become discontented and complaining. I believe You have placed in my heart a deep desire (want-to) for union with You. But somehow, I have made it into a duty (have-to) and thus have lost the joy and fulfillment it would bring, as well as having the desire almost vanish.

*****

When I was teaching teenagers, certain difficult topics came up and I asked the Lord for clarification.

Sexuality is My wedding gift to man and woman. It is a great gift that is meant to be opened only after the vows have been made. But just as the tree of the knowledge of good and evil was in the midst of the garden of Eden in plain view, so this gift is prepared long before it is given – and just as that tree was growing and developing and

looking good to eat, My plans for it were never realized because man ate of its fruit before I gave it to him to eat. So, it is with sexuality. It is there – it looks attractive and ripe, but until man has reached the maturity to handle its fruit, it causes him harm rather than the good it is meant to bring to him. But if the gift is good, the giver is better. I give the gift to those who make a covenant according to My plan. I have other gifts for those who are not in a position to make such a covenant. I am not the unfair one who withholds good from My people – I am the One who gives good gifts to them – but they have to have the responsibility to care for the gift I give them and handle it well. I give the gift at the right time, but many take it when it is not yet theirs, and their lives are thus made so much more difficult. Sexuality is good, children are good, love is good, but I, the Giver of these gifts, am better. And if the Giver is left out, the gift is easily misused and becomes a curse instead of the blessing it was meant to be. Sin is the misuse of gifts.

*****

Lord, last night You gave me such insight and revelation that I was overcome with joy and thanksgiving. I was contemplating the predicament of a friend who could not forgive someone who had sinned against her and left deep emotional scars. Through her emotions, that sin wounded and hurt every time her memory is triggered. Feelings of anger and having been wronged, and a desire for revenge, flooded her. She re-lived the whole thing over and over, bringing torment to her and all those close to her. The sinner seemed totally unaffected; my friend continued to be victimized. Her negative emotions drained her energy and her health.

We do not naturally want to forgive. We feel that the sinner does not deserve to be forgiven, and that we are entitled to revenge. We want the sinner to humble himself and admit his wrongs. But Your ways are completely the opposite. We Christians must forgive every sin, no matter how great and whether or not the sinner has repented. We are not entitled to take revenge.

Jesus taught us, "Forgive us our trespasses as we forgive those who trespass against us ... For if you forgive men their trespasses, your heavenly

Father also will forgive you; but if you do not forgive men their trespasses, neither will your Father forgive your trespasses" (Mt 6:12, 14-15)." Let's go to Jesus. Was He sinned against? Yes! Was He wrongfully accused? Yes! Did He suffer physically? Yes! But did He rehash and relive the wrongs that were done to Him? No! Why not? Because He immediately forgave His offenders. Did they deserve to be forgiven? No! Did they repent before they were forgiven? No! Was He able to forgive completely? Yes! Did He seek revenge? No! Did He threaten them with retribution? No! Was He powerful enough to punish them? Yes!

But it isn't fair! And even when we try hard to forgive, we can't seem to do it very well. But we must. For when a sin is committed against me, it has the power to continually wound me through my emotions. It is like a living, destructive thing. It lives as long as I remember it and am affected by it, like a germ, or a mad dog, or a villain in a movie. If I fight back in natural ways, it only grows stronger and can prompt me to sin as well (anger, attempt to harm the one who sinned against me, etc.). But if I forgive the sinner, then the sin loses all power to wound and hurt me. It is like a dead thing.

So why did You forgive, and why do You insist that we forgive? We are all sinners and deserve just punishment. Separation from You for all eternity (Hell) is the just punishment for our sins. It is our common fate, for even if we repent, we cannot offer sufficient atonement to God. But in Your loving mercy You, Father God, allowed Your beloved Son, perfect Man and true God, to atone for our sins, to satisfy for all sinners for all time Your perfect justice. Through Jesus' atonement, we can repent and be forgiven. But in our turn, we must be merciful and extend our own forgiveness to those who have sinned against us.

We withhold God's forgiveness from ourselves as long as we do not forgive (even if we are repentant and deserving of forgiveness, unlike the person who hurt us). I believe Jesus died for my sins. But what about the sins of my friend's offender? Did Jesus die for his sins? Did He pay the price for what has hurt her for so long? Yes! Did He forgive that man? Yes! How could He? How can she? How can she, or any one of us, forgive someone when every particle of our being screams "No!"?

When Jesus died on the cross, He who was without sin became sin. "For our sake He made Him to be sin Who knew no sin, so that in Him we might become the righteousness of God". (2 Cor 5:21). When Jesus died,

He was the sin. He took upon Himself that sin that was committed against my friend and He died on that cross. With Him, that sin died also, and has no more power to torment her. When I see Jesus on the cross, I can see that sin dead and powerless. When I see Jesus risen again, I no longer see the sin, for He has cast it in the depths of the sea, and He remembers it no more. (see Mi 7:19).

So, where does that leave me? Through forgiving my offender, I am accepting Jesus' payment to me to right the wrong the other has done to me. He never commands us to do anything He does not empower us to do. He invited us: "Come unto Me all ye who are weary and heavy laden, and I will give you rest. Take My yoke upon you and learn of Me for ... My yoke is easy, and My burden is light" (Mt 11:28-30). As we come to Jesus, He will heal our wounds and we will be free of these burdens.

But there is more. If I accept Jesus' payment, I find that He is much more generous than I can imagine. When I accept His payment, I give up the right to hold anything against the offender. What are the benefits?

1. The cycle is finally broken. The sin is paid for, it is dead, powerless, and cannot torment me any longer.
2. The emotional drain of anger and hatred is stopped. I have new energy, health, and joy.
3. I can see Your goodness more clearly because I look for the ways You are blessing me.
4. My own sins can be forgiven, and I need not live in guilt.
5. I have a new ability to love because I have experienced more of Your infinite, unconditional love.
6. In future situations, I can quickly crucify that sin, accept Your payment, and avoid being continually victimized.
7. You will reveal more and more of the benefits as I continue in Your love and forgiveness.

The only way, then, to stop the vicious cycle is through forgiveness. I realized that You, Father God, revealed this to me not just for the sake of my friend but also for my own hurts and those of other friends that still require forgiveness.

But my forgiveness cannot simply be a one-time statement. Each time I remember the hurt, I have to re-forgive until the memory no longer hurts. This can take a long time, but God blesses our efforts and does indeed heal us.

*****

In my spiritual life, I often faltered and failed, and then thought I needed to start back at the beginning. I was constantly upset with myself for neglecting personal prayer. The Lord had to show me that I could not measure my relationship with Him on my own terms.

You measure wrong. It is not a ladder you are climbing that, if you miss a rung, you slide back to a previous low. It is a journey with hills and valleys. Progress is not measured in the height but in the distance traveled. There are peaks and there are depths, but I am with you through them all. Hold fast to My hand. Do not be discouraged. This is all part of My plan. As your earthly father has said, "Only those who work can make mistakes." Enjoy My love, approval, and pledge to stay with you, and continue the journey into My Kingdom. I have been nearer than you know. And you have more benefits than you can yet see. You have passed a dark night and the brightness of day now begins to dawn. Enjoy the dawn.

It is good that you know there are two kingdoms at work in your world vying for your attention. It is time for you to choose more often to give your attention to the Kingdom of God. You are defeated so often because your focus has come off of My Kingdom and you have been distracted by the kingdom that discourages, upsets, and tears you down. Remember that I do not do these things. I have come that you might have life and have it more abundantly. Choose Me and My ways. Choose to believe the good I give you rather than the evil you see in the world. Refuse to believe the discouraging thoughts that attack you. Look for My ways and thoughts and words. Come dwell continually in My Kingdom. When you find yourself on the outside, come back in. I do not shut you out. I invite you back over and over again.

*****

Lord, I have noticed that often when I confess my sins, I find I want to go back in a very short time because another sin has popped up.

This is My grace. The cleaner you are, the more obvious a spot or wrinkle becomes. This is progress in the spiritual life. But be careful here. I am the One who is cleansing you. I will show you your faults according to My plan. Do not meddle in My work. If you give in to introspection you can do more harm than good. Go on in My love.

I have been told that any sin manifests itself in action and I should focus on actions in confession to get to the root of the sin. I think I have been doing it backwards. I've been looking for the roots. It is hard to chop down a tree from the roots up with only a handsaw. Lord, let me start on the outermost branches. Open my eyes to the obvious and give me the grace to get rid of my obvious sins. While I was upset over my pride, I indulged myself in eating things I could have left alone, and I remained lethargic and inactive when there is much to be done around the house. Lord, You told me to stop worrying about what I ought or should do and focus on what I *can* and *will* do. This is why the road to hell is paved with good intentions. It is Satan's trick to get us so focused on the impossible that we ignore the obvious. Lord, this is a great and wonderful revelation, at least to me.

So, Lord, today open my eyes to the obvious things I can change. Let me *do* what I can and not worry about what I cannot. Let me begin with small things. Lord, I also see that You are teaching me things I need to know so that I will not feel so inadequate and undisciplined. The first lesson is that when I spend time in prayer, I can expect to gain something from the time invested. I need to come asking, seeking, and knocking, and expecting a reply, a finding, and an entrance. Lord, You have touched me deeply today. You have taught me, and with the teachable heart You have given me I was able to receive Your teaching. Let me put it into practice. Thank You, Lord!

I realized how spiritually weak I still am as a result of past sins. If some of those temptations were to come now, I could so easily fall into the same sins again. You showed me that this is why I need to make reparation for sin. Reparation repairs the weakness and instability caused by the fall into sin – sort-of like my ankle that was broken many years ago. The surgery and cast and therapy back when it happened fixed the break, but it was scarred and painful and not quite moving as well as it had before. Physical therapy now could give me back the range of motion I would want – that would be reparation. It could be painful but helpful. If I do not exercise through physical therapy now, my arthritis will make it more painful as time goes on. So, the surgery was like confession – the break is fixed. The cast and crutches and nine weeks of not walking on it were like penance. The physical therapy then and now is like reparation. Without reparation there is weakness and pain and an inability to fully function.

Lord, I have had a wrong impression of reparation. I somehow saw it as a debt we owed You because You were offended by our sins. I never thought of it as a repairing our own brokenness and weakness that is caused by sin. Thank You.

*****

In the fall of 1995, I restarted my teaching career with one Algebra I class each morning at Bishop Ireton High School where my youngest son, Steven, was beginning as a freshman. Since I needed to transport him to school daily, and I had a large van, I accepted several other students to transport them to and from the school. The mornings were not a problem as the parents dropped their kids off at my house, and we went straight to the school. But after two weeks of trying to be kind and accommodating, I found it was too difficult for me to take them all to their homes. I was driving for over two hours every afternoon, and then still had to go back to retrieve my own son from after-school activities.

Lord, today I need to get in touch with the parents of the students in my carpool to let them know I cannot continue to bring their kids home. Lord, I would like to be the accommodating mother hen who helps all, but You did not call me to be a bus driver. This has become burdensome and I believe it is because you do not will for me to take on this responsibility. I ask that in Your providence, You would give each family an alternative.

Maggie be assured that I am with you. I do know your heart and its ways. And I am purifying you. You know that all that is good comes from Me, but just because it seems good, it is not necessarily

My will for you. You have heard that the greatest enemy of the best is the good. This is an example. It is good to serve others by giving rides. It is good to serve well by taking them lovingly all the way to their houses. It is good to do all this without wanting much money for it. But it is not good that you have no time for your own responsibilities because you have to spend two to three hours on the road transporting other people's children.

Lord, this is a pattern of disordered activity for me. Many other times in the past as well as this "bus" thing, shows how I jump into things without thinking or asking You or anyone else. Then I find myself in a mess.

Maggie, this is true, but before you get too hard on yourself, see My love for you and My pleasure that you are not reluctant to do things you think might be My will – you are willing to take chances – only those who work make mistakes. You are looking for a big sin behind this. It was not your pride or anything bad that got you into this mess but using the talents and gifts I have given you. Remember that I prefer that you act rather than fail to act out of a fear of failure. This will pass and you will be wiser for it. Be patient with yourself.

*****

After having an opportunity to see the play "Beauty and the Beast" I prayed:

Lord, last night as I was about to go to sleep, I was thinking that spiritually, You, Jesus, are Beauty and we are the Beast. You tenderly teach us to be more human, or actually divine, and by redeeming us change us from our beastlike characteristics (sin) to be fit for You. Your love transforms us – it is not dependent on our perfection. Lord, continue to change me and draw out my love for You. Thank You that it depends more on You than me – You are so much more dependable.

*****

Sometimes the strangest thoughts lead to a revelation:

Lord Jesus, what a night! Thank You for getting me up at 2:30 and giving me such a marvelous time in Your Presence. Your love and care and gentleness and infinity overwhelmed me. The thought of infinity – that the Trinity has no limits, that I am created with a beginning but no end, in the image and likeness of God, that there is infinity in my future – You have to guide me through it. It was almost like the movie *Fantasia*. My mathematical background helped me visualize it all. First, a line – no beginning or end – that is You. Then a ray, with a beginning but no end – that is a human, such as me. Then the line became a plane and then all of space – no limits at all. But the ray could move around and explore space in many directions, always with a beginning but unlimited as long as it was directed by You. So good!

Last night you began to ponder darkness and light.

Lord, I did notice that when I first turned off the light, the darkness was great – very dark. The only thing I could see clearly was the time – the numbers lit up under the TV. As my eyes adjusted, the light from the street was enough that I could see to walk throughout the house without bumping into anything. This reminded me of Psalm 139 – that even darkness is not dark to You.

One of the thoughts was the necessity of darkness to bring out the brightness of the light. The night has its own lights, but they are different from the lights of day. This will all unfold. Just be aware of the lights and darknesses in your life.

*****

Lord Jesus, I need one of those long conversations with You where You explain things to me.

What would you like explained?

I'm not even sure of that. I have been reading about Your perfection, Your being and infinity, and the Trinity and such mysteries and I am once again like a puppy with its head cocked trying to understand, but not capable of understanding.

What do you do with a puppy that does not understand? How do you calm it?

By loving it and petting it.

You do not try to explain to it – it will not understand. But your love and gentleness – it does understand that, and the questioning soon ceases and is replaced by trust.

So, if I focus on Your love and gentleness, then I will no longer need answers or explanations, but a trust will develop that will be more satisfying than questions, answers, or explanations?

Yes.

So how do I focus on Your love?

Come and simply receive it. I will guide you. Be open, be quiet, be at peace. Let My love wash over you and do not be afraid.

I will try, Lord.

Thank You also for letting me know that I can again appreciate and enjoy silence, solitude, and most of all Your Presence. So now let me actually do that.

Don't sanctify it or fear it. Find a balance. See both activity and solitude as My gifts to you at different times. Enjoy both the silences and the noises in your life. I can be found in both. The key is to relax and enjoy whatever comes.

Abandonment, surrender, submission, and sacrifice all sound like negative words, but that is a limitation of the language. There is a freedom and a joy that comes with them that the world cannot see. My ways are not the world's ways. Look for the joy I tuck into all that the world considers undesirable. In that joy you will find Me calling you with great love.

Blessed are the poor in spirit, for theirs is the Kingdom of Heaven. When you are poor in spirit, you know that you have nothing of your own. You realize that everything you have has been given to you. You see the Kingdom of Heaven as the source of all the gifts you receive. And as you receive them, the Kingdom is yours. It is given to you – not all at once – just as you need it.

Blessed are those who mourn, for they shall be comforted. No one wants to mourn. It is not fun or pleasant. It involves pain – deep pain – pain that is so intense that it seems like it cannot be comforted.

But the comforting does come, little by little – a card, a flower, a dish of food, a prayer, a smile, any act of kindness gives comfort. And those who mourn and receive these acts of kindness are comforted. I have taught you to take comfort. You have learned to receive My gifts. It is important to be able to receive. I am behind every good gift given to you.

Lord Jesus, thank You. You have spoken and I have heard You. You have answered my prayer. I do thank You. Does love begin with gratitude? If so, I have begun to love You. And I am grateful for that as well.

My peace is your guide. This morning the wind was too strong outside. You came where you are sheltered and it is peaceful here – the wind is just as strong around you, but you are sheltered. Find that place of shelter in Me, that peace you now feel. The storms will come and go. But I will protect you as you stay close to Me. And I will guide you and you will do greater things yet, but not in your own power.

Lord, it seems so simple – all You want is that I should be happy! Truly happy – not just feelings of pleasure or comfort. True happiness involves accomplishing what is good, knowing it is good, the peace and joy of being loved by You, and confidence that with You all will eventually go well. I think today You have made me happy!

I am not hard to find. Be at peace.

*****

After a vacation visiting friends and family, the Lord asked:

What have you learned about love?

Well, I was surrounded by love most of the time – so much love expressed in so many ways – yet I was impressed by the fact that all love originates in You. You are Love, it is Your idea, and You are in every act or thought or word of love, those of others as well as those of mine. Whether we are aware of You or not, You are there.

That is a good lesson. It also follows that I am in all goodness and kindness, gentleness and peace and joy and patience, and faithfulness and self-control. I am there whether anyone is aware of My Presence or not.

Like You are in each tabernacle?

Exactly.

You are telling me not to worry so much about whether or not I am aware of Your Presence.

Right. Just enjoy it and take comfort in it when you do notice it – then the occasions of your awareness will increase. Now you can have many more ways of noticing. One who has never been taught that I am Present in the tabernacle would not be easily aware of My Presence there. But once having been taught and faith stirred up, from then on, every chapel and tabernacle has a new meaning. So it shall be with you now. You will find Me in many new and wonderful ways.

Thank You, Lord. I do see.

As I think about it, I see that the joy I have had in tutoring and crocheting and sewing are parts of Your loving me, and my delight and gratitude are parts of my loving You in return. Not exactly what I expected, but it is very good.

What were you expecting?

I really don't know. Some sort of warm fuzzy feelings, I think.

That does not last very long.

I see and agree. So, You are delighting me with work I enjoy, and I am delighting You by enjoying it. I think I'm getting a pretty good deal.

Does that surprise you?

Somewhat.

You are still expecting My love to be difficult or unpleasant.

I hate to admit to that. But life has its ups and downs. I guess I'm so ready for the downs that I am surprised by the ups.

The truth is you get both all the time – but when you are up, the downside does not seem very important, so you hardly notice it. The same is true when you are down – you tend to focus only on the negatives then and don't notice the good I also send into your life. Right now you have great pain, but also great joy. I am with you in both situations. I know both the pain and the uncertainties involved with all your physical conditions. But I do hold you every night, send you work you enjoy, and give you joy and peace and love.

Thank You, Lord. Is joy like love – a choice rather than a feeling? I've heard a favorite priest saying that when things look bleak, he gets joyful. That sounds like an act of the will.

Child, you are growing in understanding. Remember all the times you used to "choose to believe"? In the same way, you can choose to be joyful. The feeling may or may not be present. It is nice when it is there, but not necessary. Joy needs to be developed just as faith and love.

So, all the fruits of the Spirit are like that?

Certainly. You can be kind or good without a bit of feeling. But the feelings generally come once the will is engaged.

Lord, I need a lot of training. It seems all virtue is to be learned and drilled into one's thoughts and actions.

True. That is why I said I would never leave you. You cannot do this alone. It is why you have the Holy Spirit and the Church and angels and saints, and prayer. If My people could only see how many ways I have given them to grow in virtue!

Lord, I am undone! I am so sorry. I have not availed myself of all the help You have been giving me. My rebellion has put a block in my own path to holiness.

That is why it was so important to confess it. This, too, is a grace of the Sacrament.

I am beginning to see grace as something more real than I thought before. I kept hearing about all the graces we receive as a result of this or that good thing we do or experience, but I always took it as a nice sentiment – not anything real or helpful or truly valuable. Sort-of like perfume. Except for the grace of the Sacrament of Reconciliation – I appreciated that for some time. But You have been showering **graces** upon me all my life and I was clueless and unaware of all You were doing. Lord, how blind I have been!

Rejoice that you now see. Do not dwell on your past inability to understand these things but begin to not just *see* and *know* and *understand* but also *use* the gifts I give you.

Lord, I will need so much help!

Yes, you will. And I assure you that all you need, I will provide.

So once again, how can I sufficiently thank You?

By using My gifts. And a simple "thank You" is good, too.

Thank You, Lord.

*****

Chapter 6

PLEASING GOD

I sometimes see myself as a wild horse. When I asked God into my life, I was wandering aimlessly and kicking and scared and easily hurt. When He came, He had to put blinders on me and a harness and a saddle. He had to restrict my vision and my movements. For many years, I did not know where He was leading me, but I got used to His leading and learned that I did not get hurt as much when I let Him lead me. As I stopped fighting Him, I could receive His gifts and His love. As I grew to trust Him, He became so kind and loving and gentle that now all I want is to be with Him and be led by Him.

At one point, He took off the blinders for a little while and showed me how far we have come – and it amazed me. He also showed me our destination and that it is much nearer than I imagined. But I am not to go trotting to the destination any way I see fit. I am waiting for the blinders and harness and all to be put back so we can continue on our journey. I don't see them as restriction or punishment any more, but comfort and protection so I won't need to see the dangers ahead – He will see them and guide me safely through.

*****

Lord, I'm sure You've been giving me the affection I need, but I've been too distracted to notice. I want to please You, but I don't stop trying long enough to let You affirm me. I want to avoid needing to be corrected so much that I burn myself out. Why am I so afraid of Your correction when You have always been loving and kind? I have often said how even Your rebuke is wonderful because it is so filled with Your love and the power to overcome whatever is the problem. But now I'm trying so hard to do everything just right. I know I will fail; I seem to be setting myself up for a fall. Help, Lord, I don't make sense.

Let me let You be God, and me be Your servant or child or bride or whatever You want me to be. Let me stop trying to anticipate Your wishes and let You make them known to me. In fact, Lord, let me stop my rambling, and give You a chance to speak to me, or love me, or even give Your beloved sleep. Lord, I love You the best I know how. Please teach me to do it better.

Maggie, today I am speaking to you. You have cried out for help and today I answer you. Do not speak, just listen and obey. Today I, the Lord Your God, will touch you again and again. Just listen for My voice throughout the day. Today I will take the initiative and guide you through the day.

OK Lord, even though it's raining, I'm feeling great because You have started my day.

Maggie, now is the time to put the revelation about the rivers of living water to use. I have given you a drop of water by waking you up and speaking to you. You can take that drop, and try to hang on to it by running off and being elated that I spoke to you, but I am calling you to come back to me for more. The river shall not run dry. I have more to give you. Yes, I speak, and I expect you to obey. But after you have obeyed, I am ready to speak again, and I want to bless you for your obedience. Even your dog expects some acknowledgement when he has done what he was told. And you gladly give it to him. Allow Me to express My joy to you. Do you not know that I have created you for My pleasure? Yet you rob Me of My pleasure when you do not receive My thanks, approval, joy, and love. If you only see My hand of correction on you and not My gentle love and care, then it is no wonder that you avoid Me and fail continually. I know you were raised to do good without expecting to be repaid. But that is only half of the story. You are not to expect repayment from human sources, but from Me. I will repay!!! But just as with the water I give you: you do not have to stand in line for it, you do not have to be satisfied with just a drop when I have rivers to give, you do not have

to earn it, you do not need to be afraid of taking too much. It is with My approval, My love, My power, and My joy. They are yours at any time without limits or strings

*****

Lord, there are many things I do not understand. I guess there always will be. But right now, I wonder what good offering myself and everything that happens during the day – what good is it? I don't doubt that I should do it, but I wonder if it makes any difference. I've given myself to You already and whatever happens during the day is more Your gift to me than mine to You.

Maggie, you need to renew your commitment to walk in My ways daily. You need to give Me back your life daily because you have the tendency to give Me things and then take them back by worrying, or trying to fix things on your own, or even by inactivity. When you offer individual parts of your day to Me as a gift or as a sacrifice, you show Me love. Your love takes shape and form in these gifts and thus grows. One of your greatest complaints and fears is that you don't feel you love Me enough and that you might turn away when it really matters, as did the rich young man. As you offer Me each day and as you give Me each trial or joy or sorrow, I transform them into the most precious gifts you could possibly give. This is one way you must be like a little child. Give Me gifts often and see your love for Me grow. Know that I accept every gift from you with love and delight. I will never grow tired of them, belittle them, or refuse them.

*****

Lord, I had said a few days ago that I wanted to know Your approval of me. Today You showed me a picture of You looking down on me and saying, **"Look at Maggie, isn't she doing well?"**, sort of like the beginning of the book of Job. The other picture was also of You, Father, looking down on me with pleasure, but I was holding the hand of Jesus and simply following wherever He led me. And then came the question: "Which approval would you prefer?" Lord, I choose dependence over independence. I choose to hold Your hand and follow You rather than trying to make my way alone.

Maggie, do not expect major changes overnight. I know your weaknesses and I am patient with you. Be patient with yourself. Progress comes in small victories. But as they build on each other, you will see more. Keep holding My hand and keep coming to Me several times a day, as you have been. Write when you can write, pray as you can. None of it is wasted. Yesterday you had to deal with a difficult person. Many people are unreasonable, proud, arrogant – who try to control and browbeat others. I find your dependence and desire to be led by Me refreshingly delightful. I know you are not yet perfect – but a humble, contrite heart does wonders to My heart. Maggie, I love you and I am and will continue to be with you. I will not let go of you. Hang on.

*****

Lord, You told us that You are forming us into a holy people who will not look to the left or to the right but will follow You. You also told us that there is a wall of fear that keeps us from yielding to Your power. I recognized that fear, and the fear that no matter what I do I will not be good enough. Lord, I give You these fears. I realize they come from my youth where praise was unknown and criticism was constant. Lord, *You* do not criticize me, but I still expect it. When it does not come from You, I provide it myself.

So, Lord, I forgive my family for the rejection and criticism I suffered from for many years and I choose to trust You to teach me truth in my inward being. You have the freedom to correct me when I am wrong or need correction – for I do desire to become holy – but You also praise, commend, or thank me when I do something You approve or like. Lord, I desperately want to please You, but seldom give You the opportunity to express Your pleasure. I expect You to be more concerned with my sins than with my efforts or accomplishments of goodness. I have a negative outlook, and expect You to be like me. Lord, cleanse me of my negativism. Let me see my life as You see it. Let me accept and enjoy Your pleasure in me and let me continue to increase Your pleasure. You told me tonight that I am precious in Your eyes. Thank You, Lord, that

You look at the positive. Let me see myself as precious also. Help me to keep this focus and outlook, that I might be totally healed of rejection and fear, and I might cling to You and come closer and closer to You until that union we both desire is achieved.

My dear, dear Maggie, your heart was doing cartwheels for joy. The negativism of your upbringing has disposed you to think only in terms of displeasing your God – never in terms of pleasing Him. It is a marvelous change of focus to begin to dwell on the ways to please Me rather than avoid displeasing Me. This is the beginning of the healing of your heart – to make you aware that you have the power and ability to give pleasure to your God – often – easily. You cannot displease Me while you are pleasing Me. This is the beginning of loving Me as I deserve. Know that it is possible – possible for you. Now. Not only in some distant future when everything is better, but now, as you are – here, in this state of life.

I call you to love and to build up. Do not be discouraged at the difficulties or the long time it takes to see progress. Remember that destruction is quick but construction is slow. But building up, healing, and creating are the works I do and want you to do as well. My Father created all that is good. He is still continuing to create. I have redeemed and brought forgiveness – I continue to do so. I did only what I saw My Father doing – look to Me and do the same. Buildup, forgive, love. In this you will participate in My Father's creating of good and My redeeming of the world. No act of kindness or tenderness is too small. It may not seem like it does much, but it is a part of the building up, healing, creative work of your God, in which you are called to participate.

*****

I asked You, Father, that I might come to You and really know You the way You are – not as I have imagined You. And I saw myself as a child in my Father's arms with my head on Your shoulder – held gently and comfortably to the point that I – the child – fell asleep in Your arms. And You gently laid me in my bed and stood back and lovingly watched and admired me as I slept. Then I saw You looking at me as I was a young woman about to be married. And You looked at me with love and admired my beauty. And I saw You look at me now and You were so pleased that I would seek You with my whole heart and that I was willing to do anything to reach You. So, the walls of resistance within me crumbled, that I could know I have a Father Who knows how to love me. I rejoiced. I left that time of prayer so grateful that You had touched me.

*****

With fear and trembling, I asked You how You see me. But You are so patient and kind that You waited until all my courage was summoned.

Maggie, do you really want to know?

Yes, Lord, I suppose I do.

I see you as a bride being outfitted in a beautiful lace gown – young, radiant, and very much in love. And all the lace is not fully attached to your gown, but it is almost finished.

Is this really how You see me? What about my faults and failings?

I will perfect you – I do not see your sins or flaws, but I see the beauty I poured into You. Is it so hard for you to believe that I approve of you?

It fills me with wonder and awe, that You approve of me.

I do not ask anything impossible of you, Maggie. I appreciate and approve all your attempts to please Me, serve Me, and show your love for Me.

You are just beginning to recall My tender, gentle love for you. You had lost that focus and have turned your eyes on yourself. You want to love Me, but how can you if you only see your own shortcomings? In trying so hard to please Me, you convince yourself that it is difficult. Bring your focus off yourself and back on Me. I continue to bless you and strengthen you.

*****

Lord Jesus, thank You for Your great power and love. You had said You wanted to do inner healing, and I had memories that came to me that seemed to be candidates for inner healing. As I think about it, You seem to be telling me that forgiveness on my part is what is necessary to complete that inner healing. This makes so much sense. Does this mean that I am yielding more to Your power? Am I getting free? I need more of You and less of me.

Maggie, do not worry. The great amount of self-consciousness you used to have is being replaced by your desire to be totally immersed in Me. You used to lament how great your self-centeredness was. Now you can rejoice – your capacity for God-centeredness is very great. Whatever the sin or imperfection you find within you is the raw material I have to work with to transform you. Great pride yields to great humility. Great unbelief to great faith. Great fear to great trust and great love. Do not think your inner healing is complete – keep coming to Me for more. Just because you no longer feel the pain of those wounds, it does not mean I am finished. Each scar is to be transformed into glorious virtue. This is why I ask you to give Me your fears and hurts and sins and pain. You have never understood what I would possibly want with all that. Now you see. I take what you give Me and transform it to beauty and glory and praise and joy. Rejoice – Your God is working.

Lord God, how can I thank You enough?

By allowing Me to do this work in you and showing others that this is My desire. Now you can see faults and sins in a new light. They are greater capacity for virtue and beauty. My desire to heal is so much greater than you can imagine. Your yielding to My power is the beginning of such great things. Just as salvation must be accepted and received, this transformation must be allowed through forgiveness. It is the key to such glorious work as few have dared to imagine.

Lord, this is true meat – great nourishment. Thank You.

Yes, it is no longer just milk for babies, but something you can sink your teeth into and devour. Do it. Digest it. Grow from it. I have nurtured you and found you ready for greater things. Contemplate it – discuss it. It is good.

*****

There is one other thing. In the Gospel yesterday, You spoke of us being no longer slaves but friends (Jn 15:15). It seems to be a big adjustment. I seem to have trouble with it.

So now are you finally ready to listen?

I hope so. But I do get distracted easily.

I know. First of all, know that your God is pleased with you.

You are?

Yes, I am. I do see your struggles and your desires and frustrations. But you always come back to Me to search out My will. I will make it very clear to you. Right now, you know what you must do. When the time comes, it will be clear what changes can and need to be made. Do not be afraid of missing My plan. It will emerge and you will be delighted to follow it. As for the change from servant to friend – it, too, will work out. Be at peace. I am with you. I do guide you and protect you and hold you close. Come to Me more often, even if it is just a glance.

*****

Lord, during the night I got up to give medicine to my sick family members. And You showed me that it was a self-sacrifice, small as it was, to get up and bring it to them. In that little action, I sensed Your approval and paused to accept it. I believe You want me, at least for a while, to pause and feel Your pleasure and approval until I am convinced that it is possible to please You, that none of my efforts to do so are unnoticed or unappreciated by You, and that I am capable of being a God-pleaser. This must go deep into my being to replace the lie that nothing I do is good enough. This is hard for me.

You have provided me with a multitude of opportunities to be of service and to do kind deeds for a variety of people. And I have enjoyed doing them.

Lord, did I do well? Have I pleased You in being kind and patient and loving? Is there something I missed or should have done instead? Am

I being too much of a "Dorothy Do-gooder"? Am I being a busybody? Is my pride getting out of control again? Or am I truly following You and doing the things You want me to do and loving like You love Your people? Lord, one day I almost felt that You were saying "thank you" to me for all the things I did for others. But I am so afraid of pride rearing its ugly head again that I question these things. Yet if You were not pleased with me, You have ways of letting me know. So, until You tell me otherwise, I can conclude that I am doing well, that You are pleased with me, and that it is You who are providing me with both the opportunities for service and the strength, time, and patience to serve. Lord, let me continue, and please take each act of kindness as a gift to You. You said You would never reject my gifts, but cherish them. So here I am, Your servant, ready to do Your will. Lord, if You are indeed thanking me, You are more than welcome. It has certainly been my pleasure. All I ask of You is that You hold me real tight and don't let me go.

*****

In January of 2001, I was still teaching high school full-time, being caregiver for my mother-in-law, Mom E., who had Alzheimer's, and had been widowed for over 4 years. I had not given up my dream of being a nun so I wanted to check out the Visitation Sisters in Washington D.C. to see if perhaps I could join them when the time was right. They invited me to spend a day with them, and since Christmas break had not yet ended and I had someone to care for Mom E. during the day, I accepted their offer.

Lord, it seems I'm on a one-day retreat. I am to observe the rhythm of life here and spend time in prayer. I am on the 4th floor in the retreatants' lounge. There is also a little chapel here. I got here for only part of morning prayer and then Mass. The sisters are very outgoing and hospitable. Lord, I like it here so far. I need to be downstairs at 11:30 for midday prayers and then a dinner.

So, it's You and me, Lord. The message at Mass was that You have a plan. I want to fit into Your plan. If it is here, that would be fine – if not, then I trust You to show me where.

Midday prayer and dinner were very good. My fears are unfounded. The thought that these prayers – the Liturgy of the Hours – are said all over the world by many congregations – what a uniting force! I thought it would de-personalize prayer, but instead it adds a marvelous dimension of unity and brotherhood and solidarity. Wow!

Maggie, you see that I will guide you. Wherever you go, I will be there. You will find Me and be amazed at the new and wondrous ways I will teach you. You have nothing to fear at all. Your biggest challenge will be the waiting.

I can see that. I would gladly move in today, but that does not seem to be Your will.

Everything in good order and proper time.

I understand. And I agree as well. But thank You for this day. I was not expecting a retreat, but what a wonderful way to begin a new year. You know, Lord Jesus, I was beginning to run dry and wear out. You saw that and gave me this day to re-focus and re-charge through prayer. You knew I wouldn't do that on my own. You provided for my needs even before I realized I had them. What a marvelous gift! Thank You!

See, I do have a few tricks up my sleeve. I delight in surprising you. And your delight in being surprised is your gift to Me. Come, spend an hour in pure prayer of presence. Just come and stay with Me – and I will stay with you.

I come, Lord.

*****

An hour in Your Presence without stress – a bit of dozing – yet Your love does its work. Your peace has enveloped me once again – the apostolates of caring for Mom E. and teaching seem possible again – not a chore or a burden, but a *ministry*! Gifts from You to me and back from me to You. You allow me to do them, and my joy and willingness in doing them is my gift back to You. How rich You have made me, that I can give such marvelous gifts to my King. And to know that my gifts are acceptable and cherished! My love for You is indeed growing – thank You. I feel about seven years old – having reached the age of reason yet not quite in control of it – still full of wonder and awe and love and gratitude – wanting to please You and delighted to be able to.

You come to Me as a little child?

Yes, and that, too, is an unexpected marvelous gift You have given me.

And your delight makes it all the more marvelous a gift you are giving back to Me. Once again you came to Me expecting to wait tables at the wedding feast – and once again you find yourself being the bride. This is such a pleasure to Me to surprise you like this.

So how do I get to give You surprise presents? It's kind of tricky with You being all-knowing. But I think I have some ideas – I'll talk to Your Mother. Lord Jesus, I have really had fun with You today. You pretty much had to catch me off-guard and plan a day like this or I would have messed it up. No heaviness, no stress – just Your love. I didn't have to do anything but I got to do a lot. Thank You again.

*****

Lord, I need to focus on You better. You gave me many Scriptures that showed me that I *must* keep my eyes on You and not on my circumstances. You assured me that You will again use me and that I will be much more effective because of what You are teaching me now. This now is Your discipline. Let me submit and learn well. I desire to please You. Teach me what pleases You.

Maggie, your desire to please Me pleases Me. Your turning to Me during temptation pleases Me. You are asking Me what to do next pleases Me. Your gratefulness pleases Me. Yes, your service also pleases Me. Your willingness to pray in the middle of the night pleases Me. Your desire to become consecrated to Me pleases Me. Your care for your mother-in-law pleases Me. Your bearing the pain of the illness pleases Me. Even your crocheting pleases Me.

Lord, if I am pleasing You, why do I feel so desolate and useless?

Because you are measuring yourself by earthly standards. There is only one standard you need to use. Are you doing My will? If the answer is "yes," then you are pleasing Me. If the answer is "no," then stop it and turn back to Me. It is not difficult. It is even easier when

you keep a running dialogue with Me through the day. Work at this. It will help you find Me in all things and situations. You are clean now. Stay that way. But if you should fall, turn back to Me quickly. I will always receive you back.

I appreciate your focus on Me. I came to the earth in human form so you could relate to your God. I experienced joys and sorrows as you do. Yet there is something I appreciate even more about you. So many of My people only see acts of God as the unfortunate destructive forces of nature. But you see My work in the beauty of each sunrise or sunset, in the smile of a child, in the love of the invalid, in the strength you did not expect to bear the troubles and sorrows that come your way. You do not blame Me – you ask for My strength, wisdom, and mercy. You thank Me in good times and in bad times as well. You are grateful for the big things and the little things. You notice My blessings more and more. Your willingness to learn to forgive, to hold no grudges, to take no revenge – these also bless Me. You see how much I appreciate this? Know that as you continue to love Me these ways you are giving Me the presents I value the most. Yes, I also value your kindness to others, but My own heart is blessed by this relationship that is growing so beautifully. I delight in blessing you – I love the reaction you give Me when you receive My gifts to you. Thank you for seeing so much more of what I do for you. Thank you for looking for My grace and strength when yours wears out. Thank you for your gratefulness. It truly blesses My heart.

*****

Is it not wonderful that you can give glory to your God; that your praise brings a smile to your Father's face? You have the ability to please your God. He is not hard to please. He rejoices even at your feeblest attempts to please Him. He waits for your attention. He is delighted when you give it to Him. Even the small moments when you glance toward Him are precious to Him. You have great power to please your God.

*****

I am seeking and finding a more perfect, intimate, and complete union with God. But the more I get, the more I want, so it doesn't seem like I'm making much progress except that I am generally happier and more content despite all the activity in my life.

*****

Lord, I felt Your approval. I felt that You are pleased with me overall. Not that I couldn't improve many things, but for now, You are happy with me – perhaps even proud of me. Lord, I thank You for that. I really need Your affirmation and approval. Lord, I'm loving You more than I ever did before, and it feels good. I'm not yet to the point that I'm constantly aware of Your presence, or that I pay attention to You all the time, but it's better than it used to be and I'm grateful. I see Your hand in many things in my life, and I can appreciate Your workings. I am extremely tired now. I want to go to sleep feeling the warmth of Your love and approval. Thank You for such a great day.

*****

Lord, as I am finishing this time of prayer, I see a need and intense desire – so intense that it becomes almost a demand – similar to the desire for unity with You – this desire for purity and cleansing that there be no evil left within me at all. I want to be totally pleasing to You. I want to be washed, scrubbed, peeled – anything to get rid of all that sin which robs You of Your glory and robs me of the union I so desperately want. I want to be so much a part of You that I become invisible, doing only what You do, wanting only what You want, moving exactly when and as You move. I want holiness and discipline and order. Lord, if this is also what You want – and I believe it is – then You have a *big* job ahead of You. I have no idea how You are going to accomplish it, but I do know that You are faithful and able to finish whatever You start. I am the work of Your hands. Lord, do whatever it takes, and let it be done according to Your most perfect will. Please help me avoid getting in Your way or hindering the process. Show me how to cooperate fully with You, while totally resisting Satan's tactics. Usually I resist You and cooperate with Satan. Help me in turning this around (repenting). Thank You, Lord.

*****

Everything we need to become holy is hidden in our state in life. I'm beginning to see this. I do not need to go out to the streets to find people to feed or help. I simply need to do the best job I can in being wife, mother, housekeeper, friend, teacher, chauffeur, or whatever You give me to do.

You prefer obedience to sacrifice, yet obedience often requires some degree of sacrifice. Lord, keep my ears tuned to Your voice. Let me be attentive to You and respond to both Your commands and Your love. Let me allow You to get close enough to me.

*****

The other night I had an overwhelming sense of my nothingness. Yet it wasn't negative – it just seemed like plain truth. Then there is a Psalm that expressed it – how all of humanity put together is no more than a breath, and yet You love us so much as to become part of our nothingness to raise us to infinite worth. Today is the feast of the Annunciation – the Incarnation – You becoming one of us through the faith and willingness of Your Mother. It wasn't her idea; she simply cooperated. It was Your Father that so loved the world to send You, His only-begotten Son, out of love. Nothingness, yet infinite worth, because of love. And it has nothing to do with our worthiness or lack of it. We did not originate our creation or our redemption. Neither can we originate our sanctification. All we can do is cooperate. There is total surrender in that cooperation. So hard for us – for me. But as long as You don't give up on me, neither will I give up trying to give up my will for Yours. Right now, I surrender the best I can, and for just now, I pray with You, "Not my will but Thine be done." I don't promise You any more than just now. I have failed too often in my promises.

Lord, I recognize that this is Your marvelous grace, Your gift to me, to be able to surrender to Your will. But it seems to be no more than a theory, so I do not know what this means in my physical existence. What part of my will am I surrendering? What of Your will am I accepting? It is easy to say, "Not my will but Thine be done," but I will need grace to act when the circumstances of my life require such action.

*****

Lord, last night I realized that the difficulties we endure are nothing compared to the ones You endure from your people. We rob You of the delights we used to give You when we were more fervent, and saw that all good comes from You. We truly need You to rekindle our first love in our hearts. We have grown too used to Your work in our lives, and hardly notice it any more. Yet You continue to love and care for us, and continually invite us to come closer to You. Forgive me, Lord, for all the ways I have withdrawn from You. Help me to come back, be more ardent in my love for You, and offer You my gratitude and awareness of Your greatness and goodness.

Thank You that You care about even trivial matters. You see all the affairs of men: big ones, important ones, and small and insignificant ones as well. You are not too busy with more important matters to listen to me. You even delight in my coming to You. Lord, I want You to purify me so that I can delight You even more and serve You better, and be able to do more to please You. I earnestly desire to know, love, and serve You better – much better.

*****

Lord, I come before You to ask that I might enter into the stream of Your grace and love and will. Not on the shallow edges, but in the midst of the current of Your will that Your desire should carry me to wherever You want me. Father, I ask that You would show me ways that I can please You and that You would again give me an awareness of Your approval and delight in me. Lord, You have given me a desire to bring balance and order and temperance into my life. Fulfill that desire by clearly showing me the small steps and actions that I can take to achieve these goals. Let each time I choose to act in a way that brings order be a gift I give You that is pleasing in Your sight.

*****

I can paraphrase a character's sentiment from the movie *Chariots of Fire*: You made me a teacher, I teach well, and when I teach, I feel Your pleasure. You have given me the gift of concentrating on each individual student and how he or she is receiving the subject. You give me different ways of explaining the concepts – and You give me opportunities to tell them about You. Thank You, Lord, for using me this way and for the joy it brings me and my students and their families. Please continue to give me strength and inspiration as I go through this day.

*****

I had looked up every reference I could find on "worship," for I desire to worship You, Lord, in a way that is acceptable in Your sight. But You showed me that my awe and wonder at Your works and my thanksgiving and even my coming here to spend time in Your Presence is all part of my worship. You approve and accept my love, and in the process, I am being perfected.

You also are a work of Mine – delicate and intricate. And My pleasure – yes, awe and wonder – is when such a being chooses to turn to Me in love and adoration. This is the reason for My creation. It is why I call it all good. The evil and ugliness is no surprise. But the love, the peace, the joy, the beauty of souls that follow Me – that is what warms My heart.

*****

Maggie, I delight in your prayers. It is good for you to tell Me all that concerns you. I have been blessing you and will continue to do so. Do not forget that I am still God. I can work through joy or sorrow, plenty or famine, good government or bad government, holy and unholy leaders, pleasure or pain, all sorts of weather, every situation. Do your part, and leave the rest to Me. I do understand all of your concerns. Open your eyes and see the wonders I shall do. I continue to provide for your every need. My love for you is much greater than you can imagine. Stay at peace. I am here.

*****

Lord Jesus, thank You so much for this morning. As I was lying in my empty bedroom with all but my bed removed for the painting, I started envisioning new ways to arrange the old furniture. A creativeness and freshness overcame me. It is as if some part of me is coming back to life, not bound by the way things always have been, but with new possibilities. Then I got up and, as I did the Morning Prayer, found that today is the feast of Your Transfiguration. How appropriately wonderful! And as I went through the readings and intercessions, somehow, I imagined myself dancing with You.

*****

Shortly after entering the convent with the Little Sisters of Jesus and Mary, I became terribly homesick.

I am feeling very guilty that I have been neglecting You. I am also feeling lonesome and homesick and wishing I could hold those I love at home. But even if I were at home, that would not be likely. So here I am, before Your tabernacle, needing Your love and care and wanting to love You the way I love my family.

You're not really sure what you are feeling, just that it isn't the way you want to feel.

That's pretty much it, Lord. I don't know what I want, but I want something I don't seem to have.

No, you do have it, but you don't see or feel it. You want My love, which you do have, but for it to satisfy you, you want it in a form you recognize as love.

Yes, I think that may be what my problem is.

You have skipped prayers lately – and are again doubting your love for Me.

That is also true. I don't know if I am rationalizing that the things I do for others are as good as praying, or if I'm simply failing in my devotion to You. I sort-of enjoyed missing Morning prayer today and Evening prayer the previous two days. Yet I don't mind the prayers. It does not make sense.

You were expecting maybe it should?

I guess I was. But I should know by now that I don't always make sense.

I can handle that. I can love you even if you don't make sense. I can love you through your tears even if you don't even know why you cry. It is good that you are here. As much as you wish you could hold your kids as you did when they were small, I want to hold you. I know your pains, your fears, your uncertainties, and I also know your strengths and your abilities. I am not disappointed with you.

*****

Lord, how do You want me to spend this time with You? How can I console Your heart?

You already have. By listening and being willing to take instruction, you give Me great joy. You have honored Me tonight in coming to Me and honestly presenting what you saw as a problem in your life. And you showed your love for Me by your willingness to obey. I do not require hours of meaningless words. There are times when I will call you to pray without actually understanding the prayer – I will understand it and that is enough – but right now that is not My desire for you. Relax. I will not require more of you than you are able to give. I do not find fault with your generosity. I only want for you exactly what you have cried for through many years – perfect union – total union with Me. It is impossible without a continual awareness of Me. I am a good and gentle teacher. You will learn. Do not be afraid.

*****

How can we ever appreciate Your sacrifice enough? Will we even realize the magnitude of what You have done? How can we properly respond?

Maggie, you are beginning to see clearly. You also know My mercy and love. You know I do not ask for the impossible. I want you to come to Me daily. I want you to simply spend time with Me.

You need no eloquence or great agenda. Just come and sit with Me. If you have nothing to say, say nothing. If you have something to say, go ahead and say it. If you have questions, ask them. But come. I have removed all external obstacles. The internal ones will also go. This is a time of grace and learning for you. Grace because the obstacles have been removed. Learning because, if you persist, you will learn to come to Me easily even when the obstacles come back. Feel My hand upon you. I have set you apart for this purpose. What you have seen as exile, I gave you for your healing. The illness was simply My grace to help you stop the destructive ways in which you were heading. Now your weakness and loneliness are My grace to cause you to come to Me, that I can become your All in All. You once wondered if you had any beauty at all. Then you thought you had lost it all. Your King still desires your beauty. I see the beauty of a soul filled with grace. I see a repentant heart. I see an effort to please and a desire to love and serve. This to Me is true beauty that only grows more radiant with age.

Lord God, You are so good to me. All I can do is offer You my life – I've done it before and I do it again.

*****

Lord, I really want to honor You.

Just your taking the time to pray honors Me.

Once again, You take me by surprise. You treat me so well, as if I were a celebrity or someone important. It seems backwards – I should feel honored that You allow me in Your Presence – but You say *my* presence honors You. Your ways are definitely different – marvelous, but different. So, if my just coming to You in prayer honors You, let me do so more. What a privilege to honor the Living God! I have always loved to make others feel good – but to be able to make You feel good or honored, that is such a powerful concept.

Maggie, here is another one. When you love Me, I feel loved.

I'm trying to imagine that.

You can. You have often felt loved. It is a good feeling.

Yes, I know – but that brings me to Your love. Could taking time to *feel* Your love and enjoy it be a good and acceptable response to it? I've always felt that my response to Your love was so inadequate. I respond better to my cat than I do to You.

You see, you are learning. Yes! That is a great response, and it stirs up your own love for Me. This generates a marvelous cycle. Not all cycles have to be vicious.

Lord, there is a big smile on my face.

Mine, too.

*****

Lord Jesus, due to a cold, both sleep and breathing are difficult right now, so I thought the best use of this time would be to spend it with You. I've been wanting to spend time with You, but it seems wanting and doing are different. Oh, I've been praying regularly the formal prayers, the Morning and Evening prayer, but none of that seems personal enough. I've been saying other devotional prayers, but these don't satisfy me either. I guess that's the problem – I'm trying to satisfy *me*. Could You change that in me? Get my focus off me and put it on You? To try to satisfy You, not me.

*****

After an illness when I could not attend Daily Mass, I was so happy to be well enough to be able to return.

Maggie, I, too, am delighted to have you here. I told you that all you need is a desire to love Me. You have had this desire for a very long time – and now that you have not been able to attend daily Mass the desire has blossomed. This is very pleasing to My Father. You have asked, "Father, make us One." You are already seeing this fulfilled. It is the Father's desire to make all His children One. Today you saw your life as a tiny bubble. As your life touches another life, each bubble joins the other, and the two bubbles become one larger one. As others join, the bubble becomes larger. The unity is in knowing

and understanding more. Yet the most important unity you need is to be One with your Triune God. You saw the deep devotion of many others this morning. Their devotion to Me touched you. It touches Me, too. It is that devotion to the Trinity and to My Mother that also unites. It is good. It is very good.

*****

It is marvelous to consider myself Your bride again. That is what I want to be. You allowed me to see myself that way many years ago, but at that time Rae was still living, and I did not understand. Then when I was accepted as a postulant with the Little Sisters, I thought that was the way it would happen. But when I was sent home, I was confused again. With the Consecrated Widows, I thought I had another chance. Now that I have heard a teaching on the Mass as the Marriage Supper of the Lamb, I am beginning to dare to think of myself as Your bride once again.

Maggie, I could not leave you thinking that your husband had to die for you to become My bride. The marriage I desire with you is spiritual – not physical. It is in a different realm than human marriage. But there is sufficient similarity that it is a good image of My relationship with you. Whether or not you are married on a human level does not affect the reality or possibility of your spousal relationship with Me. Be at ease about that. The intimacy I desire with you is beyond human marriage – but a human marriage that is centered on Me is enhanced and also enhances the spiritual relationship. As you come to Me regularly, you will see and understand better. Do not be afraid to enter into this relationship. You have felt that it is very near. You need not be afraid. It is good.

Lord, it is so good that I can please You. That is a definition of love – the desire to please the Beloved. Lord, I have had this desire for a long time.

And I have accepted your love. Now you need to see that I also desire to please you. Love is not a one-way street.

Lord, I humbly accept Your love as well. The thought of You wanting to please me is difficult for me to comprehend.

I know. But it is time you allowed yourself to relate to Me as you truly are – you are no longer simply a child of God – though you will always be that – but now you are also My spouse. Your consecration is a reality.

I have only looked at my consecration as accepting new duties.

I know. But it is much more than that. It is a relationship of love – both ways. Every time you thank Me for anything, you need to see that I have succeeded in pleasing you. And every time you pray or speak or act kindly to someone, you need to understand that you succeeded in pleasing Me.

Lord, I thought I knew much more about love than I do.

It is delightful to Me that you are still willing to learn.

So, I have pleased You again?

Indeed.

*****

Maggie, you desire to please Me. What you don't seem to realize is that what you desire is already taking place. Your love, your desire to please Me, does please Me. Believe it! Trust Me to let you know if you need correction. But in the meanwhile, enjoy your Father's pleasure and relax in My love.

*****

Thank You, Lord, that You are perfecting me. Please help me to cooperate and keep coming back to You even when I have failed. Also let me come to You in thanksgiving when I have done well, for it is only by Your grace that I can make any progress in holiness. That is what You desire for me, and I so greatly desire it as well.

*****

Lord Jesus, this morning I came to You and it was a marvelous time of communion. You took over, and I was able to stay in the fellowship of the Holy Trinity. You assured me that this is the union I have sought for so much of my life, and it was indeed what I desired. The song, "You gave me beauty for ashes, the oil of joy for mourning, a garment of praise for the spirit of heaviness, that I might be a tree of righteousness, the planting of You, Lord, that You might be glorified" (paraphrasing Isaiah 61:3), came to me, and it touched me that, when You give gifts to me, I am blessed but You are glorified. Lord, it is such a privilege to glorify You.

*****

Chapter 7

CREDIT TO GOD'S NAME

Once I had car troubled, took the car to the nearest service station, the mechanic fixed it, and presented me with the bill, which I paid. When I got home, I realized that the bill was incorrect. It said $5.71 when it should have said $57.10. I quickly returned to the gas station, found the mechanic, and explained that there was a problem with the bill. He was expecting me to complain, but when I explained that he did not charge me enough, he exclaimed, "You are a Christian!" I replied that I was, indeed, a Christian, and did not want to cheat him. This experience showed me how great it is to be a credit to God's Name.

*****

A few years later, I was following the Spiritual Exercises of St. Ignatius, and was praying, usually at night, realizing how far I was from where I would like to be.

Lord, I want to thank You for the way You have been speaking to me through the night. I am seeing more and more how far – very far – I am from where You are calling me – how disordered my life and thinking and affections are. I still resist discipline in every form, and am not much of a witness for any aspect of Christianity. But You, Lord, are not rebuking me. You are not angry with me, You are not even disappointed in me. You are not forcing me or nagging me, pushing or pulling me. You simply invite me. Right now, You are inviting me to lay aside those things (foods, activities) that do not help in praising, reverencing, and serving You. I am the one disappointed with myself – not You. But the way I am presently doing things is not helpful to my peace of mind or my serving You. It is not that I may not do certain things, it is that they are not helpful for the end to which I was created. You are also calling me to take more care of my appearance and my language that I may indeed be a credit to Your Name. So here I am, Lord, right now I accept Your invitation.

*****

Though my life was busy as wife and mother and math tutor and helper to my husband's side business as a soccer referee, I often wondered if the Lord had anything else He wanted me to do.

Lord, I do not know if You are calling me to any other ministry than just wife and mother, but even if You are not, I need Your power to do a decent job of it. And if You do have any other part for me in Your Kingdom, I certainly need more of Your power. I have seen that You anoint and use *anyone* who is willing to be used by You. Lord, I'm willing. Anoint and use me. But Lord, please purify me first so I do not bring dishonor to Your name. I want to do those greater works You spoke of, but I want to be so united with You that I would know exactly what You want done and how to do it. If my time has not yet come, or if Your will for me is just to be behind the scenes, then please give me the grace to accept that and the patience and perseverance to do exactly when and what You desire of me. Lord, I am Yours to do with as You wish. All I ask is that my love for You should become an all-consuming fire, united to Your all-consuming fire of love. I want nothing apart from You. And through Your love, let me love and do good to my family and all those around me.

Maggie, I see you truly trying to do the best you can. I see a willing servant, a trusted friend, a child of God. You are precious to Me. By name I have called you, you are Mine. I do not find fault with you. I lead you and empower you to do the work I set before you. I am pleased that you are coming to Me for strength and direction. I will not disappoint you and you cannot disappoint Me. I know you inside and out and I love you completely. Continue to be cautiously

unafraid. This is My work that you are participating in, and I will bring to completion what I have begun.

*****

The evening of October 31, 1995 seemed to go quite normally. Rae was home from work; our son Karl was away at college, and the other two sons Raeme and Steven had been out refereeing and came home tired. Since it had been a busy day, we ordered pizza. Rae even went out to pick up milk at the grocery store that evening. Later, as we were scheduling referees, Rae received an irate phone call from a parent about the game our two sons had just refereed. When Raeme overheard the conversation, he motioned to his Dad to let him talk to the lady. Rae and I listened with trepidation mixed with amusement as Raeme feigned respect while quite sarcastically apologized for being such a terrible referee.

As evening turned into night, Rae and Raeme continued assigning referees, Steven worked on his homework, and I went to bed before any of them. Close to midnight, Rae came into to bedroom to get ready for bed, but complained of a terrible pain. He paced between the bedroom and the bathroom, thinking it must be indigestion from having eaten one more piece of pizza than he should have. By this time, I was fully awake, and asked him, "Are you sure you are not having a heart attack?" He answered, "No, my heart is beating just as steady as it can, and besides, this is the same pain I had last Sunday." I had not known about his pain on Sunday. By now he was in a cold sweat, and as I was trying to figure out how to help him, he said, "The pain is letting up, but I think I'm going to pass out." And he did. He began a very noisy, labored breathing, and I knew, though I had never experienced such a thing before, that he was indeed having a heart attack.

I screamed for Raeme and Steven to come quick, and called 911. While waiting for an ambulance, I struggled out of my nightgown and put on street clothes. We did what we could to make Rae comfortable. Just in case, when the boys were not in the room, I leaned over Rae and kissed him.

The paramedics came, did the best they could, discovered that their oxygen tank did not work, put him on a gurney, and loaded him into the ambulance. Raeme decided he should stay behind and watch the house, so Steven and I got in the car and followed the ambulance to the nearest hospital. On the way, Steven started saying the Rosary frantically. I joined him with equal fervor.

When we got to the hospital, Rae was taken to the emergency room we went in to the waiting room. I filled out all the paperwork. When I asked how Rae was doing, I was told that they were still working on him, a good sign.

But soon someone came out and asked Steven and me to come to a separate room. I knew that was not good news. We were told that Rae had died. As the shock penetrated, I called Raeme and Deacon Rick Fisher. We were allowed to stay awhile with Rae's body. I could only look at his face. Steven noticed that his cold hands had curled in toward his body.

When Deacon Rick arrived, he anointed Rae. I was very grateful, though liturgically proper or not, as Rae wasn't Catholic, he did what he thought best.

When there was nothing left to do there, I drove home. We were numb from shock. When we reached the house, we three had to figure out what to do next. Raeme had called Karl at Indiana University; he was coming home as soon as he could get a flight. By then it was about three AM – it was unreasonable to call anyone else.

There were many questions: How do we tell Rae's mother? How do we manage getting the car pool to school? Do we even go to school? What about my students? Who else needs to be called and when?

As we were facing all these questions, I felt the power of God coming over me. It was as if He was strengthening me by pouring something like concrete over me spiritually, standing me up straight and bold. I declared, "I want to go to school and be the one who tells my students." The thought had come to me that my ninth graders needed to see how someone deals with tragedy. I was aware how often teenagers take their own lives over less serious problems, and I thought I could be an example to them as they saw that I had confidence that God would care for us through this.

Raeme and Steven tried to get a little sleep, and left me to pray. I had had a very good teaching on losing a loved one. It came to me at this time and I remembered a parable we were told at seminar: If one day someone comes to your door and hands you a $100 bill, then day after day continues to do the same for many years, but then passes by your house and goes to another house, can you yell at him and demand your $100 bill? I realized that I had been given over 27 year of marriage to Rae, how great a gift that was, and I had no right to be mad at God for no longer giving me this gift. I decided right there and then that I would only give thanks to God for all the time Rae and I had together, rather than be upset about what we would not be able to have. I spent much of the rest of the night thanking God for Rae, and for the strength He was giving me.

When morning came, I had had no sleep at all. Raeme had had about an hour, so we decided that he would drive the van pool. Rather than calling all the parents, we met them in front of the house as they came to drop off their children. We explained that Rae had died during the night, and we would take the kids to school that day, but would probably not go to school for a week. They were all very compassionate and loving and understanding.

Steven did not wear his uniform, but just as I wanted to tell my students, he wanted to tell his teachers. Most of them were compassionate, but he did have to deal with one who was not. As I approached the door with two sons beside me, my vice-principal happened to be there and saw that there was a problem. She asked what was wrong, and I told her that my husband died during the night. She exclaimed, "What are you doing here?!" I replied that I wanted to be the one to tell my class. She understood, and let me go on to my classroom. Two of the students in my class were also in my car pool. But they stayed very quiet, and did not tell anyone.

When the bell rang, and the morning announcements were over, I stood in front of my class and said, "You know that I start each day with a Scripture and a prayer, and I'm not sure where it is in the Bible, but it does say that God is husband to the widow and father to the fatherless. Last night my husband died, and I won't be here for about a week, but I wanted you to know that God will take care of us." At that point, my voice cracked, and my vice-principal was at the door ready to take over my class. I left with some of my students crying, and she handled it better than I could have.

Kindness, care, and love just poured into our lives. I felt like my arm had been ripped off of my body, and every word or act of kindness was like a blood vessel being sealed off so I would not continue to bleed or hurt as much. The arm was gone, but there was continuing soothing and healing. Some people sent cards, some sent money, some sent flowers, some brought food. We were truly blessed.

I handled grief differently than I expected. I did not cry much, but felt I needed to take care of all the responsibilities I had. Occasionally the tears would come, but I kept myself busy and tried not to think too much. It was not until I went to a three-day Holy Week retreat at the retreat house I usually attended, that I had time and space to work on my grief. I was expecting a retreat like I had attended for at least two years before, but things were different. Instead of the usual retreat house staff, there was a guest retreat master, Fr. John McHugh, S.J. who was to conduct the retreat. My spiritual director was also present, but stayed in the background.

At morning prayer, I knew I was in trouble the moment Fr. John McHugh said, "fantasy exercise."

He wanted us to imagine ourselves as a rose bush. Then he led us through John 15 ("I am the vine, you are the branches"), considering ourselves as being a branch of that bush. But when he came to the part "ask anything," pain and defiance rose up in me, with much crying. I arrogantly screamed in my thoughts, "I want my husband back – what are You going to do with that *anything*?" I immediately realized that I don't normally speak to (or yell at) You like that, so I tried to stuff it back in but it was already out and the tears would not stop. "Ask anything" – I don't ever ask for things I'm not likely to get. I carefully assess things – I don't like being told *no* when I ask for something – but You say ask ANYTHING.

That evening I prayed:

Lord, You have graciously brought me through the tears and pain of this day. I went to cry at the feet of Your Mother – and when I had cried a while, You sent me another widow who has been one for 18 years. We talked a long time, and it helped. Then this afternoon the tears flowed again after Fr. McHugh's talk – that's twice in one day that he got to me. So, I went to Confession to him. It was good. I cried all the way through, but he was not upset by that; he was very affirming and kind. Then after dinner we had Holy Thursday Mass and my feet were washed. And then we had Eucharistic adoration. Now it is time to sleep. Once again, if You wake me, I will come in the middle of the night. Good night, Lord, and thank You for this day.

The next morning, Good Friday:

Lord, You did wake me during the night and I came to You. And You showed me how You prepared me as much as a month before Rae died. The cliff I was at the edge of – I think I have jumped from it, and You were there to catch me and carry me to the other side. Now I am climbing a new mountain, but it feels just like the old one.

Lord, Fr. McHugh has left me in a river of tears three times in a row now. For morning prayer, he did the "Pieta exercise." He had us imagine Your Mother after Your body was taken off the cross, how she held Your body, remembering all the phases of Your life. And there I was, holding Rae, and the tears would not stop coming. Before I came to this retreat, I had spent some time at the school chapel, which has a floor-to-ceiling crucifix up front, and I either saw spiritually or felt as if Rae's coffin was in front of the crucifix. During this "Pieta exercise," I felt that Your Mother and I exchanged the ones we were holding. She took Rae, and I took You. I thank You for the privilege of having been able to love my husband so well. The whole time Fr. McHugh was talking about You, I saw Rae instead. But You and he are in union now – and whatsoever I did for him, I did for You.

My own spiritual director, Fr. Steve Garrity, and I had a good talk the next morning amid my tears. He instructed me to spend the rest of the day as a hermit.

I will go to the chapel and stay so I can totally focus on You. We agreed that You are doing something really significant in my life and that this is indeed a time of grace.

Lord, You answered my angry question of yesterday through the outdoor Stations of the Cross I prayed on my own. I used a little booklet my friend Veronica had sent me a long time ago. When I came to the thirteenth station, the one where Your body was taken off the cross, I read the response I was to make:

I beg You, Lord,
help me accept the partings that must come
from friends who go away,
my children leaving home,
and most of all,
when you shall call them to Yourself.

Then, give me grace to say:
"As it has pleased You, Lord,
 to take them home,
 I bow to Your most holy will.
 And if by just one word
 I might restore their lives
 against Your will,
 I would not speak."
Grant them eternal joy.

Everyone's Way of the Cross, by Clarence Enzler (© 1970, Ave Maria Press)

Through my tears, I surrendered. I no longer asked questions or made demands arrogantly. You took Rae, I gave him to Your Mother, and in return, I received You.

I was able to hold back tears until the afternoon liturgy when it came to the veneration of the cross, with the hymn "Were You There?". Lord, Your death and Rae's death somehow mingled this week; I can't separate the two anymore. You also showed me how Rae taught me to love. I never understood a father's love – not even my own father's – until I saw how Rae loved our sons. And his care and protection and genuine concern for me and his acceptance of me despite my flaws – so much like You. He loved much; he loved well.

*****

For the next couple of years, I did the best I could and kept busy, but often complained to the Lord that I did not make sense.

Maggie, I know you and love you even when you don't make sense. There is no commandment that "Thou shalt be sensible and rational at all times." You see and understand a little better now, and you can act accordingly. I met you in the formal Ignatian prayer. I also meet you in the informal armchair writing you do. I meet you in chapels, in outdoor walks, at Mass, and many other places. I meet you in your work, your kindnesses, and even in your pain. You do recognize Me often and know I am with you. Don't give up. I am not the one upset with you. I still love you and accept you – irrationalities and

all. This week, just come to Me anyway and any time that you can. I will comfort and console you. You are still in pain and mourning. Two years is not long enough to take away the sting of that loss. Be more patient with yourself. I hold you close and love you. Now go back and sleep, and rest in My arms.

*****

Jesus, You saw fit to wake me, so here I am. I offer You this day. Let me do whatever gives You glory today. Please open my eyes that I might see You, open my ears that I might hear You, and open my heart that I might love You. This was my first prayer many years ago that I wanted to speak out at a prayer meeting, but I was too nervous and self-conscious to do it then. I have no such fear any more – thank You for that. Of course, I don't go to a prayer meeting with 500 people either. But You have given me boldness and security, and so many things are easier now. Twenty-two years ago I came to You full of fear and worry and anxiety and insecurity and bitterness and resentment and a critical, negative outlook on life. You have changed me and have healed me of all those things. You changed my relationships to loving and kind ones and You have given me many gifts, ministries, and opportunities to serve You and Your people. You gave me a love for serving and a joy in helping others. You have given me an intense desire for union with You. You have given me great insights and understanding and compassion. Thank You.

*****

In teaching both math and religion classes I started each class with a Scripture and a prayer, and often the students would add their special intentions to the prayers. The students in the math classes thought they could get away with less math if they asked me some faith-related questions, so we often spent ten minutes or more on these questions. They thought they were getting away with "wasting" math time, but I was delighted to spend that time answering their questions and teaching them more than just math. I think the students received religion better in my math classes than in the religion classes.

During those first few minutes of prayer and discussion, I had related to my students the story of Leonard and Anne. Students in one of my classes came to school one day with flowers, cards, and small gifts for Leonard. I was so touched by their kindness that I wrote a letter to the editor of the BI Word, the school newspaper. It was printed on October 15th with my picture and the heading, "A letter from a beloved teacher":

I know a couple who has had a very difficult time the past two years. In fact, they are very good friends of mine. Their names are Leonard and Anne Philpott. I have known them for many years and they have helped me many times when times were tough for me.

Two years ago, Leonard had a stroke and became paralyzed on his left side. He had to have brain surgery and we did not know whether he would even survive, but he did. He was even improving and could walk again with help. But last October he had a severe brain hemorrhage and had to have brain surgery again. This time, we seriously doubted whether he would survive, but we prayed. My math class also prayed, and miracle of miracles, he lived.

But this letter is not really about Leonard who is doing better than expected even though he is severely brain-damaged. It is not about his wife, Anne, who lovingly cares for him day after day. It is about a whole lot of marvelous BI students who have adopted Leonard even though they have never met him. These students have been praying for Leonard, ask about how he is doing, and really care. Last year, they unexpectedly came in to school with flowers, cards, and gifts for him while he was still in the hospital. What joy I had while taking these things to the hospital – all the while bragging about the kindness of my students! Today, I was given more cards and another gift to take to him. Marvelous cards, and many signatures – these things prove how kind and wonderful high school students (my BI students) really are. Their prayers and care have certainly been encouraging not only to Leonard and Anne, but also to me.

I am so proud to be a teacher of such caring and loving students. I want to thank everyone who prays for these friends of mine and also thank them for the cards, gifts, and pure Godly concern.

*****

While I was teaching full-time, I was also caring for Rae's mother, whom I called Mom E. I had "kidnapped" her when she could no longer live alone, and always had someone at the house to stay with her. I had the night shift, and she often got up and wandered through the house thinking she was in a past part of her life and could not figure things out. I was given the wonderful gift of being able to wake easily, and be completely alert, so I could guide her back to bed and console her that all was well. But this particular evening, she had lost consciousness and we had to call the paramedics. Later I prayed:

Last night I was able to have a really good time of deep communication with Steven. Thank You for that. We both realized that this was the second time we had looked death squarely in the eye, and that it was so similar to his father's death that it brought back all the feelings and circumstances of that tragedy in our lives. I see so many reasons to thank You – that we were all there when Mom E. fainted. We could do what was necessary, the emergency people were able to come, their equipment worked, she did not die. I was able to give her comfort and reassurance and I did not have to go to school yesterday. I have good friends that I can talk to about such things, and my sons are so good and caring in such situations. But, Lord, I still am not very good at turning to You in a crisis. Yesterday when I finally did pray, I was not able to receive any comfort or help from You. I was still looking first to people.

Maggie, I am not the least bit upset with you. This is a learning process. You naturally look for help and support from physical sources. You have to learn to look for and receive the help and support that you cannot see or hear with your physical senses. Do not be discouraged that you are not yet at the goal. You need to see the process in order to be able to lead others through it.

So, I didn't blow it?

No, child, you are on the right track. Be patient with yourself. I am with you.

Thank You so much. Let me try to sleep a bit more now. Please hold me tight as I do.

I am here.

*****

Lord, thank You for all the times and ways You have saved me, and all the places You have prepared for me, and all the ways You have provided for me. Lord, last night I heard that St. Teresa of Avila said that many don't make it to the higher levels of prayer because their desire is not strong enough. You have given me a very strong desire for union with You. I do not know how far along I am, but I know I want total union with You and I want to be totally committed to You. I still don't fully know what that means, but I know I want it. You put the desire into my heart, and You are faithful to fulfill it.

Maggie, I have taught you much these past years, but there is yet much more. You are correct. I did put that desire into Your heart, and I will fulfill it. I have been fulfilling it, and will continue to do so. Your capacity for Me must increase. This does not happen quickly. Be patient – it is happening. Let your contentment grow and, yes, let your self-discipline also grow. Do what you can to reclaim your house and keep working on finding Me and coming to Me and asking Me for all the graces you need. I cannot refuse you – My love for you is so much greater than you could possibly imagine. Keep asking, keep seeking, and keep knocking. Your asking, receiving, seeking, finding, knocking, and entering give Me glory and pleasure. Yes, you must respond to the answers. When you ask, prepare to receive; when you seek, prepare to find; and when you knock, prepare to enter. Nothing is impossible.

Lord, I will keep asking, seeking, and knocking; and I will be more careful to stick around to receive Your answers, find You and Your gifts, and enter through the door You open. It is so good to belong to You.

*****

As I see almost certain persecution of Your Church on the horizon, I also see that I must come to know Your touch so completely that it is all that is important. That I can be so secure in Your arms that nothing else matters. And if I have this trust and attitude, it is so pleasing to and appreciated by our Father that it makes His heart glad that He created all. Even just one such love makes all of creation worthwhile to Him.

And, Lord Jesus, that is how You accepted the Cross. Total love, total surrender, total trust, total contentment regardless of the pain – no self-pity, no anger, no revenge, no fear, no worry, no regrets – just love, trust, faithfulness, even joy and peace and all the fruits of the Spirit. You showed me that this is not only possible, but how beautiful it is both from Your perspective and mine.

*****

Chapter 8

WALK, TALK AND ABIDE

Often on a retreat, I was given a particular Scripture to meditate on. These were my reflections or conversations with the Lord on these occasions.

JOHN 3:1-3

Nicodemus – you must be born again – and again – and again. I feel like I'm just starting out discovering a whole new world. I am to love You here, now, in the lowliest of low estate of Your handmaiden – sick, crippled, widowed, now jobless, less income than I expected, housebound – definitely of low estate. But You have regarded it, and this is what You want for me right now. This has become Your perfect will for me. This is the best possible condition in which I can love You and become what You know I can become. It is out of Your infinite love for me that You have provided this situation for me. So I will stop fighting it, I will stop wishing it was over, I will stop plotting and planning what I might do when it is over, and enter into living it and loving You in it, and learning how to find You in it. I will stop whining about how much I don't like it and submit to Your will.

I remember the day in Budapest (I must have been about six or seven) when I was walking home, I tripped and fell, skinned my knee, and started crying. Then brand-new idea popped into my head. I suddenly realized that I did not have to cry, that crying was neither helpful nor necessary. It was a brand-new way to handle being hurt, go home and take care of it – wash it, bandage it – and go on. This is how I feel now. I have found that fighting, complaining, and all the discontent I have been struggling with is neither necessary nor helpful. It is time for a new approach. One I still have to learn – but one I can have help with – rather, a Helper. You are my love, my help, my guide, my constant companion. You are God, and I am not. What You want is important; what I want is not.

I surrender the best I know how. Death to self sounds much easier than it is. It seems I have found a way to run from You even when I couldn't run any more. But for now, I have stopped and am relieved that I did not manage to get away from You. No retirement from the Christian life; rather, keep growing and maturing and being born again. I have often wanted to know what You want of me, what can I do that I'm not already doing, and You say, "**It is not the doing that is important. Just stop and enjoy the company.**" You want Mary and I'm trying to be Martha. I'll stop now. I want to give You a chance to talk. I have gone on and on.

Maggie, I love you – even when you go on and on. You are right – it is another new birth. Behold, I am doing a new thing. You do perceive it. New possibilities are right in the situation where you are. Explore them. Search out the adventure, live it, love it. Fear not! Go ahead, be happy. It's OK, and not impossible. Each death brings a new birth. Practice now. How can you love Me now?

I don't know.

Think about it. How do you love a God?

By keeping His commandments.

Which commandment can you keep right now?

The first one?

How?

No strange gods?

Yes, which gods?

My likes and dislikes?

Good! Keep going.

Love You with my whole heart, soul, mind, and strength – I can't do that if I don't like where You put me.

So now what?

I have to re-assess – change – not liking my situation?

Can you do that?

I don't think so – at least not by myself.

Bingo!

I don't have to do it by myself?

Getting warmer!

Ask for Your help whenever I don't like something?

Good – go on.

Ask to see if it is to be changed or accepted? Or not important enough to worry about?

See – not only do you have an answer, but you now feel My Presence.

Yes, I do. Thank You.

So now put away the books and pen and enjoy My love and Presence and go to sleep.

Aye, Aye, Sir!

*****

John 14:7-14 (He who believes in Me will also do the works that I do; and greater works than these will he do because I go to the Father.)

My response to Your Presence is not good. I am treating You poorly. I don't understand. I remember many years ago walking down one of these hills when You spoke to my heart and said, "**I love you,**" and my response was a monotone, "That's nice." But You kept repeating it until I realized that my response needed to be more positive and enthusiastic, and eventually You brought me around. Right now, my response to Your Presence and love is at the level of, "That's nice." Is it fatigue? Or frustration with the slowness of my body? Or is it some sin lurking in the deep dark corners of my being that Your light is now exposing? Lord, whatever is in the way of a loving and tender response to Your love? I suppose my petition is just that You clean me up so I can love You as You deserve. Give me back a grateful heart and put a right spirit within me.

Lord, if You are to cleanse me these are the words that will do it. What "greater works"? I can't even do small works in this condition. Ask anything? No, You don't mean *anything* – You mean anything that is already Your Will. So now my sin has reared its ugly head. I thought this one was gone when You brought me through accepting Rae's death – but here it is again. Resentment – I resent that the lame leaves our churches and prayer meetings and healing services still lame, the blind leave still blind, the deaf leave still deaf; where are these "greater works"? I pray for a co-worker – I don't even know if he is still alive – I pray for healing, but if and when healing actually comes, it is so slow and usually partial. Where are these "greater works"? What can we do that we are not already doing? We are told that You already paid the price. So why do we see so few results? Lord, I don't want to cause You more pain – I want to soothe Your aching body. I do believe You are Who You say You are. I do believe that You and the Father are One. But the "greater works" and "ask *anything*" – to me they are harder sayings than eating Your Body and drinking Your Blood.

So, are you leaving?

No, Lord, I agree with Peter – to whom else could I go? *You* have the words of everlasting life. I will serve You whether I understand or not. I will thank You for all You do and say I choose to believe that You do love me and that I can also learn to love You, even if I don't understand.

Do you want to understand? Often when you don't understand you keep probing until it makes sense.

Yes, but those did not hurt. This one hurts. What must I do?

Let Me wash your feet.

But I can't even walk down to the river anymore.

I know that.

So how are You – the invisible – going to wash my feet?

Do you want me to?

Yes! More than anything. But with that washing, I also want to be cleansed of this resentment.

Wait and see what I will do.

Later that day:

So, Maggie, are you still angry with Me?

No, Lord, and I know I had no right to be angry with You in the first place.

But you were.

Yes, and I'm sorry. I see now that You are frustrated with our inability to do the "greater works" – when Your disciples could not cast out the demon from that man's son, You showed Your frustration. I should have simply asked You what You meant; instead, I got angry.

And now, where are you?

Well, I'm not hiding, and I'm not running away.

That's progress.

I think I'm ready to face You and more humbly ask what You mean about the "greater works" and "ask anything."

Remember My servant Job?

Yes.

He had similar problems – he did not understand either.

Then You asked him where he was when You created the world.

But I'm not asking you that. I do not need to put you in your place. You already know that I am God and you are not.

Yes, and I also got a glimpse of what I (we) would be like if everything I (we) asked for was done as I (we) wished. The pride and arrogance would cause more harm than the original problem. I have such pride and arrogance, and when it appears, I am horrified at its ugliness.

What did I mean by "greater works"?

That You have planted the seeds and we get to bring in the harvest. But only if we do it in Your Name; on our own, we mess it up.

Actually, I say, "He who believes in Me will also do the works that I do; and greater works than these will he do, because I go to the Father." I also say earlier, "The words that I say to you I do not speak on My own authority; but the Father who dwells in Me does His works." You see, it is not even My work or yours, but the Father's. I do what I see Him doing. What do you see Him doing?

I don't even see Him yet.

Neither did My disciples. They said, "Show us the Father." They missed the whole unity aspect. My Father and I already have that unity. This is why you so desperately want union with Me, yet you know that you have no clue what it is. There is the phrase, "In My Name" – that means in union with Me. For 25 years, you have been works-oriented. You learned a lot, did a lot. Some things worked, some didn't. But I am calling you to be God-oriented. Do you see that it is a higher calling? Without Me you can do nothing. Even with Me you can do nothing unless it is the Father's will. For I will not do anything unless it is My Father's will.

So that is why that book of the letters of St. Francis de Sales, *Thy Will Be Done* was touching me so deeply?

Yes. This is a great truth. You have begun to see that My Father's will is most important. Search for it. Ask for it. Knock on the door.

You did not say believe in the works – but believe *Me*. That union between You and the Father is more important than the works. The works cannot exist without the union. Once again, I have been climbing the wrong mountain. No wonder I've been exhausted for 25 years, I've been pushing the cart up the hill while the horse is on the other side. So now what?

Keep looking for My heart. Get to know Me. The union you seek *is* the Father's will for you.

*****

Psalm 51

This, the greatest of the penitential psalms, is King David's prayer of repentance after the prophet Nathan reproached him about his adultery with Bathsheba and murder of her husband. Having been named after Mary Magdalene, I have learned to repent often. When I asked for cleansing, this Psalm always did what I needed.

I could almost recite this psalm by heart. Lord, You are so gentle and kind. And I have been so slow and stupid. All You ever asked of me is to keep coming to You. Every time I did, You welcomed, loved, uplifted, encouraged, taught, or helped me in some way. But I didn't keep coming to You. I would get distracted, or lazy, or somehow forget – and days, weeks, sometimes even months would go by when I hardly prayed, except for prayer meetings and Sunday Mass. You never let me completely forget, but my failures far outnumber my successes.

Maggie – enough! I may count the number of hairs on your head, but I do not keep count of failures. Yes, you have failed, but I am bigger than your failures. I do not want you to wallow in remorse. Yes, you need to know your sins and sinfulness. But now it is time to go and sin no more. It is not My intention that you feel bad, but that you get better. I came to save sinners. I've saved many better than you and many worse. I want you to come to Me daily. You are doing it now, and through this retreat let it become a deep-rooted habit. Look to My patience. I have not struck you down in anger. I have not condemned you, and I do not dwell on failure. Repentance is good. Remorse has its place, but do not stay there – come up higher. I give you grace to do what is good and helpful.

*****

Isaiah 30

I was amazed, for I did not realize how it began: "Woe to the rebellious children," says the Lord, "who carry out a plan, but not of My spirit, that they may add sin to sin" – that's just verse 1! I was reminded of all the grandiose plans I have had over the years but have indeed added sin to sin in my failures. It goes on and on about looking everywhere else for help except to the Lord. How guilty I have been of this! I'd read any book, listened to any tape, sought out any counselor, done everything except the simple answer God has already given me. The "Egypt" referred to is all the old ways of formulas, striving, seeking authoritarian answers, and self-degradation. All have brought shame. But verse 15 is the *key*: For thus says the Lord God, the Holy One of Israel, **"In *returning* and rest you shall be saved; in quietness and trust shall be your strength. And you would not."**

Lord, all my plans are useless, but Yours will work. I was also reminded of the parable of the evil spirit being cast out and the place clean and empty and then it comes back *with company*. Lord, my way of ordering my life is to first get everything in order and then invite You in. But that is not Your way. You choose to enter into the disorder and disaster and fill the place first with Your light and goodness so there will be no room left for sin and evil and disorder. My way is backwards. But I have been holding on tenaciously to this way. You want me to embrace Your way and rest and trust You quietly. Lord, there is not much quietness in me – except when I'm in Your Presence. The whole chapter of Isaiah 30 speaks to me, even though most of it is Your rebuke. You do it out of love, and also send grace and power to repent. One of the translations I read says "repentance" instead of "returning." That works, too.

Isaiah 30 also reminded me of Your covenant, that You are my God and I am one of Your people, and that this is an ongoing relationship, lasting forever. I shall never outgrow my need of You.

I was told to engage in a "prayer of presence" for as long as I wished before dinner and then go home. This I did and I was overwhelmed by Your kindness and generosity, Lord. You have given me so much and all You asked of me in return is to simply be with You. Nothing difficult or impossible, just be there. And it was so good to be there in Your Presence.

*****

Luke 5:1-11

The first miraculous catch of fish and the call of Peter

Lord, Peter left everything to follow You, but You are not calling me to leave everything to follow You – You are calling me to stay where I am and follow You.

Maggie, I am calling you to stay where I have put you, but not where you are. I am calling you to leave everything that is not helpful to Your service of Me. That was the same call to Peter. For him, it meant leaving his sinful ways – for you it means the same. For him it meant to put out his nets when I told him to, even though he thought he knew more about fishing than I did. For you it means that I will tell you what to do and when, even when you think you know what you are doing. Following Me is not a one-time decision to leave everything else. It is a moment-by-moment response to My call and direction. It is leaving things that are keeping you from fulfilling My desires for you. Did Peter sell his boat and stop fishing forever? No. But he was no longer considering himself a simple fisherman (a sinful one) but now became a disciple – an Apostle. You will continue to be a mother, a teacher, and everything else you are, but you are to be My disciple (disciplined one). All I ask of you is to come, follow Me. I will show you the way, one step at a time. I will give you all that you need for your journey.

But, Lord, I've already committed my life to You. Why do You ask me again?

Just as I asked Peter three times if he loved Me, so I will ask you repeatedly to follow Me. You need to decide daily to follow. It is not just a one-time choice. Choose today Whom you will follow (obey). Then tomorrow, choose Me again.

Lord, I am ashamed that You need to ask again.

Maggie, I do not love you less by asking, but I know you and how easily you forget that you have a God who is willing and able to lead you. You rely on your own understanding and your own devices and then wonder what happened to your relationship with Me. You have

to rely on Me. There is no other way than to choose to follow Me daily – not run ahead or lag behind or look to the left or to the right. I invite you to choose Me one day at a time. And today, I require an answer – for today, will you follow Me?

Yes, Lord, today I will follow You.

Good. Go on about the business at hand. Straighten your house, plan your dinner, take care of your responsibilities, and I will be with you, guiding you.

Thank You, Lord. Welcome back to the control of my life. I do love you, Lord, and my love for You will grow.

*****

Psalm 23

You took me through Psalm 23. You prepared a table before me in the presence of my enemies and gave me all sorts of food I like. There wasn't a single calorie – spiritual food does have its benefits. You gave me only things I like – no lemon or mint or green peppers or onions. The tea was just the way I like it, with just a hint of a fruit flavor, and the finest desserts, just a taste of so many. No salad, for I have had enough of that. And my enemies were no bigger than the insects on the table – an ant, a spider, a wasp. But they could not hurt me, for You protect me.

Then You accompanied me on a walk down to the lake and I sat on a bench. The beauty of everything was so evident. You told me to seek Your face in the trees, the sky, the lake, the grass, the breeze – for You are there in all those things. And though I did not see Your face with my eyes, I understood and rejoiced. You told me that You loved me, and I told You how good it was to be told that. You agreed and told me that You also liked to hear those words. I told You that I loved You and we took turns saying why we loved each other. I remembered many things You have done for and with me – and You reminded me of many ways I have served You and ministered to You through what I do for others.

*****

Walk

Lord, my one-track mind is getting narrower. When I started walking yesterday, I could no longer communicate with You. There were too many other things distracting me. The exercise was good, but my praying stopped.

Maggie, that is why the greatest commandment is: to love the Lord you God with <u>all</u> your heart, <u>all</u> your soul, <u>all</u> your mind, and <u>all</u> your strength. Your relationship with Me will take <u>all</u> your attention. That is why you have had such a hard time this summer. You have had many stimuli and could not focus on Me. Your writing down our conversations serves as a way to focus. It slows down your mind enough to hear Me. But you have been afraid that pencil and paper will become a bondage for you. You thought it ridiculous that you can't pray without your notebook in hand. After all, none of your friends have to write down all their prayers. To a man who is crippled, a wheelchair can be confinement or freedom, depending on his outlook. The blinders on a horse are not put on him out of meanness, but to help him concentrate on his course. But man has a way of twisting My blessings into curses and thinking of curses as if they were blessings. When you were prayed over at your Baptism of the Spirit, you were given the Scripture: "Do not look to the right or to the left." This is because I know you well and know how easily you can be distracted. This is not a fault of yours, it is the nature I have given you. There are and have been many times that this is a benefit. But other times, this has to be overcome in order to move ahead. When you were younger, you needed a church or a chapel to be able to spend time with Me. Not because you thought I only stayed in chapels, but because you could concentrate there. Now you have found that you can concentrate with pencil and paper. I have told you before to go ahead and make use of anything you find helpful. I simply desire to have fellowship and communication with you. I am not concerned with what you use in order to hear My voice. I want you to hear and understand. You would not think less of anyone because that person used a hearing aid to listen to you. In fact, if he couldn't hear you without it, and refused to put it on, then you might be upset because he valued his appearance more than your communications. So be content to write. When you are faithful in

small things, then I am free to give you bigger ones. In eternity you will see Me face to face. Then you will need no help to hear Me, see Me, or understand Me. But for now, you need all the help you can find. Don't be ashamed of needing help. Be grateful that you are getting it.

Lord, I am truly grateful to You. You really do know me better than anyone else, better than I know myself. Now I see that we cannot compare ourselves with others. You have made each of us unique, and I am no less valuable to You than anyone else because my gifts are different. You are the Giver of the gifts, and all Your gifts are wonderful. Thank You for the gift of notebook and pencil.

*****

After a retreat, life became busy. As Lent was about to start. I also decided to walk the two-mile trail through the woods at the local national park each day. By Easter, I was able to walk the two miles in a little over half an hour. I was proud of that.

I was taught a couple of new ways to pray using the Rosary. The first one was to pray for fifty people and five countries. At the beginning of each decade, on the Our Father bead, pray for a country. Then on each of the Hail Mary beads, pray for a person, family, friend, enemy, or someone who is in need of prayer.

The other new way of using the Rosary was to pray the Examen. The Examen is a prayer said usually at the end of a day, promoted by St. Ignatius of Loyola, that is more than an examination of conscience. It is keeping track of how God is working in one's life as well as how one is doing in his or her walk with God. Using the decades of the Rosary, I was to think of ten things I am thankful for, then ten gifts of the Holy Spirit I am asking for, ten things Jesus and I did today, ten things I am sorry for, and finally ten things I am looking forward to tomorrow.

I often used these ways of praying on my walks as well as the traditional way of saying the Rosary. Sometimes I went into deep intercessory prayer for someone in particular, like my uncle Laci, while on my walks. More often, it was my immediate family that I prayed for. But I spent at least a half-hour in prayer and exercise all through Lent.

*****

Lord yesterday was truly a day of grace. At Mass at the prayer of the faithful we were asked to think of one thing we would like a saint to intercede for us – what do we want from God? I usually have so many things run through my mind at such a time that I never come up with just one thing. But yesterday I instantaneously had an answer – and it did not come from my thinking: total union with God! After Mass, I had some time, so I walked on the retreat house grounds down to the Potomac River and, with a boldness that is not characteristic of me, I shook my fist at Heaven and declared: "Lord, I will not be satisfied until I have total union with You." Then I remembered that several years ago as I was walking down the same hill and You told me that You loved me. At that time, I realized that my response of "That's nice" was not very good. Now I realized that total union with You is Your idea in the first place and now I am demanding it. Funny, isn't it?

*****

Lord, I don't know how to approach You. You have done such wonderful things. You have spoken to me so gently and tenderly. Yet I have not responded very well. Early Wednesday morning I walked through Fort Washington Park for the first time in quite a while. You met me and walked with me and allowed me to cry and pour out my fears and disappointments and You comforted me and assured me that You will supply all that I lack. I came home renewed and refreshed and able to face the day. But yesterday I was back to feelings of helplessness and yet You met me and allowed me to cry again and sat next to me and let me express to You (and You alone) my need for tenderness and touch and compassion.

Lord, keep drawing me closer to You. Every time You do something wonderful, I seem to shrink back and stay away from You for several days. Lord, am I thinking (or feeling) that I'm only entitled to a little of Your kindness? Do I think (feel) that once I've had my turn, I need to go to the back of the line and wait again for Your love and goodness? I wouldn't think much of a person who treated me that way, yet I act like You would treat me so. Forgive me, Lord. Your love is so incomprehensible that I cannot understand it. But, Lord, You are so gracious to help me get rid of my misconceptions. I come to You now for Your kindness and love, and when I receive it, I'll try not to go away clinging to the little I have received, but stay and keep receiving until I'm so full that I have enough overflow to give away to others. Lord, I want Your river of living water, not just a cupful.

*****

Lord, I'm still struggling. I have done badly for several days. Fatigue is severe, and the house is in chaos. Yet You encourage me to go on – not to be consumed by failure but to turn around and start walking again with You. I accept Your invitation. I can see You almost holding me up as I continue. You proceed to heal my hurts and I can walk straighter and better. In fact, as I stay with You, I get younger and more energetic all the time. But if I get away from You, I get old and feeble and bent over with all my cares and sin. But You are ever willing and able to get me back on the right path. So, Lord, I thank You for Your vision and parable this morning.

Maggie, I love you. I see your struggles. I am closer than you think. And I am willing to take hold of you and lead you. You are willing to come My way. I will be there to talk with you and help you choose. When you fail to ask, I will not turn away from you. You will find Me again. And I will gladly guide your day today. I am right here. Lean on Me as the day goes on.

*****

Lord, I just watched Your sunrise. It was beautiful. Thank You that the weather is turning wonderful. Today I need to work inside but I will open as many windows as I can and praise You while I work. Lord, I long for Your peaceful, quiet Presence that I'm used to on my walks. Yet I also desire to hear Your voice, so I invite You to walk with me and talk with me today. Or am I responding to Your invitation to walk with You and talk with You? Either way, let's have a great time together.

*****

Lord, I went for a walk in the rain at the retreat house. I got wet going to the car to get my umbrella, but I was warm enough anyway. It was getting dark, but I walked to the statue of Your Mother and, on a whim, went up close and held my umbrella over it and me. And her hand was so close that I held her hand and with tears asked her to help me come closer to You. On the way back, one of my shoes came untied, and I asked You whether You were trying to wash my feet. So, I took my shoes off and let You wash my feet with the rain and walked in every puddle I could find. Then I went back to the field behind the retreat house where Your statue is, and tried the same umbrella thing with Your statue, but that did not work well. Yet I felt that You appreciated the effort. All through the night, I was aware of Your Presence and kept reminding myself that You are in me. I was able to pray well before going to bed and slept pretty much the whole eight hours. The awe and wonder of Your great love are still with me. I thank You.

*****

Talk

I need to come before You and pour out my heart to You and allow myself to fall to pieces so You might put me back together again. At some point early in my marriage, I felt like there was a bucket inside me that was full of tears, and every time something happened to jar my life even a little, I burst into tears. The bucket was full and could take no more. That is how I feel now. My bucket is full. Yet instead of bursting into tears like I used to, I seem instead to be filled with malaise. It's as if I am building up the bucket so it can hold more, instead of emptying it, and now it seems too heavy to lift in order to empty it.

Perhaps that is what Confession is about. The bucket is really full of sin, not mere tears. It is filled with wrong responses to the natural irritations and problems of life. It is filled because my wrong responses should not be openly expressed. They are what I am ashamed of or wish I could have handled better but didn't. So, they sit there in the bucket and, as I go through day after day, I add to them. I've not before thought of sin as simply a wrong response. When I have read St. Thomas

Aquinas' explanation of emotion, I have been intrigued and excited. I wanted more, but as my days got busy, I didn't follow up.

This all started last week when I heard a teaching about the punishments for sin. A quote of St. Thomas Aquinas said that the consequences of sin are, first, an increase of temptation; then, if the temptation is given in to, a disposition toward that sin; and eventually a compulsion to that sin. I'm sure I've been told this before, but somehow, I really heard it this time. As I look at addictions, I can see the progression. And virtue is built the same way. Resistance of temptation weakens its strength and builds the strength of the soul.

Perhaps the Sacrament of Confession *is* the emptying of the bucket, doing penance a washing out of the bucket. Through prayer and Scripture, we learn how to respond properly to situations, and our buckets won't fill up as fast.

Lord, You are amazing. I came to You full of sadness, ready to cry and complain, and now I don't remember what was bothering me so much. I am filled with joy and delight that I have another nugget of gold to share, and all the things that weighed me down less than an hour ago seem to have lifted. Thank You so much, Lord Jesus for Your teaching and healing.

*****

Lord, I've been watching my emotions lately – would You show me how to keep them under control?

Maggie, I, too, have been watching your emotions. They are easily controlled by others. A book, a play, a TV show, a motorist on the road; they can all change your emotions. However, emotions in general are not bad. You would rather take your chances with an emotional person than spend your time with one who seems to have none at all. Yet, you don't want them out of control, either. There must be a balance. You must allow yourself to feel the emotion, recognize it, and then control your thoughts, words, actions, motives, and attitudes. Don't deny or squelch the emotions themselves, but your relations to them are under your control.

This seems very difficult – if not impossible.

On your own, it is. But I have come to show you the way. And I stay with you to help in each situation. As you are more aware of My love and presence, you can turn to Me and learn how to handle each situation. No general formulas or laws, just a close walk.

Lord, I'm in awe of Your ways. They are so much better than ours.

Maggie, I am opening your eyes. But I choose to do it slowly, a little at a time. Be patient; it is for your own good that I do this. You know of the brightness of My light – you do not want to see it all at once. But as long as you want to see it, you will in time see. I promised to reveal Myself to you, and I am faithful to my promises. Your part is to keep My word. If anyone loves Me, he will keep My word, and My Father will love him, and We will come to him and make Our home with him. There is a different level of seeing, hearing, knowing, and loving when you live with someone. This is what I have put into your heart as a desire. This is what I long to fulfill. Ever since you were a child, you begged Me for a "best friend" that you could share your innermost feelings with. None of your friends met that need. When you got married, your husband did not meet that need. When you became a Christian, none of your Christian friends met that need. I am the only One who can meet that need. Food cannot meet that need. Animals cannot meet that need. Possessions cannot meet that need. Only I can. But you had to try all the other sources. You have known for many years that I alone can be that Friend. But you have searched for so long, and became so accustomed to not finding Me, that when you finally found your answer, you passed Me by and kept looking. You have forgotten what and why you seek – you only know the search and the disappointments you have experienced. I call you to STOP LOOKING. Begin to rejoice in and enjoy the Friend you have. I am with you all the time. I understand your deepest thoughts and feelings. I care about all that you care about. I love you more than you have ever been loved. Begin to digest that. Begin to believe it. Begin to act on it.

*****

Lord, I'm confused and have an overall malaise, yet I have no real reason for it. I'm not in serious sin and I'm being used by You in various ways. Your love for me is easily seen, and today even the weather is wonderful.

You told us to come to You as little children and trust You again and enjoy Your Presence. But I just wanted to curl up in Your arms and cry. I don't even know why I want to cry, but I still do.

Maggie, you need not apologize for your feelings. I do not want a plastic smile pasted over a sad heart. I have not forbidden your feelings; I simply want you to come to Me with them so I can be a part of your life. For Me, you do not have to be logical or reasonable or anything other than honest and real. I can handle your confusion, sadness, inconsistencies, and everything that others in your life would find difficult. I will delight in accompanying you through all the aspects of your life.

Lord, do You mean that I do not have to control these things?

That's exactly what I mean. That is why I said for you to come to Me as a little child. A child laughs when he is happy and cries when he is unhappy. But none of it lasts long. He is easily comforted. You have been working too hard, thinking that I am interested only in your work and accomplishments and your growth or learning or improvement. I love you much more than that. You need not perform for Me. I can accept you with the negatives included. Does that mean you should stop improving and working and learning? Of course not. But let it come naturally. I will correct you when necessary, but do not always be looking for a heavy hand. My love for you is so much better than that. Go home now and enjoy this day.

*****

Maggie, do you believe that I can still heal people?

Lord. You can and You do, but it does not seem to be very often. Is it our lack of faith? Or does a healing have to be rare, otherwise it would become commonplace, ordinary, or natural?

Many times, I said, "Your faith has made you well." But other times it was the faith of others. Faith is an essential aspect of healing. Prayer is another. It cannot become manipulative, but if

you don't ask, why should it be given? If you ask without faith, it is an insincere request. But a healing cannot become a right to be demanded either. It must be received as an unmerited favor. After the Fall, one consequence became aging and decay. All healing and recovery come through grace.

So, it is only through Your generosity that our lives are sustained at all. Sort-of like how I see my family's coming to the United States, as Your mighty work. All life and healing, even of a small cut, is a mighty work of Yours.

In this life that is so.

Lord, I thank You for my life and all life, for all healing and joy, and most of all for the ability to know You and see Your workings in my life and in the lives of others.

*****

Please help me to stay calm and in Your Presence.

Maggie, I see your heart. I see your love and your care. I also see your struggles. All will be well. Together we will cross every challenge. I will be very close today. Just reach for Me and I will touch you whenever you need Me.

Lord, I seem to need You every moment.

That is a good thing. I want to be needed every moment. This is another aspect of My personality I have given you. You also like to be needed. The difference is that I will not grow tired of your need, while with people's needs can easily wear you out. Your strength is finite; Mine is infinite. Go in My strength and remember that I delight in your neediness of Me.

Thank You, Lord. You have put a smile back on my face.

And you have done the same for Me.

*****

Maggie, I see your struggles and I still draw you to Myself. I appreciate that you keep trying and keep coming back even when you are sure you have failed. So today, you are listening better. Today you can turn to Me and feel My love and Presence and be encouraged that I will not forsake you. I don't want to take all the pleasure out of your life – but I do not want you to be a slave to anything. Freedom is not easy, but it is what you were created for. But love and relationship give form and substance to the freedom. Be patient with yourself. Believe it or not, this is a time of training. You are not just passing time, waiting for the next important part of your life's journey. This is a part of the journey itself. It may not be your favorite part, but you can only see the progress when you get to look back. But you don't always have time to look back; you need to look where you are going, or you fall. It is that tightrope again. But if you keep your eyes on Me and keep hold of My hand, I will guide you and keep you safe. And even if you find yourself having let go and fallen into one of the chasms on either side, just reach out and call out and I will grab you and pull you out of whatever mess you ended up in. And I will clean you up and love you still. Be assured that I do love you.

Lord, right now I really feel Your love – yet I lose track of it so easily.

Don't worry. Just enjoy it for now. You will find it more readily as you take the time to explore and enjoy it. Go now and let this day be a really good one.

*****

Lord, You showed me that my psychological needs, which I thought were imperfections at best, or sins at worst that I should even desire them – things such as attention and honor and thanks and approval and acceptance – are not evil. They were given to me and to everyone by Your gracious hand. And if these needs are not met by those whose job it was to meet them, then the hunger grows. But the hunger is not sin, though looking for it to be satisfied by human means can be. You want to satisfy these needs. You give me all the attention I could ever want – You even hear my thoughts. Nothing I do escapes Your attention. You honor me with Your Presence, You give me Your very Body and Blood, You encourage my every step, and You notice every good thing I do.

You thank me for the smallest of kindnesses – I used to be embarrassed when You thanked me for things, but now I see that You desire to thank me. No one's approval but Yours is important, whatever You approve is truly wonderful, and it does not have to be any great thing – You are not stingy with Your approval. Acceptance: You created me, You know everything about me, and You love me with an everlasting love.

So next time I find myself looking around to see if anyone notices what I do, I need to look to You, for You see all of it and You alone can purify my motives. If I do things to please You, then that is the best; if I do things to please others, it may be OK, but I can do better.

How freeing this is!

*****

Lord Jesus, thank You so much for waking me before the alarm clock was ready to ring. It seems we both like this hour.

It is quiet and I am happy for the company.

Actually, so am I. Thank You that You are always available as my Companion.

Maggie, I am always here, and there, wherever you go. And I love being with you.

Lord, in that case, I invite You to be a part of every moment.

I accept the invitation. The more difficult part is keeping you aware that I am with you, in you, all around you – and still available as the day gets in full force.

Is this why Brother Lawrence taught that Your Presence must be practiced?

Exactly.

Lord, we were told we have to find our own rhythms of life. Like what time of day is best for prayer. It seems my best time is now, but the duration that seems comfortable is 20 minutes.

For the first phase, that seems right.

You mean there are phases of prayer?

Certainly. In every meeting there is the initial "Hi, how are you" part. Catching up on everything since the last time. Then there is the part where the real purpose of the meeting is discussed.

Lord, what is the real purpose of our meeting?

Ah, there is a good question. Can you come up with a few purposes?

I guess I can – to get to know You better, to deepen my love for You, to see what Your will for me is overall and particularly for this day, to honor You as my first priority. I suppose those are my goals for coming to You at 4 AM.

And what about My goals for drawing you here?

Lord, I never thought of You having goals and desires for our time together.

Sit a spell and think about it. When you see that you are not here simply because you chose, consented, condescended, had to fulfill a duty, were expected to come, needed to come, or even wanted to come – but instead that I have called you, invited you, empowered you, desired you, pushed and pulled you, awakened you – what could possibly be My reasons?

Wow, Lord, You love me that much?

And more.

That brings a whole new dimension to prayer.

So it does.

It's not about me – is it?

Yes and no. It is about My love for you – not about your designs and plans and agendas. But it takes time for you to see things the way I see them. I am not busy, busy, busy. There are times of quiet Presence. And there are times I do enjoy letting you go on and on about your plans, desires, activities, concerns, and feelings. Do not think of Me only as your Boss, but as a true and close Friend with Whom you can discuss any topic whatever.

Lord, this will require time to digest. But it is so marvelous. Once again, the pressure is off of me. You are the initiator of our relationship – I simply respond.

That does not belittle you, though. It shows how greatly I value you, to desire such a relationship.

I see that, and I am very grateful. Lord, You have given me a great grace – a marvelous insight – I now see as if the scales have fallen from my eyes. Thank You.

You are most welcome. I am delighted as well. Go and enjoy this day.

*****

Thank You that some of the high-school students only have little problems. Thank You for the boy who came to me with problems in geometry, that we were able to make progress, and that he seemed to understand by the time we finished.

You see, not every problem is so great. My child, I see all the problems – big and small in your life and in the lives of those around you. You see that you cannot handle them all. There are very few that you can solve. But you can be My hands or voice of gentleness, and even if the problems remain, My people will have been touched by Me through you. Keep your focus on Me and continue to love and serve My people. I call you at odd times – but even if you come late or reluctantly, you come. You are also listening better. Fight discouragement. You have some time coming up this weekend. I can help you make the best of it.

Now, child, it's time for you to lay all these burdens down. Your own and everyone else's. I am big and strong enough to handle all of them.

*****

Lord Jesus, it seems You have to give me insomnia to get me to pray. So here I am. Mom E. seems to be better after passing out again. I really want to go away on a retreat. Advent starts tomorrow. I want to work on my relationship with You. I would also like to go to Confession.

Trying to escape from home again?

I'm afraid so. And I don't even have a legitimate reason.

Near-death situations are not legitimate?

You mean this is OK? That I want to run?

As long as you run TO Me and not AWAY from Me.

And I thought I was wrong in this restlessness.

Well, yes and no. The restlessness is quite natural. What feels wrong is that it took you so long to come to Me about it.

Oh – it's the dirty pitcher again. The cooking and the caring were service, and I didn't come to You right away, though I was aware of and grateful for Your Presence and strength and provision.

True, but you needed to let Me console you and build you back up after that took so much out of you.

Yes, I see that now. Lord, is it like when the woman with the issue of blood touched You – You felt power go out of You? Is that what happens to me? When I serve You, power goes out from me? And I need it restored by being in Your Presence? Kind of like a rechargeable battery?

See, you now understand something more clearly about Me. I needed recharging, so I went to pray to My Father.

Wow! You are revealing Yourself to me.

Yes, I am, and that energizes you.

*****

As I have tried to pray without talking, I do not know if I was correct this morning when I thought that not needing to talk between You and me was progress. Lord, I am confused.

Maggie, I am still willing and able to talk with you. I have not changed. The changes are all in you. And there have been many changes. Since you were taught about the prayer of Presence, you have lost your husband, your children have grown up and married, you cared for your mother-in-law, spent two years in the convent, cared for your mother, and had other changes. You wonder why you are confused?

Yes, I am working in your life, and you don't have as many questions as you used to have. We don't need to constantly be talking but talking is still good. You still hear My voice, and as you know, I also hear yours. I will call you to more study when you are ready. Right now, be patient. Trust Me to lead you when I want change in your prayer life. I can get through to you in many ways. Do not belittle the peace you have been feeling. Do not work yourself up into discontent again. Let Me lead you.

Thank You, Lord. I can make a problem out of anything, can't I?

Yes, but I love you anyway.

*****

Lord, You have allowed me to offer several pains to You for the salvation of souls. I have some particular souls in mind, and You already know who. I hope to contact some doctors to see if any of this pain can be fixed. In the meanwhile, I will continue to offer it all to You as raw materials for whatever good You wish to make from them.

Other than that, I can offer You my adoration. Lord, You deserve all honor, glory, praise, and thanks. You have been so good to me. Let my life be a continual sacrifice of praise, thanksgiving, honor, and glory to You. In my life, Lord, be glorified.

Maggie, it is true, I do welcome you. It is not that you have left Me, but I do appreciate your desire to spend time with Me daily. I also accept your pains and disabilities. Do not belittle these gifts you are giving Me. They are precious to Me. Stop now and receive My love. I shower it upon you.

Lord, I feel my cup being filled and running over.

Yes – and every time you come to Me to let Me fill it, it grows and will be able to hold more. That is the advantage of living vessels. And the more love I can pour into you, the more you will have to give others. My blessings are upon you. Would you come to Me in the morning as well?

Yes, I will come, and then will You give me direction for the day?

I will indeed.

*****

Lord, I have begun cleaning my house; I ask You also for a thorough cleansing of my soul. I want to be clean and pure before You – that is the grace I ask. Lord, You can make my soul beautiful. And my desire is to be beautiful in Your sight. I want the end-product now, but You seem to be more interested in the process. No quick fixes, just long, hard work instead.

Maggie, have I not been cleansing you all these years? Have I not been preparing you for Myself? I will not stop or give up. But now you see that it is possible. Yes, it is. Your house can be cleaned and organized and ordered. Yes, it will take a lot of work and a long time. But it can be an enjoyable time of work. You will see the progress and you should rejoice at each new area that is done. This is what I do. I rejoice at each new accomplishment in your spiritual life. You are right, no quick fixes. Do not rob Me of My joy by your impatience. Let Me enjoy your progress bit by bit. I already have the finished product in sight, but you need to see it a little at a time. It is for your good. It is worth doing it well.

Lord, I surrender and yield my desire for instant perfection. It was impossible anyhow. But I still want perfection and beauty and purity and total union with You. And if You have chosen to give it to me a little at a time, I can savor each crumb to the fullest with You. Thank You for Your great patience and love that You should want so much pleasure for me. Your ways are so much better than ours, and Your thoughts – how marvelous they are!

Lord, You just showed me that I have looked upon cleaning house as an unpleasant chore, to be avoided as much as possible, but that You want me to see it differently. Again, I yield. Your ways are much better. Help me to remember this, and act on it. You prepared me for this long ago. I used to get ridiculously happy every time You convicted me of sin because I knew that with the conviction would come the grace to overcome the sin. Now You want me to take pleasure in the work of cleaning, ordering, and fixing up my house while You do the same to my soul. It is to be a joint venture and may take many years. But as I do it with You, the union I so ardently seek will be formed.

*****

Lord, we sang about building You a resting place. Let me prepare my house and my heart as such for You. But it will not be I who prepare it, but You and I together. Purify my heart and let me continue to yield to Your most wonderful and perfect will. Thank You for the great grace to see what You desire and the joy of being able to accept it instead of fighting and kicking and screaming. What a great grace to willingly and joyfully accept Your will when it is different from anything I imagined. Lord, this stems from the faith and knowledge that You are good and loving and want only what is the best for me. Let me see Your goodness and love behind every circumstance I find difficult and embrace You by accepting Your will for me.

So now do you see the progress? Do you see that I have been laying the foundation for years?

Lord, I do see it. Thank You for showing it to me.

I have also given you a real and concrete way of showing your love for Me. Your acceptance and willingness to do My will is an embrace. Your coming to Me whether you feel inspired or not is a wonderful kiss. Do not judge your prayer time as good or bad: leave that to Me. Just come. I will do great things with what you might consider insignificant. As to your complaining, do not be afraid to express your real feelings and circumstances to Me. Though I know and see all, I want you to continue to tell Me what is going on inside you. This is relationship. This is love. I, too, will tell you more and more as you get closer to Me. Be encouraged. What you long for is happening. The union you seek began long ago. You will soon see more signs of it coming to pass. I do love you and am with you.

Maggie, I have been cleansing you and I will indeed send you. I have a plan for your life, and I know how hard it is for you to wait for it to unfold. But wait you must. Trust you must. I also had to wait and trust. Trusting also means being still. Not a lack of activity, but an assurance that I am working and have things under control. Keep coming to Me, leaning on Me, and taking refuge in the Trinity until you are sent forth. You need to be built up before you can be sent. This is a time of being strengthened.

Lord, I feel terribly weak and feeble.

That is why I need to strengthen you. Just as I came to call sinners who needed Me to heal them, I come to strengthen the weak.

*****

I started my prayer with a list of things I needed to do.

So, these are my plans for the day, what about Yours?

I plan to create a few things, clean up several people's messes, forgive a lot, teach a few who are listening, heal a few, welcome some into My kingdom, chastise some, bless many. The usual – yet it is never boring to Me. People are so interesting when you love them. Have you noticed that?

Yes, Lord, I have. That is why I could teach the same course over and over again, but it was still new and interesting because of my students.

But you wanted to know if I had any plans for you.

Yes. Yours are pretty interesting.

They are indeed. It is good for you to consider what I do all day. It gets you out of self-centeredness. That is one of the goals of finding Me in all things. Also, keep account of when you and I do things together, and when you forget to include Me in your activities.

Maggie, your sight of Me will improve, but do not expect even that you will be aware of Me. Just come to Me often – your awareness will grow. I do not want you discouraged if you think you have lost your focus. It will come and go – but in time you will learn to keep it on Me. This is a process, a journey – do not be so anxious to be at the destination that you miss all the beauty and joy along the way. I am the Way, not just the End. So come, begin this day – see, the light is beginning to come. There is much to be done.

*****

Lord, I thought I could focus on You, but distractions abound. Let me try again. Better yet, can *You* try again. You lead me in focusing on You. I'm sure that would be better.

Maggie, right now your attempts are counted as if they were successful. I appreciate that you have not given up. I will still wrap My arms around you, and eventually you will feel it. I know how difficult it can be at times to pray – why do you think it often took me all night?

Lord, You have me smiling again.

That is good. But your awe and wonder at the sunset also counts as prayer. As does your care and gentle kindness to your mother and Julie. Relax in My arms tonight. Be content that I am pleased with you and that I am in you as well as with you and for you.

Thank You, Lord.

*****

Lord Jesus, I did get glimpses of You yesterday, but somehow this is not yet penetrating into my being.

Maggie be patient. Finding Me is the first step – even that is difficult right now. Wait until you get better at that before you take the next step.

OK, Lord, I'll keep at this. It just seems like such small steps.

I know. You want instant holiness – automatic union – that is not My way. Destruction is fast – construction is slow. My way is building up, not tearing down.

Lord, that is such awesome truth.

*****

Lord, we need to talk – and yes, I'm willing to listen. But when I don't write anything down, I feel like I never took prayer time at all. Yet writing is so much slower.

Maggie, why are you in such a hurry? "You are anxious and troubled about many things; one thing is needful" (Lk. 10:41-42). Just come to Me and relax. Enjoy My company. Listen if I talk, talk if you want to. I am not the One driving you. I was on the earth for 33 years and only in public for three years. But is there a record of Me being in a hurry? Yes, I want you to get things done, but don't rush.

Lord, You are right. You are able to tell me whatever You want in the time we have, or you can increase the time I have. Please help me to use my time wisely.

*****

Lord, I read in a book last night about You being a debtor to me. That did not compute. I can see life from the other side – as I am indebted to You for everything, for I have nothing except what You have given me. But to see You as owing me anything? It is a different concept.

That is because you do not see your relationship with Me as a two-way situation. You have been focused on you and what you should or should not do. My covenants always include what I will do as well as what you need to do. But when your focus is only on your part, I get left out. What I have given you is truly yours. No debt on your part. What you give to Me is your gift as well. No debt on My part. But the covenant itself means that you owe Me, and I owe you. You owe Me allegiance: do My will, be Mine. I owe you protection, guidance, provision. If you will belong to Me, then I will be your God. In this case, "be your God" means what I will do for you. In that sense I do owe you something – by belonging to Me, you are entitled to many things. You often beg Me for what is already rightfully yours.

*****

It seems that when I have had a really meaningful time with You one day, the next few days I have nothing more to say, and prayer is more difficult. I expect that is the reason my prayer life has been so sporadic over the years.

Maggie, there is a big challenge in keeping prayer both spontaneous and real, without becoming rote or routine or meaningless. Personal prayer should be personal, and yet some structure is helpful. But you see how structure can become restrictive as well. It is always a balancing act. A routine time and place for prayer is good but should not be the main focus. The Person to whom you are speaking is the most important. Once you feel you are in My Presence, you have much less trouble. But often, you don't make it there.

Yes, and I am usually ashamed of that fact and find myself reluctant to seek Your Presence the next time or for many times thereafter.

I know. We need to work on that. You have many helping tools to get you into My Presence, but you seldom think to use any of them. You still want to "barrel into prayer." The preliminaries are definitely helpful. You see them as a waste of time. They are not.

Guilty as charged. I will try to improve that, Lord, but I will need Your help. I had a hard time deciding to actually try to come to You just before I started today. But I was afraid that if I did not start, I would again go a long time before I tried again. I really want a continuous daily prayer life but sabotage myself so often.

Don't take all the credit. You do have other forces that discourage serious prayer. Every time you do come it is a victory. Begin to see it that way.

That sounds very helpful. Thank You, Lord.

*****

Lord, last night when I saw the Crucifix on my wall, I realized that I have not really even tried to spend time alone with You in quite a while. I need to again make this holy hour a priority. I have no excuses. But I ask for help. Thank You that You are here ready, willing, and able to give me that help.

Lord, it has been a long time since I have really listened to You or conversed with You.

I know. I've missed that, too. But fear and unbelief and pride have gotten in your way. They are also the cause of that sadness that keeps trying to overwhelm you.

I see that now. But I have started to fight that.

I know. And I have been right with you in the fight. This month you have spent a lot of sorrow in re-living the past. That is not necessary nor helpful. It keeps you from truly appreciating or living in the present.

So how do I stop that?

Like you did this morning. When thoughts that cause you grief come, choose to think of what is directly before you instead.

I think I can do that.

I know you can.

Lord, I actually feel love for You right now – thank You.

It is not your love that is lacking. You simply are not sure how to express the love you have.

That is true. I read how others can go on and on about their love for You, and I seem to be tongue-tied. But give me a person who needs love and I'll do almost anything.

And you do it unto Me.

So, it's OK for me to be so people-conscious?

I gave you that gift and you have used it well. I am not complaining.

But how do I bring a balance to the Martha and Mary?

You don't. I do. You think everything has to be done by you. But I am the One in charge.

You mean I should relax and let You take over:

I do mean that. Just for a little while, take more time to see, enjoy, admire, be in awe of any beauty you see. Would you do that for Me?

Of course, I would.

Then that is your assignment. Now consider your holy hour complete and enjoy the rest of the evening.

Thank You, Lord. Stay with me.

I will.

*****

Lord Jesus, You are already directing this day. I haven't been able to sleep since a little after 4:00 AM so I finally gave up and got dressed at 5:30. Since then, You have been instructing me to do one small thing at a time. I averaged one set of grades; I now have two done out of five. I would have continued, but I thought You wanted me to stop. I cooked breakfast and put in a load of laundry. Now I am eating and will work a bit on the mail and paperwork next. Your directions this morning seem very clear – thank You for that.

Maggie, do you see that no-one else could pay as much attention to you as I can?

Yes, who else could have the patience to watch me do these things and know exactly what I need to do and how to proceed?

And not criticize but encourage?

Yes, especially that.

Do you begin to see My love for you?

Yes, and the cherishing – I am beginning to feel cherished. Thank You for that also.

Do you also see how you are listening to My voice and doing exactly what I tell you even though your own tendency is to do it differently?

Yes, I would have continued with the grades, but now I will be glad to get back to them whenever You tell me to do so.

And If I had told you to keep at it until it was done?

I would have done it, but it would not have seemed as easy. Thank You again.

You see, I don't want to wear you out. I am on your side.

Why do I so often act as if You weren't? It is the same with children – they act as if their parents and teachers were their enemies rather than the ones that are on their side.

It is that fallen nature. The real Enemy can conquer so much more easily if there is infighting among the ranks. It takes maturity to cooperate and work together. This is true in big things as well as little ones.

That gives me things to think about – as well as something to teach about. If our kids could see how they treat the people who are on their side, it could make a big difference in their lives. It is good to know your supports as well as your enemies.

Congratulations! You have now received a teaching as well.

*****

Maggie, I love you whether you listen to Me or not. But when you listen to Me, you are happier.

Lord that is so true. Right now, I feel Your Presence, and I am delighted.

I, too, am delighted. Tell My friends how delighted I am when they seek to hear My voice. I want only good for you. I want happiness for you. I want to be a major part of your life. I can guide your every step. But you have to want Me to guide you. You have to come to Me, ask Me, listen to Me, and act on what I tell you. You would not direct those you love in a wrong direction. Neither will I. And you are one that I love. I know you love Me and want to please Me. I am pleased when I can communicate with you and when you know that I have touched you. Allow Me to hold you close and brighten your day. That also brightens My day. Let My peace envelop you. Draw near to Me, and I will draw near to you and delight in you as well.

Lord, Thank You so much. I've often said that even Your rebuke is wonderful. I tend to get stuck in places. It took me so long to come out of the negatives – thinking, words, and self-image – that I was afraid to visit that area again, lest I get sucked back in.

Don't forget that I am with you. You need not fear anything in My presence. I will bring you safely through any place I bring you. Not only will I bring you safely but remember that I have a purpose in leading you through that place – and My purpose is good and for your benefit.

*****

Lord, I started out OK, but seem to have gotten lost.

I can tell you how it happened. It was your hope of getting more done while you had help available. The weather did not cooperate, and you had to give up your plans. Then things snowballed into that lost feeling.

I tried to be content that some things got done, but it didn't take, did it?

No, it didn't. The rest of the day, you just went through the motions, but your heart was not right.

It's that strong will and wanting my own way, isn't it? So, what should I have done differently? I need to know because tomorrow is likely to be similar.

You need to admit your disappointments and ask My grace to redeem the situation. Ask how good can be brought out of your foiled plans. Ask for My plans. It is not that the computer game you spent several hours playing is evil, but you had no joy in playing it. If you had occupied yourself with something you felt was My will for you, you would have been happy to do it. You have learned to be habitually unhappy.

Lord, that sounds ridiculously funny, but unfortunately it is true. I take no pleasure in the things I do unless I feel I'm doing some good for someone, unless it is out of the ordinary.

You just hit a key here. Start taking pleasure in ordinary things. Note the significance of the words "take pleasure." The pleasure is there for the taking. You took pleasure in the beauty of the snow for a little while, but then you didn't anymore. There is pleasure for the taking in so many ordinary situations. A negative outlook robs

you of these pleasures. If you concentrate on what you can't do or shouldn't do, you lose the ability to see the possibilities that are still abounding. Give Me the pleasure of taking pleasure in the life and situations I give you. Remember that I live within you. I feel what you feel. Let Me feel some pleasure.

*****

Lord Jesus, it was so much better today because I chose to enjoy my day. I didn't do anything extraordinary, but I did things for better reasons, and I did them happily and willingly.

You see, every day can be like this. When you didn't know what to do next, you looked to Me. It was not difficult. Do not be afraid to enjoy life. It is true that I suffered, but not until it was time. I enjoyed My life – I had fun and continually looked to My Father for what to do next. He was in Me and enjoyed what I did. He said He was well-pleased in Me. He would not have been pleased if I did things simply from duty or because I had to or ought to. Remember in the lives of your sons when Karl danced for joy in the snow, or the pure enjoyment of Steven when he bought his super Nintendo, or listened to his music in the car and just really enjoyed it, or Raeme playing with the kittens – remember your joy in seeing them enjoy life? So it is with Your Father in Heaven. He gives you life because He wants good and enjoyable things for you – and He takes pleasure in your joy.

Thank You, Lord. It is so good.

*****

Thank You for putting up with me.

Maggie, I not only put up with you, I delight in you, and tenderly love you. You feel like you have so much more to do and more to learn and far to go but take heart – you are on the right road and I am with you. I know how much effort it takes for you to do all these things. I see and I receive your offerings. I hear your prayers. I bless

you abundantly and I will continue to perfect you. Keep doing what you are doing. You will become stronger.

*****

Maggie, you are still reluctant to turn to Me for help, aren't you?

I guess I am. Why is that?

Because most of your life you did not have anyone to turn to for help. You had to fend for yourself. Even in your illness, you tried to keep going on your own. Relying on others is frustrating at times and simply does not work at other times.

So, it makes sense that I'm reluctant to ask?

Yes, it does, but you can't stay there.

I can accept that. So, I should keep trying, but not get too upset at my failures?

Right. And remember that asking Me for help is different from asking others for help. I am always available and willing.

Lord, You really encourage me in this. Thank You.

*****

A thought was running through my mind about self-discipline vs. obedience. It seems like I want to have someone *visible* to obey in my life, and I'm blaming my lack of self-discipline on the lack of such a person. But then there is also the aspect of being social and needing more approval. I don't have much of that, either – at least on a human level. I'm having a lot of difficulty looking to You for these things, and that frustrates me.

Me, too.

Lord, the last thing You need is frustration from me. I'm so sorry.

Let's get past this.

OK, Lord, lead on.

How real am I to you?

Real enough that I don't question Your reality or existence anymore. I know You are. In fact, I get upset when I encounter a wavering on this in others, especially in books.

Being an all-or-nothing type person, your belief in My reality is total.

Yes, but my actions do not correspond.

Exactly – thus you have great frustration. You need your actions to flow from your faith, but when that is not happening, you shut down.

And being overly dramatic, I think all is lost.

The good news is all is not lost. There is a training involved and necessary here. Just as your students need to re-train their ways of looking at subtraction as adding a negative number, you have to re-train yourself and practice to let your thoughts, words, actions, motives, and attitudes flow from your faith and not your flesh.

It sounds so simple – but the practice is so different from the theory.

That's why you need Me constantly by your side.

And I suppose I can't be perfect at it immediately.

Right. This is what you need to ease into and can use as the Advent project. Use this next week and a half to come up with ways that your actions can flow from your faith – and then do that.

Lord, that sounds really good. Is it OK to get others to do it, too, and help me with it?

By all means. That would bring unity and purpose and accountability, and it would help you with that social need.

Thank You so much, Lord. I accept this as a challenge.

I knew you would – and I am pleased.

Lord, it is still so great that I have the ability to please You.

Yes, you have – and in your more negative moments, remember that I also attempt to please you at times. Look at Thanksgiving from that point of view. How please-able are you? Can even a perfect God

please you? It's all a matter of focus. Is it the dark cloud or the silver lining? The silver lining is impossible without the cloud.

Wow, Lord, that is quite a new perspective – at least for me. Thank You.

It is truly My pleasure – see, you have given Me pleasure again.

Lord, it really feels good to give You pleasure – is this how prayer can become a delight rather than a chore?

Do you now see your God jumping up and down for joy? This is My silver lining – to have you understand something that has been bothering you for a long time. The cloud is the difficulty and inconsistency of your prayer life; the lining is that prayer is mutual love, communication, pleasure, and yes, union between you and your God.

So that union I so strongly desire is nothing more than continual prayer?

Oh, it is much more than that, but once your thoughts, words, deeds, motives, and attitudes all flow from your faith, continual prayer or union or giving and receiving pleasure on a spiritual level naturally flows from that.

Lord, I feel like the woman at the well again – are we talking about living water?

Exactly. Do you want some?

With all my heart.

I'm Yours.

Yes, You are – and let me hold nothing back from You. Let me be completely Yours as well.

Is this not total union? Is this not what My heart and yours have longed for?

Lord, how can I thank You?

By doing it – and letting Me be continually a part of doing it. I do not expect you to do anything alone – in fact, you can't.

*****

You inspired me to some moderation in a most delightful way. At Mass, my mother handed me two chocolate-covered marzipan bars. After my second tutoring job, I was about to open one of them when I wondered how many little squares they were portioned into. it was 16, so the two of them made 32 little squares. Then I checked the calendar. There were seven days left in November and 25 in December, totaling 32. By this time, I knew it was You inspiring me. I realized that if I ate one little square each day, I could have a truly enjoyable moment – perfectly legitimate and in great moderation. Those two chocolate bars would last until Christmas – an "Advent calendar" for me! A gift from You! My Advent is a little longer than that of others – that, too, is Your gift to me. So, I broke the chocolate into the 32 little pieces, ate one, thoroughly enjoyed it, and put the rest in a freezer bag and froze them. Today I will get to have another small piece, so with Your help that will be the only chocolate I will have today.

And if I can do all this out of loving obedience to You, or as my offering of growth in the virtue of self-control, would that be an acceptable Christmas gift from me to You? And if, with Your grace, I can accomplish this, there are bound to be good results – which could be Your gift to me.

Maggie, the plan is good. Go ahead and begin today. But let Me decide what My gift to you will be.

That's fair enough. But would You accept a daily offering of this discipline? And if I can do more, would You consider that a little unexpected surprise gift from me? After almost two years, this is the first idea I have had of how I can give an all-knowing God a surprise gift.

Maggie not only would that be acceptable, but it would be most delightful and pleasing to your God to receive such gifts from you. And your delight in giving such gifts will be another gift as well. This is love – this is one of the ways you can love your God. It is good. Notice that it is not overambitious. Neither is it too little. It leaves room for more without it seeming like a burden. It is offered with joy and the joy is itself a greatly acceptable gift.

There is an addition to your parable of the pitcher. It is the "how" of the cleansing. You understood the "why" and the "what" and the "who" and the "where," and though the "when" was not completely clear, you know that it needs to be done as soon as possible. But the "how" was not specific. You are cleansed and re-filled whenever you present yourself to Me in prayer. You can ask, or just come to Me as you are. Speak to Me of whatever you want. Think of yourself as a child who has just completed a "masterpiece" of finger-painting and presents the finished product to the parent. Your ministry is the painting. But you are still covered with paint, and as I the parent accept and admire the work, I also proceed to wash you, and help you clean up the supplies so they will be ready to use for the next masterpiece. You may be totally unaware of the cleanup process because you are busy discussing the work or the plans for the next one. But it is very good. And guess what: you have now spent over an hour in prayer this morning. How about that?

Lord, it is wonderful. Thank You so much. Once again, You prove that no one can out-give You. Thank You for a marvelous prayer time.

You are most welcome. And thank you for spending more than an hour with Me.

Lord, You too, are welcome. Help me to listen for Your call if You call me to come back.

*****

Lord, I am always so impressed with Your gentleness and tenderness. You, who have unlimited power and authority, handle us with utmost care. It reminds me of the day I took the kittens to school. The gentle, tender way some of the boys held those kittens – especially one of the burly football players was so beautiful – so loving and kind. If I ever teach again, let me tell my students how they remind me of You when they are like that. In fact, that would be a good thing to tell my sons, as well. Help me to speak good, encouraging things to them.

Maggie, here is another change I am calling you to. If you are looking for good things to say, you will be less likely to say things you regret. I am not a God of negatives. I do not delight in criticism.

I find good and build on it. Learn of Me. Most people do not see that. They see righteousness and justice only from the point of view of where it is missing or might be applied with destruction involved. Yes, some things need to be torn down, but My work is to build the Kingdom of God and bring it close enough so My people will enter. It is good – it is lovely – It is full of love, joy, peace, patience, kindness, gentleness, goodness, faithfulness, and self-control. Find these qualities in the ones I give you to teach, starting with your own sons. Tell them when you see these fruits of My Spirit in them. Let them know that you see *Me* in them. And look to Me and My Mother for examples.

*****

Three things to remember: 1. That Jesus will always be there. 2. That He wants me – really, Lord? You want ME? I know that I want You – But You also want ME? 3. That He needs me – You need ME? I know that I need You – but YOU need ME?? How can this be? Yet You have created me and so You must have wanted me – and You went to great lengths to preserve my life and bring me to this land. *You want me!* And what I do for You – *You need me?!* So now my question is: how can I respond? How can I satisfy *Your* wants and needs? How can I hear You better? How can I see things from Your perspective? Help me, Lord. I truly want to do things to please You. That is why I am here.

*****

I was told that the word sacrifice means "sacred offering." That makes my whole day a sacrifice when I offer it to You in the morning. And my body can be a living sacrifice simply by my offering it to You to be used for Your glory. Lord, I do that now. I offer You my body for Your use. It seems so simple. You make what I offer You sacred. My body becomes sacred, my day becomes sacred, my work becomes sacred, my prayers become sacred, my joys become sacred, my sufferings become sacred, and my praises and thanksgiving can become sacred. Anything I offer You becomes a sacred offering – sacrifice. Wow! What power in prayer! And Your Presence just came over me as if to confirm this.

I offer You my sons, my husband, and my class as well, but are they mine to give You? Will You make them sacred? Perhaps not completely, but maybe my dealings with them and my time with them could become sacred. This is important – I can only offer You what is mine to give. Yet all that is mine came from You in the first place. You give me a gift, I offer it back to You, You make it holy, and bless me more. Lord, let me offer You more today than I have ever done before.

*****

I realized I need to come to You with all my problems. I had started out like Smokey the Bear stomping out campfires in a dry forest. So, I "gave" You a boot for stomping out the fires, then I realized You don't need a boot – You can squeeze a cloud and put out all the fires. I gave up worrying about them. You lifted my spirits. I gave You all the brokenness and strife in my life; You took it and did wonders. Thank You!

*****

What struck me was Your Mother's attitude through all the changes in her life. How did she handle Your Ascension? She finally got You back after all the pain of Your Passion and You leave again – how did You tell her? And then she had to wait about 20 years to join You? Yet as I contemplated all this, I could not imagine her attitude to be like the one I've been struggling with. She was probably grateful for life and did not live in the past or the future. That attitude is what I seek now. To live in, embrace, and be grateful for the present. Where You put me is where I shall delight to be, for You do it out of perfect love. Finding You in all circumstances isn't really "finding," but focusing on Your love as the creator and manager of the circumstance. And love is never boring or distasteful.

Maggie, you are getting it. This is a very important lesson for you. But though the theory is beautiful and understandable, the practice is much more difficult. There needs to be a "finding" before the focus can be placed. Keep at it, you are definitely on the right track. This is the way – walk in it.

*****

Lord, I do thank You for today. I took my mother-in-law on a trip to the Chesapeake Bay. The weather was marvelous, the trees are turning beautiful colors, the water was a delight, and we even saw a flock of geese flying in formation. We had a nice dinner. But when we got home, I was unsettled. Nothing satisfied me, so I guess that was a call to prayer. I blew that one.

At least you know you blew it. Next time, try Me. I promise to be surprisingly refreshing and satisfying.

You're making me smile again.

I know – I like doing that.

Lord, do I make You smile sometimes?

Quite often.

Could You let me know sometimes?

Sure – how about now?

Really?

Yes.

You are right – You are surprisingly refreshing and satisfying. I wish I could dance with You again.

You will.

In this life or the next?

Wait and see.

Lord, am I too casual with You?

I have not complained. I don't want you to be so formal that you see Me as unapproachable. Neither do I want to be treated rudely.

I think my rudeness is ignoring You so often.

No, it is not rudeness – you are not yet at the place where you can be as aware of Me as you and I would like. But keep at it, it is coming.

Lord, I don't want to offend You in any way.

I know. But you do have to learn to walk that tightrope in so many aspects of your life. You can't live in the past and you can't live in the future. There is always an abyss on either side. Pride and discouragement – unbelief and presumption – too much work or too little work – boredom and frenzy. The list goes on and on – the tightrope is that straight and that narrow. The good news is that I'm willing and able to safely lead you across. Sometimes I use others in your life, sometimes I use others from My life – like My Mother and saints and angels. It is meant to be a great and glorious adventure, but only when you know Me well enough to trust Me and turn to Me for help the first instant you need it and know that I can and will be there. This is why I hate fear. Awe and wonder are good – fear and dread are not. If you need to be a bit casual, that is so much better than constantly feeling unworthy.

Thank You for speaking to me tonight.

See, you make Me smile again. I am delighted that you can understand Me even a little bit.

I guess not too many even try.

Right! Yet that is the purpose for which I create people – to reveal Myself and My love to them – it is so refreshing when someone is willing to receive.

Lord, I'll receive.

Now there's a case when I don't mind you volunteering.

Lord, for You, I gladly volunteer for anything.

I know. Right now, receiving is what I really want you to do. That means waiting, that means not doing much on your own. It means watching and being ready. It also means recognizing what you are to receive – more work there than you expected.

*****

Lord, the morning went well as long as I was alone – I kept asking You what to do next. But once Mom E. was up, my attention was no longer on You.

Now you see why I have given you so much solitude. This is a major step in the right direction. Rome wasn't built in one day.

It felt so good, though. I got to do so much that I really wanted done, and still did as much crocheting as before. I wasn't bored or restless or wasting time doing useless things I don't even enjoy. Thank You, Lord. The Mass confirmed all You and I discussed yesterday. The most important thing is why we do things. When I did things – ordinary things like housework – because I felt Your inspiration to do them, it was so much better than doing them just because they needed to be done. Please keep me concentrating on the relationship between You and me rather than the work I need to do. Your love for me came through every task You had me do – and my love for You made me want to do an even better job than I would have on my own.

Would you like to do it again tomorrow?

I'd love to.

It's a date.

You did it again – made me smile.

Yes, and so did you.

I wasn't expecting to be dating these days.

I know. It isn't possible when you are discontented, but once you see your life as an adventure, even in your present condition, there are so many possibilities. Many years ago, you told a lady that her loneliness was My way to have her to Myself; so, her relationship with Me could grow. I have also chosen to isolate you so I could have you to Myself. That union you so desperately want is to begin here and now. It can grow by leaps and bounds now. You don't have to wait for it, and I don't have to wait any longer, either.

You mean You – I can hardly say it – desire me? It isn't just me wishing.

Where do you think your desire came from? Why were you created except for union with your God? You believed you had a God-given purpose in life – that is true – but it is the relationship – not something you have to do. Yes, you do things that grow out of the relationship, but it is not the things you do but the relationship

that causes you to do them that is most important – the "why," not the "what" or the "how."

Lord, why did it take me so long to see this? And why is it so easy to forget?

Now that you do see it, it will be easier to remember. But there was a lot of work that had to be done in you before your eyes could be opened to this. Some people see it sooner, some later, some never. The important part is to not just see it but live it.

I will certainly try.

That's all I ask.

*****

Lord, yesterday I heard that prayer must be a two-way conversation. Thank You that, most of the time, it has been in my relationship with You. I get long-winded occasionally, but Your patience is wonderful.

Maggie, it is good that you listen. Sometimes it is more difficult to listen but keep at it.

Right now, I am having a difficult time.

I see. Try joyfulness.

OK, Lord, I choose to smile, and I choose to relax and welcome You. And I am joyful that You are here.

See, it works every time. Right now, I want you to Myself.

You do?

That surprises you.

I thought I was pretty dull company today.

And My love is supposed to grow dim because you think so?

I see, Lord. I'm sorry. Thank You for Your great love.

Allow Me to exercise that love.

Lord, it is so good to be loved by You.

Think of My love in the Trinitarian sense. If one loves Me, and you do, then We come and make Our home with you, and We have. You will find Us right here.

Lord, how can I make You more comfortable?

By finding Me – Us – here. Your faith tells you that it is true, but it is quite different when you try to put that faith into practice.

Lord, this puts a new face on "seek and you shall find."

Yes, it does. Seeking and finding, but not in physical terms. This is no game of pretending – it is real though not physical. You know without seeing and listen without hearing, yet you understand. You feel but not through touching. You can ask without speaking and you will receive. And knocking can simply be a desire. It is not magic. It is the spiritual world. Enter in. Rejoice like you have never been able to rejoice before. You see the Spirit is teaching you. The Father is holding you. And I – your Spouse – am with you and continue to remain with you. I receive you, love you, desire you.

Lord, I can only thank You and accept with great joy.

That is all I ask of you. You delight your God – all Three Persons.

*****

Lord, one of the verses in my prayer this evening was, "If you hunger for holiness, God will satisfy your longing, good measure and flowing over." Lord, I do hunger and long for holiness – true holiness – not just appearances. It says You will satisfy this longing.

I will, but you will not see it. You will not suddenly feel you have arrived at holiness. On this side of eternity, you will always have room to improve. But if you leave the results to Me, great progress can be made.

Lord, I will gladly leave the judgment to You. Remember, Lord, many many years ago I thought You told me that I have enrolled in Your school, and You would teach me.

I remember it well. And you have learned many lessons.

But my attendance has been sporadic at best.

True, but neither of us gave up completely.

It seems I have begun again.

Yes, but now it is much more than school. You are espoused to your Teacher. What did Mary Magdalene call Me at the tomb?

"Rabboni" – meaning teacher.

But was she relating to Me simply as her teacher? No. And neither can you. You and I both desire and long for total union. Now it comes at moments. The time will come when it will stay for seconds – then minutes – then hours – and eventually for eternity. But once again, leave the progress to Me.

I shall try. So, I should not expect report cards?

Right. You did not get any in your marriage to Rae.

This relationship is truly spousal?

Did you doubt it?

Well, actually, I saw it more like holiness – to be desired, but always with room to grow. I've heard of the purgative, illuminative, and unitive stages of prayer, but thought I was simply going back and forth between the first two.

Not leaving the judgments to Me?

I suppose not.

So repent.

Gladly.

You are forgiven.

That was quick.

Why dwell on it?

Thanks.

You're welcome.

Lord, we're actually having fun.

Yeah, ain't it great?

It is indeed.

One of the reasons you had trouble persevering in prayer was that you were expecting only heaviness and correction. So often you were surprised or amazed that I was gentler and kinder than you expected.

Lord, how true that is! Yet You have proven over and over that You are so much better and greater than I expect.

So now give Me even your expectations. Allow Me to love you as I desire.

Gladly, Lord.

This way each day can be exciting, for you will not know what blessings, graces, and gifts I have for you.

As I have offered You my prayers, works, joys, and sufferings, I have been focused only on the works and sufferings.

So now focus on the prayers and joys. The work will continue on its own. The sufferings will also come and go. Dwelling on them is not helpful. Dwell on prayers and joy.

Lord, there is joy again. I really need more joy in my life.

How well I know!

You restored my joy through a trip to Texas.

It was time to lighten up. Remember My yoke is easy, and My burden is light. You were heavy-laden. But you came unto Me and now I give you joy as well as rest.

Lord, I really do appreciate it.

Stay with me, kid – there is much more.

Lord, Mom can't seem to rest as long as I'm up.

I know. I'm working on her as well.

Thank You.

But it is *you* that I am communing with here and now. Do not think you are unimportant to Me. And do not get puffed up either. Accept My love for you. It is real.

Lord, I do accept. And I am so grateful.

It is good.

*****

What can I do for You?

Maggie, stay with Me a while. Take an extra minute or two after Mass to be with Me. Hold My hand, touch My face. Sit beside Me.

Lord, there is a gentle sadness in that request. You have held me and stayed with me countless times when I needed that. Of course, I'll stay with You, Lord. I want to hug You, hold You tight. It is such a beautiful privilege to console You.

You are a consolation to Me. In a little while laughter will return. But now, let Me rest in your tenderness.

Come, Lord, rest as long as You want. I am here.

*****

How is Your day? It looks like You have provided another beautiful day. Thank You. Lord, the thought that You might answer that little question "How is Your day?" is overwhelming. You have much greater issues to deal with than I do. Though I would never really understand it all if You did answer, the mere idea of being a confidante of God is so high above my expectations – yet that is what You desire me to be. That is what a friend does – listens to the plans, troubles, joys, thoughts of the other. You do that for me, and it only stands to reason that I should do that for You. I would like that. I do not expect to be told great secrets, but if I can somehow in the tiniest of ways be there for You to tell of Your days, wow, it would be such an honor. Such a small part of a relationship, yet so overwhelming: to be a confidante of God!

Yes, Maggie, I am calling you to such a relationship. There were a few in Scripture that were able to have such a relationship with Me – Enoch, Abraham, Moses, David, John the Baptist, Mary Magdalene, John the Apostle – in fact, all the apostles, including Paul – and of course Joseph, and most of all, My Mother Mary. That is what the prophets were – confidantes of God. What made them so? They listened to Me. They were able to step aside from their own lives and issues enough to focus on Mine. Do come to Me and ask Me about My day. I will not tell you more than you can handle, but I will tell

you more as you listen more and can leave your own world enough to approach Mine. Yes, this is a part of what I call you to become – a confidante of God.

*****

Late evening at the prayer meeting we heard this word:

Listen, my daughters, to the joys of My heart. I have the joy of receiving My faithful ones into My kingdom. I have the joy of showing them the glories of heaven. I take great joy in providing for your needs. I take great joy in calling you to be co-workers with Me, and even greater joy when you accept the call. I am a God of great joy. See and share My joy. Receive My care, My comfort, My provision, and My great joy.

*****

I want to please You. I want to be what You desire. Perfect me as You see fit. Let all my iniquities fall from me. Let me become the beautiful bride that blesses Your heart and attends to Your desires.

Maggie, I am doing it. I shall finish the work I have begun. I shall not abandon the work of My hands. Even you shall marvel at what you will become. I am the Lord your God. I have chosen you as the Persian king chose Esther. Right now, you are being prepared. This is your time of instruction to learn the ways of royalty. Your beauty shall be radiating from within. It will be a true treasure to your God. Remember that I am the One who does this. Allow Me to guide your steps and do this work. Step back and see that I do it better than anyone else possibly could. Do not direct My work; allow Me the freedom to do it as I wish. Be the clay in My hands and let Me mold you according to My design. I assure you, the result will more than please and amaze you. I have glorious plans. You cannot imagine them. See what wonders My Father had done with the submission of the one who became My Mother. It took her acceptance and her willingness to become what He desired to make her. Learn from her.

*****

Holy Spirit, I invite You to lead me in prayer. I will start with psalms, but there are two elements I want to take care of first. I offer this day and this time of prayer to You. Father let it all be an act of love. Second, I ask for what I want. I dare to ask to be Fathered – to be allowed to be dependent and cared for by You, that I might feel Your touch and approval and be strengthened by Your love.

Psalm 68 and all the psalms in the sixties – Lord, I needed to see a bigger picture. These psalms show Your greatness and splendor and majesty. I tend to think of You on a much smaller scale. You are holy, mighty, glorious – yet loving, gentle, kind. How marvelous to belong to such a God?

Maggie, it is good that you see Me in a different light. There is more of Me than you can comprehend. But I reveal Myself to you as you care to listen. I show you My love. It is total and complete. It will not change but you only discover bits and pieces of it as you are able to digest. Take what you need. Today you need nourishment and sustenance. Take it, it is yours.

Lord, I see how vast Your provision is – it's like a feast fit for a king, and I am an ant. Yet You tell me "take what you want."

That's right. What you want to know is – what do I want or expect from you in return? Love only wants love back. Gratitude is a beginning. Dependence is a step in the right direction – but love is the journey and the destination. You wanted to know how to love a God back during your senior year in high school. Now, more than 30 years later, you are still discovering the answer. Self-sacrifice is just a part. Enjoyment is a big part. Right now, I invite you to enjoy My company. Hold My hand today. Let's walk together and just enjoy the day.

Lord God, I thank You. Father, I am strengthened and feel Your approval. The awe and wonder are back. Jesus, I will walk with You this day. Whatever the day brings, You and I will handle it. Holy Spirit, thank You for leading me into such marvelous prayer.

*****

Maggie, believe it or not, there is progress. Your prayer life is improving. You wanted to make it a priority – it is. You have not given up; you are seeking Me and My ways. You are doing loving and kind things daily. Can you improve? Of course! But you are working on it. Be patient with yourself. When focusing on your own shortcomings you must remember that My love for you does not depend on your perfection. I accept you as you are and love you as you are – but I am helping you to become better. Relax and rejoice even in the disappointments. These are your temptations – resist them by remembering My great love for you. You are redeemed, cleansed, adopted, and very much loved.

How do I respond to You?

Maggie, it is not difficult. It is very simple. First, you relax. This is not painful, this is joy. It is what you want more than anything in the world. It is what I want more than anything else in the world. You asked Me to "take and receive." Now I ask you to take and receive My love and My grace. I give it all to you. You asked, now receive, for I am giving you what you asked for.

I accept and take and receive Your love and Your grace.

This is not an instantaneous thing – it is the same journey you have been on. You were created for this. You were created as a living container of love – My love. This is your purpose in life – to take it and to give it away. The journey and the growth are how to be able to receive more and more. You may be a thimble to start with, but you are to grow as big as a reservoir, or even an ocean. I have enough to give – there is no shortage – but you must grow and expand and continually receive and pour out. You shall no longer be a pitcher but an ocean. If you continually receive and pour out, then the cleansing will also be continuous. Hold on tight – this is about to get exciting. But remember – FEAR NOT!

OK, Jesus, I fear not. Back at Loyola, I had gotten a picture of the transformations that must take place. It may be silly, but here's how I see it: When I was before the tabernacle there, I told You that I wished I could become small enough to get in there with You. And You answered, "But you don't need to. I have already become small enough to come into You as bread and wine." So the way I see it now, when You said, "If anyone loves Me, he will keep My word, and My Father will love him and We will come to him and make Our home with him," You and Your Father and the Holy Spirit now become small enough to come and live in my heart. But in prayer, smallness is traded. You become BIG and I become small. And as I learn to pray without ceasing, You will stay BIG but will still be in me. I will grow as I pray. Does this make any sense at all?

Does it to you?

I think so.

Then use it. Whatever is profitable, go ahead and use it.

Sometimes I hide in You and at other times You hide in me. I need You, and You need me to reach some folks who are not seeking You even though You are seeking them. You are right. It is an adventure, a joint venture. Thank You so much for Your great patience.

My child, I rejoice. You have made your Father celebrate – I am so glad to take My rightful place in your heart.

Father, I welcome You. The place is clean and ready for You. Bring whatever You want or need. If I can be of help, let me know.

I have angels to do all I need. See your Father dance – for it is MOVING day.

Jesus, is He often like this?

This is but the beginning. He is full of joy. And so am I. I have also longed for this day. Come – dance with Me.

Where?

Out in the hall – it'll be great.

But I can't dance.

I'll teach you.

What if someone else sees?

We'll deal with that if it happens.

How about music?

Let My joy be the music.

How could I refuse …

*****

So, Lord, how are You today?

Maggie, I too, am rejoicing. It is good that you have found feelings for Me but remember that love is not dependent on or consists only of feeling. You have faithfully done many loving things for Me over the years. Even your continual struggles with prayer and Scripture and all the other fights you have waged over the years are evidences of your love that are very precious to Me. I see your love in many ways; it is there, and what is even better is that it is growing.

Yes, Lord, I see that You are right. Let it grow strong and big.

It will. And do you see contentment growing?

I feel it.

*****

Lord Jesus, I'm afraid to ask You how You think this day went.

Do you think I am so critical that you couldn't handle it?

No, that would be me, not You.

So why are you afraid of what I'll say?

It doesn't make sense, does it? I have been told that I had misplaced guilt. Could we deal with that?

Do you want to analyze it or get rid of it?

Don't I need to know what it is in order to get rid of it?

Perfectionism and legalism.

But don't we humans need to work toward being perfect as our Father is perfect?

Be – not work toward.

I still don't get it.

Who are you? Or rather, whose are You?

Yours. But often it doesn't show. I get caught up in so many things that I forget or lose awareness of You.

When you were married, did you have to work at being aware that you were married? Or when you became a mother, did you have to work at the awareness of your motherhood?

No – it came naturally. But I often wondered and worried about whether I was a good enough wife or mother.

Did you do the best you could?

I think so.

Then that is good enough. Did you ever deny being a wife or mother?

No.

Neither do you deny that you are Mine. Did you make mistakes as wife or mother?

Plenty of them.

Did they diminish the state of being a wife or mother?

No – so my mistakes do not affect my being Yours?

Not at all. What are mistakes good for?

To learn not to do it that way anymore – to try something different.

See – it works in math and in My Kingdom as well. But if you are convinced that you are no good at math, you are likely to accept your mistakes instead of learning from them.

Oh, and if I think I'm a failure in obedience or prayer or self-control, I am not learning from my mistakes but wallowing in them.

This is why I want you to avoid discouragement, and why you need to focus on how much I love you and on how you cannot be separated from My love. There is fear behind all the striving, not love. Instead of fearing mistakes and failures, be assured of My love and power and help and guidance and face each mistake as a tool for learning and a stepping-stone for holiness. You have learned to graciously make mistakes in math – now do the same in your faith. You are not laden with guilt or shame when you make a mistake in math, even though you really know better. But once aware of the mistake, you do not leave it uncorrected. That is the perfection I want of you. And

all My mercy, grace, love, help, power, and everything I do to assist you are available to you. And I also have great confidence in you.

It now makes a lot more sense. The exercises, the diet, the cleaning of the attic, these are corrections of past mistakes. I need to keep working on them. Caring for Mom E and tutoring are the work I'm involved in. But all of it is blooming where I'm planted if I don't give in to defeat or discouragement and keep looking to You for all the help and love I need.

And remember that you cannot do it alone, nor should you even try to do it alone. I offer you so much help. Use it.

So, prayer is not so much a duty as a help? Like homework?

Right! But unless a child does homework on a regular basis, he will not make that transition from having to do it versus needing to do it in order to learn the subject well. Then once the training is over, and one is in a profession, the practice and learning that seemed like a chore when it was called homework become a most pleasant and important aspect of the profession. As long as a child thinks he is doing homework for the benefit of the teacher, he is missing the point. It is with good works and the practice of virtue. Do you do these things to impress your God? Or are you learning the perfection you were created for?

So that goes for Scripture study as well?

Of course. You learn to be like Me by seeing and studying what I am like. This is why the will of My Father is so important. It is His will that defines your purpose in life and the means to attain it. His will for you is very good. It is worth pursuing.

Lord, I think I've grown tonight.

Yes – maybe a couple of centimeters.

*****

I've been pondering the child vs. adult in Your kingdom. You encourage us to come to You as little children, and that we can only enter the Kingdom of God if we are like little children. Yet we are to grow to maturity and not stay in our infancy as Christians. There are certain qualities of childhood that we must retain: trust, obedience, unsophistication, unpretentiousness, dependency. But to do the work of the Kingdom, we must not only grow in these qualities but also acquire adult virtues, including, patience, responsibility, faithfulness, self-control.

You are the One maturing, redeeming, and sanctifying us. The child in us will thrive naturally in the proper environment, and that environment is Your Presence. So, the grace that I desire today is to stay in Your Presence more and more each day, to climb in Your lap and stay there, and soak in Your love and mercy and goodness. Then I must pick up kids, make dinner, and do whatever else I need to do. Thank You that You are always available.

*****

Personal prayer has again been missing in my life. So here I am realizing that, despite all the other things I try to do, I have again been avoiding You.

Maggie, you want total union with Me, but you still can't seem to believe that it is possible, or if it is, it is very far off in the future.

Lord, I am guilty as charged – help my unbelief.

I do help you in so many ways. Do not be afraid to write. You have learned St. Augustine's realization of his need for Me. He wrote, "You were within, but I was without." He meant that I was trying to get his attention, but he was not looking within his heart but was distracted by other things. I am within your heart and your life. But when you avoid Me, you are without. Your writing brings you within. It is not the only way to come within, but it has often worked for you and you are more confident of hearing My voice this way. I will welcome you any way you come to Me. Let My love drive away all your fears and uncertainties. I also desire total union with you. All My blessings are not a substitute for My love. Any of your strivings are not a substitute for your love, either. The prayers and Mass and service are to bring you into My arms and bring Me into your life. They are not an end in themselves. I am the only Way, Truth, and Life that can satisfy you. Allow My love and My life to penetrate your being. Rest in Me.

Let me rely on Your grace and Your love to meet all my needs. Grow my faith to believe this is possible.

Maggie, when I called My disciples "O ye of little faith," it was not a rebuke, but a term of endearment. The ones of great faith, the centurion, the woman healed of the issue of blood, they did not follow Me and live with Me and receive all My words. My closest friends were the ones of little faith. Yes, their faith did grow to greatness, but they needed a lot of help. When you feel like your faith is feeble and small, know that it endears you to Me even more. It is not My admiration but My life and My constant help you need. And it is not only available to you but My greatest desire for you.

Maggie, first of all, I am so glad you came this morning. You might not see, hear, or feel what I am doing in your life, but I am working. The desire for total union and constant awareness of My Presence is coming to pass, or rather being fulfilled.

Lord, I feel like I stumbled on a brick and wanted to build a city with it. Yet, You are building that city. It is simply taking a lot longer than I imagined.

Exactly. Total union with Me is taking a long time and much work. But I put that brick in your path and you took it and did not let go. Now your city is coming along. It is good.

Thank You, Lord.

*****

Abide

Lord Jesus, this morning I believe You are calling me to prayer, the way You used to do it long ago.

Maggie, it is true. I am calling you. Much has happened in the last week and a half. There is much on your mind and though you want to include Me in your life and though you want to give Me the controls, you are slipping back into some old ways.

Yes, Lord, I see what You mean. I am beginning to worry rather than pray, and I am filling my time with trivia rather than coming to You.

Exactly! You have been more aware of My action and direction in your life, but instead of drawing closer to Me, you are becoming a spectator.

I see. I have been watching all that You have been doing, in awe. I have been grateful, but I have not come to You to talk about it – instead just watching and trying to stay out of Your way.

I do not want you out of My way; nor do I want you missing My way. When you felt there was not enough activity in your life, you knew that much was missing. Now that there is enough activity, you are trying to step aside and just let it happen. But you are afraid to really take part in it.

I see and agree. I feel like I am seeing my own life from the outside. My patio door got replaced, Geri went to Winchester, Jodie (formerly Sr. Joanna) had a good weekend here, and several of us former sisters took a trip to Emmitsburg and it went well. Carol (formerly Sr. Carol, Jodie, and I had a nice lunch together; my prayer group friend Jeanne's ordeal at the hospital passed; I babysat; the kids were OK. I'm there, but not completely – sort-of numb, no passion.

And it does not feel quite right.

True. But it is better than the way it was before things started happening.

Yes, it is better, but if you are not careful, the pendulum will swing back to the frenzy of too much activity, too much responsibility, and still a missing relationship with Me.

I see the danger. I'm also feeling Your loving Presence more strongly than I have in a long time. Thank You.

You are welcome.

*****

Lord, You called me this morning not to rebuke me but to help me. I see and appreciate that. I am listening, but I do not see the remedy. I see the problem; I don't see that I can fix it. And now I see that I can't just sit back and watch and expect You to fix it, either.

Do you see Heaven rejoicing? By George, I think she's got it! This is a joint venture. You cannot do it by yourself, and neither will I do it by Myself. The joy is in the companionship. Not just the results, but the process. Not just the destination, but the journey. Walk with Me, talk with Me, and abide in My love. Don't walk past Me, don't lag behind, don't just watch, and don't show off expecting Me to stop and watch. Don't talk all the time, stop and listen. But don't expect Me to do all the talking either.

This is what it means to abide in Your love?

It is. Securely in My arms, neither afraid nor arrogant. Knowing I can carry you if necessary, but that you can walk with Me.

It is a great thing to be able to walk, not grovel, or crawl, but securely walk hand-in-Hand.

You do see and understand.

Lord, thank You! Thank You for calling me tonight – for speaking to me on a higher level.

You mean more like an adult?

Yes, I feel much more grown-up.

Because you don't feel scolded but helped.

Yes! You and I are on the same side – not struggling to control nor competing against each other – working together.

To improve something worth improving.

Wow, Lord, that's quite a compliment.

But true, nonetheless.

Thank You, Lord.

*****

Lord, I'm at Your service – what can we talk about today?

It seems you had more joy today.

Yes, Lord, thank You for that. And I even took an afternoon nap.

You are rested, warm, full, staying with your Lenten aspirations – all is well. Now you can work on serious matters.

What serious matters can we work on?

How about love?

OK Lord, what about love? Suddenly I feel Your Presence.

Stay with that feeling a bit.

You are demonstrating Your love for Me?

Yes. I am. When all the impediments – physical, emotional, etc. – are taken care of, it is easier for you to recognize and accept My love. Yet it is there and available all the time. I want you to grow in awareness and be able to enter into My love – first at times like this when all is well – but also when there are problems, irritations, discomforts, distractions that inevitably come. Find My love as a refuge that you can enter into – be it for just a moment or for longer periods of time.

So, this is the safe and secure place I have heard about – I thought it was somewhere within myself that I had to find it. I thought it was just a nice idea – not reality.

This is what it means to abide in Me, and I abide in you.

Lord, I like it – a lot.

I'm glad. This is what I want for you, to be able to know My love any time, any place – and to desire it always. It needs to be so much a part of you that nothing – no one – can take it from you. It is My gift to you. A gift that is ever new and is never spent. The burning bush – the living water – the fountain that never will run dry. And it is yours.

Lord, thank You. I accept Your great gift. I realize that I do not deserve it – have not earned it – am not worthy of it – but I gratefully accept it and will try to use it often. Please keep reminding me to do so.

I will.

*****

Lord Jesus, I have so much to thank You for. At some point this afternoon I believe You spoke to me and showed me my unbelief. It brought both conviction and joy in that You seemed to give me the power to overcome it as well. You said that I did not believe that You would actually dwell within me. That You will actually initiate the closer union I so desire – it seems I have been expecting it to come about through *my* efforts. Yet everything I am being taught says that You want this union much more than I do and that You make it happen and all I have to do is respond. Today, You showed me that I had not truly believed this. But by Your very speaking to me, I could see You drawing me closer – and my response is joy.

And a very good response it is! I rejoice when you respond to Me with joy. I want to draw you completely into the Trinity. For now, you will be aware of this relationship only for a few moments. But that is the goal, I dwell in you and you abide in Me. Remember the verse you memorized long ago, "If any man loves Me, he will keep My Word, and My Father will love him, and We will come to him and make Our home with him." You are doing all you can to keep My Word. Now believe that the Trinity can, wants to, and does live in you. No longer just outside, but within. And you are dwelling within the Trinity. Not because you earned it, not because you are perfect, not because of anything you do or have done – simply because your God loves you.

Lord, I understand and thank You – please continue to drill it into me until it becomes as real to me as Your existence. Once I did not truly believe that, but now I have no doubt. You have proven Your love for me as well. But now this is much greater. How can I respond except in awe and wonder and joy and thanksgiving?

That will do just fine.

*****

Today at Mass after Communion, I realized Your Presence within me. I told You how it humbled me for I know I did not merit it, and tears came to my eyes.

That is also a good response. You see, your natural responses are right on track. All these years you worried about not being able to love God, yet you can and do love Me very well.

I guess my frustration came from the expectation that I had to produce the love and union with You. You gave me the desire, but I did not know how to make it happen.

You cannot – it is not your job. I initiate, you respond. I provide opportunities to love others. I also provide opportunities to die to self. You need not manufacture any. I will provide.

Thanks, I guess. Dying to self is necessary, I know, but not pleasant or easy.

But it is coming along. Hang in there.

Thank You, Lord.

*****

Lord, the hymn at Mass today, "Here I am," touched me deeply, but not as one would expect. I sang only the refrain – the words moved me to tears. They are meant to be understood as You speaking to us, but You showed me ever so tenderly that they are the words of my life to my husband, children, students, mother-in-law, my parents, friends – the word "lover" changes to "mother" or "another," but the great grace You have given me in my life so far has been availability. I was there when they needed me. I have comforted many by being there and doing what I could. I am now available to You. I want to say to You, "Here I am." I pictured You as a small child that needed comforting. Here I am, ready to hold You, protect You, and soothe Your wounds. This is what You have allowed me to do to countless others. The grace I ask for today is the grace of continued availability – first to You, for whatever You desire of me – and also to the others that are or will be a part of my life. Is this not a part of union? Also, I ask for the grace to hear and respond to You as You say to me, "Here I am."

Availability – abiding in love – they are very much the same, aren't they? Once again, keeping commandments is equated with love. Apart from You I can do nothing. Apart from You, I can *be* nothing. Through that hymn, You allowed me to see that I have been able to bear much fruit. I have comforted many. That is fruit. I have been kind to many – kindness is a fruit of the Spirit. Your Father is glorified by that?! How wonderful! My illness – pruning so I shall be able to bear even more fruit? Could it be? I am not yet all dried up but can still bear fruit? I feel like Sarah, being told that she was to bear Isaac. Lord, I don't care what fruit You plant in me as long as it is good. I will gladly do or be whatever You desire. I was content to wait tables at the marriage feast of the Lamb – but You called me to be "Bride." It seems I thought all was over through this illness. Though no one mentioned death, I saw it as a real possibility when I didn't know why I could not walk and was in such great pain. And even though You kept assuring me that You still had great plans for me, I was afraid those plans were not for this life. Sort of like Martha when You said Lazarus would rise again. So, am I at a resurrection already? I don't mind. Really. But I wonder if it is that easy. Can I really skip the pain and suffering now and say, "been there, done that"? I wouldn't mind. Really. But if not, here I am, ready to do Your will.

*****

Lord, I think yesterday went very well. I was able to serve You in many ways.

Maggie, I, too, am delighted that the day went well. But you are again assessing success or failure by what you *do*. Today I want you to focus on who you are. Your identity is not wrapped in just your doings. You may continue to do all the things you did well yesterday, but today focus on who you are. See what that will do to change your perspective. Avoid pride as well as discouragement. Explore your littleness or insignificance as well as your uniqueness and infinite worth in My eyes. You will see strengths and weaknesses. Accept them without judgment. Ask for help to overcome the weaknesses as well as to build on the strengths. I gave you both – so you can work on them. View them with neutrality, and thanksgiving. Do you now see detachment forming? This is what I want for you. It is good. At the end of the day, see how you did with this and let that be the focus of your Examen – it will make the Examen much more interesting.

Wow, Lord, this is really good stuff. I feel like I'm already on retreat and You are my Director.

Good. Keep coming. There is much more.

*****

What keeps you from knowing Me more? What keeps you from loving Me more? What keeps you from serving Me more? From seeing Me, from hearing My voice? I reveal Myself to you in so many ways. I want to be known by you. I desire to be one with you more than you crave that union. I am not the one who blocks it. Search your heart and see what is blocking what you and I both desire. Is it fear? Is it some inordinate attachment to earthly things? Is it resentment? Is it bitterness? Is it rebellion? Search your heart and I will help you get rid of all that blocks My love. Can you even imagine what it would be like to have love flowing freely from Me to you and back from you to Me? This is My plan for your life. It is good. It is very good. Let Me till the soil of your heart to break up the paths, remove the weeds and rocks, and let it be the good soil that will produce in abundance. I desire to do this. You only need to allow Me to do it.

Maggie, I will make use of you and the talents I have given you. But remember that I did not create you only to be used. Dwell more on My love. Enjoy the pleasure of your God. See the beauty and glory I have for you even now, even here. When you work, I am by your side – laugh and enjoy the work through fellowship. We are in this together. You are not alone. When you rest, rest in your Father's arms. I will give you rest. When you have others around you, they are My gifts to you as well. When difficulties arise, as they must, know that I am with you and will guide you through. The purpose I have for your life is much greater than just service or usefulness. But I will show you little by little. You will look back in awe at what I will accomplish through you – but it will not seem like any great thing as long as you just concentrate on My love and companionship. Yes, it is possible. Rejoice in this day.

*****

Lord Jesus, here I am struggling at prayer again. My mind is wandering in many directions when I really want and need to focus on You. Some of my friends think that I am going through spiritual dryness, but I wonder if it is instead something, I'm either not doing or doing wrong. The whole idea of just "being" and not "doing" is very difficult for me. If I am here to "just be" in Your Presence, shouldn't I at least be aware of You? I am occasionally, but I want to be constantly aware of Your Presence – at least while I am here in adoration. But so often, I seem to lose track of You and get lost in my own thoughts. It does not seem to be any form of prayer at all. Yet, Lord, You continue to love and bless me so wonderfully. You deserve better than what I have so far given You. How can I praise and thank and worship and adore You better? Am I looking for more consolations at prayer than I am supposed to? Am I looking to "feel good" at prayer? But shouldn't prayer be a delight? To be with You, the Lover of my soul? I enjoy "just being" with many people. Why do I find it so difficult "just being" with You?

It takes time and perseverance. This form of prayer is new to you, at least on a regular basis. Before, when you tried the prayer of presence, it was only occasionally, and your life was so hectic that a bit of peace and quiet was refreshing. Now you think you have had your fill of peace and quiet, so it is not very exhilarating. But what you thought of as peace and quiet was actually the pain of loss and a bit of depression.

You cannot have constant activity. You need to discover true peace and quiet in Me. Not boredom, not avoidance of things you cannot face, but resting in My arms and knowing you are loved and accepted and cherished. Not criticized, not prodded to do better or be better, but accepted and acceptable as you happen to be. It is time to stop striving. Your eyes don't have to be good; your legs don't have to work well; you can simply come, and I will love you. And once you can relax in My Presence, you will love Me back. Even now your gratitude is expanding. Be patient. I am.

Lord, I am beginning to understand. Thank You ever so much.

You are most welcome. Now go and relax. I love you.

*****

Lord Jesus, it is still such a struggle to spend a whole hour in prayer.

Maggie, on a retreat, an hour a day does look easy. But in your life with many other things going on, it gets more complicated. Also, praying in a chapel is easier. But none of this is impossible. Listen to what you tell your students about prayer. It is conversation – it is relationship – it is a time for consolation and for working things out – for love. Human beings need love. I provide that love in many ways. You also need to come to Me to receive My love. It is good to have a set time and place for prayer. But it is also good to come to Me every time you can or need a touch of My love. Sometimes it is only a sigh or a glance or a little passing thought. But it is prayer. Be patient again. In math, understanding is very important – in love and relationships and matters of faith, it is not. And even in math, sometimes you only understand after you know and have practiced a while. Don't worry. I'm not leaving you – and I won't let you wander too far away from Me. I'll take split seconds of love from you and treasure them – and you will see My love also – like sunrises and sunsets and hugs from your students. Be not afraid.

*****

Lord, You know I would do anything You ask of me – at least I would try – but all You wanted was my company. I don't know why that surprised me so, but it did. I owe You thanks and praise and worship and service, but You wanted my companionship. I didn't need to say anything, do anything, even think anything; I just had to be there. I was somewhat embarrassed, felt quite unworthy, but I knew that was all You wanted of me, so I did the best I could to just sit in Your Presence and be with You. If my mind wandered, I would return to feeling Your Presence and realize that I simply had to *enjoy* Your company. And I did. You didn't give me any great revelation, no teaching, no correction, just let me know You wanted my company. What a boost to my drooping self-esteem! The Creator of the Universe, the King of Kings, and the Lord of Lords desires my company. WOW!

Maggie, you are right. I am no longer teaching you to listen to Me in the middle of the night. You have learned that lesson. Now, you might only need an occasional review. But now, the emphasis

moves to hearing My call in the daytime. This is a harder lesson for you. You were always easily awakened and quickly alert at night. But now I want you ready to hear Me in the daytime – to be able to drop everything and come to prayer or to come to Me in the midst of whatever you are doing. This will take lots of practice and a great deal of patience. This is a great step toward that total union you want.

You already have experience with this concept. When you were helping your husband with referee assigning you had to react to the ringing of the telephone this way. Often, you had to stop whatever you were doing to answer the call, and either make a note of some change, solve some problem, or just spend some time talking to the person on the line. It was not usually unpleasant. You grew to love the people and did not mind the work involved because you loved your husband, and this was helping him. Now, the focus is to change. Some of the process will be the same. I will be calling you to come and spend time with Me. You will have to be alert to My call. It may be a quick call, or one that takes some time. But you can call Me as well. I do not ask anything of you that I am not prepared to do for you.

Also, this is something to give form to the Examen at night. See how you do in listening for My voice. There will be days that you feel you did not hear Me at all. Yet I will show you that you heard, answered, and did what I asked without even noticing. There will be times when you miss the boat. There will be times that you hear, but do not want to answer. There will be times when you hear, answer, but don't want to do what I ask. And there will be times when you do it even if you don't want to – and that is true submission. This is a time of learning. If you hear My voice while you are busy, I will tell you when to stop, or to slow down, or most anything else. But remember that I am good and loving and kind and patient. I am no tyrant or slave driver or playing mean games. This is all a part of a GOOD plan. You will not do much that is different from that you have been doing. But your focus will be to listen to My voice and obey. You will not find it too difficult. You will really enjoy the rewards.

Jesus, what an adventure! I think I am ready.

*****

As you are struggling with health issues, remember that I am with you regardless of how you feel. I also suffered, so I understand. My love, care, provision, and comfort are there for you. Take the time to enjoy My gentleness as I cherish your every glance toward Me. Healing takes many forms. You have experienced much already and will still have more. I am not finished with you yet. I appreciate your endurance. My hand is upon you. My love for you is total. Rest in My arms.

Maggie, My healing often comes in layers. Some of the things that bother you now happened many years ago. When you broke your ankle, the initial healing involved setting the bones, bandaging the wound, and stopping bleeding. Then there was a long period where you could not walk on that leg. Through much work and therapy, the ankle was better. It worked for twenty years. But then something else went wrong, and more healing was needed. In fact, more surgery was needed. Then the next level of healing was necessary. It was not complete. The ankle still swells and hurts daily. But you have gotten used to it, and hardly think of it. Spiritual healing is similar. There are some injuries that have been completely healed. But others can give you trouble even years after you thought all was well. You have serious rejections in your life. You need to come back to Me with your pain. You need not be embarrassed that it hurts again as you thought it was healed long ago. I know your hurts. I feel them as well. I long to comfort you and continue to heal you. Do not jump out of My arms thinking that all is done. I have more to do. I do not want you to stay in pain. I can and will help. Turn to Me with *every* problem and pain. Only I can understand and heal. I even understand your reluctance to seek My help. You think it is your fault that the initial healing has somehow been insufficient or has worn off. No. I have more work to do in you. Allow Me to do this work. My love is much gentler than you think you deserve. Come to Me. Rest in Me. Delight in Me. And I will come to you, hold you in My arms.

*****

How do you enter into My rest? The Israelites in the desert coming out of Egypt were not able to enter into My rest. But you can enter into My rest by abiding in Me, relying on Me, trusting Me, believing that I am in control and only want what is best for you. What is My rest? Is there any record in Scripture where I worried, rushed around not knowing what to do, or gave up? No. I trusted My Father and appealed to Him and did His will. This produced the peace within and around Me. I want that peace for you. A secure resting place in My arms, knowing all will be well, regardless of present circumstances. Ask me for what you need. I will provide. Do what you need to do, and then enter into My rest knowing My love for you will always surround you.

This is a time of hope. You have come through difficult times. I have been with you every step of the way. I am with you still. I will continue to guide and sustain you. I do not promise that there will no longer be challenges or problems, but as I have in the past, do now, and will always love, protect, teach, heal, and provide for you. Bring Me all your concerns, joys, pains, successes, failures, loved ones, enemies, everything in your life. I will rejoice when you rejoice and hold you in sorrow. Your relationship with Me has grown very close, but I want even more intimacy with you. Seek My Face. Converse with me even more than you now do. Look for My blessings, gifts, and graces. They are here for you. I am here for you.

The difference between living and existing is joy. When you wake up complaining, you are missing the joy I put into each day of your life. Re-discover My goodness, provision, care, gentleness, and love. I came that you might have life and have it more abundantly. Begin with just one little bud of recognizing My love for you. Let it fully blossom through thanksgiving, and soon it will turn into praise. Before you know it, you will be in My Presence and able to receive more gifts, graces, and blessings. This is what I want for you. This is joy. I want you to abide, dwell, live fully in My joy. When you are filled with joy, I also rejoice.

*****

I wanted to just sit with You and let You hold me as I hold my cat in my lap. Let me rest in Your lap and know that I am where I belong and where You want me. Lord, when I was teaching, I knew it was a privilege to serve You in my teaching. Now it is a privilege to be with You in quieter ways. But let me truly be with You whether in quiet or in service. Thank You that whatever I am doing, I can be united to You.

Maggie, your words are not even necessary. I understand your heart. Contentment comes in small segments. But things change. That is why you need to practice finding Me in all situations. If you are securely attached to Me, you will not be attaching yourself to fleeting things or moments that pass by in your life. I alone am permanent. If you fix your eyes on Me and My love, the scenery around can change at will, but you will be secure.

Lord, it makes so much sense.

*****

Chapter 9

CONTINUALLY FILLED

*W*e are taught that when we are baptized, we are filled with the Holy Spirit. Then later, the same Holy Spirit is further released in our lives, and helps us live the Christian life. But we tend to spring leaks. We need to be continually filled to overflowing in order to bring that wonderful living water to others. I have often felt the need to ask for continual refilling.

Please help me, Holy Spirit, to meditate on or contemplate these readings. The one in Exodus was about the way Moses talked with God and it made his face radiant (Ex 34:29-35). Should that happen to us as well? Can our relationship with You be so close that it would become obvious to everyone? Does it connect with the Gospel that the treasure in the field or the pearl requires total commitment (Mt 13:44-46)? That in order to have the close contact with God as Moses did, we must have no other agenda but to serve You?

Maggie, your questions have an obvious answer. Yes. But serving your God works well only when done with love. This is why the greatest commandment does not say "serve" but "love" with all your heart, soul, mind, and strength. But do not confuse love with warm fuzzy feelings. The desire to please the beloved is a much better definition of love. Yes, the warm fuzzy feelings are nice and often follow, but are not necessary. Obedience, service, and surrender out of love are very pleasing to the Father. If He should reward these with outward radiance, that is His choice. If not, there will definitely be an inward radiance – the heart burning within.

*****

On the mind level and the will level, I trust You. But on the emotional and reactional levels, I'm not at the same level of trust. So, Lord, I need You to put me together. Fine-tune me, Lord, so I will trust You completely. You did not give me a spirit of fear, but of power and of love and of a sound mind. Come, Holy Spirit, I really need You more in my life. I need everything You have to give me. In return, what can I give You? My surrendered will? My cooperation? My increased efforts at using the gifts You have already given me? All You ask of me is my love, yet I want my love for you to grow much more and faster than it has so far. I would like to offer You much more than I am able. My love for You is so feeble and inadequate, yet You do not complain.

*****

Holy Spirit, I thank You for what You are doing. I don't understand much of it, but I trust You and know that it must be good. I have relied on my own understanding for so long that I find this non-knowing very uncomfortable, but I choose to yield to Your power and will and ask that You enlighten me as You see fit.

*****

Holy Spirit, I ask You to fill me to overflowing with Your power to live the Christian life. I ask You to stay with me constantly and strengthen me that I might use the things that help my spiritual growth and discard the things that hinder it. Come, Holy Spirit, set my life on fire with love for my God and His people. Come, Lord Jesus, and lead me to Your Father.

*****

Lord, as I'm learning more about spiritual life, I see that I had been expecting mature spirituality of myself when I was just a spiritual infant, kind of like expecting a first grader to understand calculus. But as I have started letting You control my growth; I see there has been much more growth. How silly I have been! So, Lord, I surrender my great desire for spiritual maturity. You are the Teacher, You are the Guide, You prepare the syllabus. Let me enjoy and rejoice in the present, not jump ahead nor fall behind but follow You, respond to Your direction, and seek Your leadership.

*****

Lord, I read that the Holy Spirit forms Christ within us and He manifests Himself in Christ dwelling in our hearts, and it hit me powerfully. Could it be that in the many years since I've received the Baptism of the Holy Spirit that this "deep dwelling down" of Christ has been taking place and I didn't even realize it? Have I been unknowingly becoming more Christ-like? Could it be that the things I do for others are really directed by You – not just my own attempts at imitating You? Could it have started with my attempts, but somewhere along the way You took over? I don't seem to have as much disappointment and despair as I used to. Wow! There is progress! It just didn't seem like it because I'm not trying so hard any more. And I don't need to! You are doing it! What freedom!

Lord, You are so marvelously powerful. You are in me. I asked that I might be more aware of You. Suddenly I am!

*****

Lord, You gave me a most beautiful revelation, ever so simply. You whispered to me, **"Have you ever considered self-control as a gift?"** And I realized that animals act on instinct or have to be trained. But we humans can control ourselves and resist instincts, and even our own desires. It was suddenly a case of "I *get* to, rather than I *have* to." Each of the fruits of the Holy Spirit starts out as gifts and, as we accept and use them, they take root in our lives and eventually bear fruit. But in the meanwhile, we have them available as gifts if only we accept and use them. This all came after a message at last Friday's prayer meeting, that we should use the gifts of Your Holy Spirit more often. So, Lord, I decided that I can do that. Thank You for this marvelous revelation.

Continually Filled

Maggie, stop now and receive My love. Eat your breakfast and with each bite realize that I am giving you what you asked. As your hunger is satisfied by the physical food, let your spirit be filled with My blessings as well. Do not think of your duties as separate from your relationship with Me, but as your response of love to My love. So now your breakfast has become part of your prayer. Getting dressed, you can remember the armor of God I have given you. Driving to Mass, you can remember that you are coming ever closer to Me. Making bread, you help Me feed the hungry. Giving of your time to others, you help the needy. In teaching, you instruct the ignorant. All these you do for Me. They are acceptable gifts you give to Me. Your entire day can become a prayer.

*****

Lord, there seems to be a lot of tension within me. It drains my energy and ability to accomplish what I want to do.

I see it. It will decrease as things settle in the household. You are dealing with many major changes and that is difficult. But I am with you.

Lord I seem to have a hard time remembering or feeling that You are with me.

This is why the saints had to practice My Presence. You believe now, so your faith will work, but you now need to practice what you believe. Why do athletes and musicians need to practice so much? They need to make what they know or believe become a part of every aspect of their being. Even one hour a day in My Presence is not enough. You must practice like a musician or an athlete. Practice!

Holy Spirit, would You be my coach?

Of course. I was hoping you would ask.

OK, Lord, I suppose this is boot camp.

But this boot camp can be better than you expect. You have heard of athletes whose trainers were their spouses – or skaters whose partner is also a marriage partner. Is it not comforting to have a coach who loves you perfectly and knows exactly how much you

need to grow and what you are capable of becoming and how fast or slow to take you?

Oh yes! I do understand – thank You! I will to submit. I choose to obey. I beg for Your grace and strength. I only see my weakness. You see much more. Jesus, I trust in You. Holy Spirit, I trust in You. Father, I see You rejoicing. Father, I trust in You as well.

Maggie, I do rejoice. Many years ago, I told you that you have enrolled in My school. In all those years, your attendance has not been very regular. But I have never expelled you. Now you want to be on the school team. This will not be like your other experiences with sports. You were faithful in attending practices then. Your faithfulness to practice here will bear much more and better fruit.

Maggie, I do hold you close. It really is a big step you are about to take. I am with you. This is a time of transition, and transitions are difficult. Stay close to Me. Your trust and love are growing. My forty days in the desert were not filled by simply three temptations – it was a transition of leaving behind My former life and beginning My ministry. The Holy Spirit led me into the desert, and you are being led by the same Spirit. Holy Thursday was another transition for Me – never alone but dependent on the strength and guidance He provides. Fear not. All is well.

*****

Maggie, are you ready to listen?

I think so, Holy Spirit.

I am ready to speak to you.

I am listening.

You were just thinking that you are in a better place spiritually than you were this time last year.

I was feeling very helpless last year. Now I feel that with You, I can do almost anything. There are possibilities this year that I did not see last year.

It is your vision that has improved. But this improvement is temporary. It can come or go. What is required of you now is more faithfulness. If you want more of My Presence, more of My wisdom, more of My grace, more of anything and everything I give you, it will require faithfulness on your part. You asked Me to teach you. I will teach you if you come to Me to be taught. You are embarking on an intense program of study. It will only be possible and helpful to you if you make prayer your first priority. I have already taught you much. It is now time to put it into practice. I do not generally speak to you with great manifestations. I do not need to show you tongues of fire. You can hear My still small voice. You have already been trained to listen and watch for the movements of My Spirit. I (the Spirit) am already within you. As you give Me more room to work, I will transform your life.

*****

Lord, I noticed how a distraction just came – the battle is already begun – the devil must fear this intimacy I desire with You. I choose with the power of Your Holy Spirit to turn to You and away from sin. I take the weapons of warfare You give me. The helmet of salvation, for You have paid the price for my salvation; the breastplate of righteousness, for You are righteous; the belt of truth, for You are the Way, the Truth, and the Life; the shoes of the Gospel of Peace, for You are the Word, the Good News; the shield of faith, for greater are You who are in me than he that is in the world; and the Sword of the Spirit, which is You, the Word made flesh. You had already assured me that You have given me a spirit of power and of love, and of a sound mind – other translations say self-control – I'll take both, sound mind and self-control (2 Tim 1:7). So, Lord, You have outfitted me for battle (Eph 6:11-17). Let me go and fight the good fight.

*****

Lord, thank You for showing me that I take controls that do not belong to me and that I can return them to You as soon as I realize that I have somehow acquired them. Let my trust in You grow by leaps and bounds. Let Your love amaze me throughout the day. Let me find You in many, many ways. Let me be continually filled with You – Father, Son, and Holy Spirit. I give You this day You have given me. Help me to conduct myself in a manner pleasing to You, and let me come back to You tonight and see how it went.

*****

So now you need to lighten up a bit. Let's catch the Holy Spirit and spend a bit of time with the Father.

Sort of like a game of tag?

Yes, but He likes to be caught and when He is, you are caught up in joy and peace and feel His love.

That's the best offer I have had in a long time.

That is only the beginning. My love will also encompass you, and then the Father's love is even more wonderful. Come – let's enjoy.

*****

Lord, thank You for Your compassion. Please increase mine and show me what I can do to help others rather than lament what I cannot do.

Maggie, there is much that you can do and indeed have done. Keep listening to the voice of the Holy Spirit. He will show you what you can do.

I will, Lord. Please amplify my inner hearing that I not miss any direction.

*****

Some time ago the word had come at one of the prayer meetings that the death we have to die to ourselves is a real death. I believe one form of that death is that I should now wait for Your leading and listen carefully to Your signals. I must look to You for everything. Keep teaching me this. Holy Spirit, keep reminding me to look and listen before I leap. Seal my lips so that I may not speak unless I have first consulted You. Bind my hands and feet that I may not go anywhere or do anything to which You are not leading me. Let nothing separate me from You, Jesus. Be my King, my Lord, my God, my Friend, my Lover, my Husband. Be all that I need or want. And let me be all that You want: trusting, obedient, wise in Your ways, a pleasure in Your sight, a credit to Your Name.

*****

I remember a past hurt that was painful. By now, the forgiveness has taken hold and there is no more pain in the telling of it, though it took years of choosing to forgive every time the memory came with pain. So now I choose to forgive the hurt I just experienced and will continue to do so until it no longer hurts. Please forgive those who hurt me as well, and keep giving me the grace to continue to forgive.

Maggie, I do give you the Holy Spirit. You are right. It is necessary to continue to forgive. You will have opportunities to clear up other situations as you might be offended. Keep forgiving until the pain is gone. It is a worthwhile endeavor. But beyond that, do take time to feel My love and pleasure. Let Me wrap My arms around you and know that I love you. Do not be afraid to dwell on My love.

*****

Now, Lord, I really want to pursue that deeper walk in the Spirit. Holy Spirit, please show me how and what to do or say. I guess the first step is desire – that is here. The second, also here, is the willingness. You have given me these, so there isn't anything I can take credit for. But I would like to totally yield to You and have You draw me deeper into Your love any way You will. I seem to have the time as well as the alertness, also Your gifts. St. Francis de Sales says one learns to love by loving, so I suppose one learns to pray deeper in the Spirit by praying in the Spirit. I don't know if I can give voice to my prayers – though if You want me to, I suppose I could take a chance – but it will surely start with a whisper.

Maggie, a whisper is a fine start. Do not be afraid. I am with you and will lead you.

*****

Lord Jesus, thank You for the gift of "counsel." I just read about this gift of the Holy Spirit and realized that it is through this gift that I hear Your voice in my prayer and writing. Sometimes I wonder if I will be thought presumptuous because I truly believe You do inspire me through these notebooks. But as this gift of counsel is described, it fits perfectly. You have, through my writing, quieted me so I can "hear" Your voice and come to know it. You have directed me in the day-to-day details of my life. You have continually encouraged me in my Christian journey and have brought me far along the way. I may still have far to go, but am assured that You and Your gift of counsel will stay with me until I reach the place You are preparing for me in Heaven. How marvelous are Your ways, O Lord!

*****

Lord Jesus, I had two fantastic times of prayer. The first was in the middle of the night a little over a week ago. I was having trouble sleeping, and thought perhaps You were calling me to prayer. I started with the little devotional book, *Jesus Calling,* by Sarah Young; and for July 9 and July 10, it reminded me to stop worrying and relax in Your peace. I did my best to do that, and found myself asking You to allow my love for You and Your love for me to meet and intertwine. At this, I had a vision of two vines. One was growing up from the ground, and the other was descending from above, and as the two met, end to end, they joined, and intertwined, and small shoots grew out of the combination and immediately grew leaves and flowers. It was beautiful. And You showed me that, as our love comes together, it brings forth blessings for the lives of others (the small shoots). This overwhelmed me with awe and wonder, and I felt that this was the total union with You that I have desired, even demanded, for years. I stayed in Your Presence that way for quite a while, and the joy of having received such a blessing stayed with me throughout the day.

The second really great prayer time came very early in the morning when once again I had trouble sleeping. I had been discouraged that, after such a wonderful time with You the previous week, I had avoided prayer. After tossing and turning for a while, I decided to go to my little room with *Jesus Calling* and apologize to You. This time I read July 13 and July 14. The readings reminded me that my relationship with You does not depend on anything I have accomplished or failed to do, nor on how I look or feel, but only on Your love for me. I cannot make You love me more by anything I do. Also, that the Father sees not my worth or lack of it, but Your righteousness in which I am wrapped.

Lord, this brought me such great freedom! For over a year, I have been asking to be totally surrounded and wrapped tightly within the Holy Trinity, a hiding place I can run to, enveloped within the Communion of the Three Persons of God. The thought of being completely wrapped in Your righteousness brought a picture to my mind of a wrapped present. The Father "sees" only the fancy wrapping until such a time as I am perfected and come out of that wrapping fully conformed to the image and character of You, Jesus. The Father already knows the end product even though I am not yet perfected. He loves me as if I were already perfect. Once again, I was full of awe and wonder and great thanksgiving.

Then, Lord, I received another inspiration. When we are conceived, we are enveloped in our mothers' womb. We receive all the nourishment and environment we need to grow and mature and thrive. At birth, we come out of the enclosure with all the features we have inherited from our parents – we bear their image and likeness. In the same way, when we come to You, Lord, whether at Baptism or at a later time, we enter into a spiritual womb and are enclosed in Your perfection, where we are given all we need to grow and mature and thrive until we are ready to emerge into the next stage, eternal life, perfected in Your image and character. The song we used to sing at the prayer meeting now has a new and deeper meaning: "He gave me beauty for ashes, the oil of joy for mourning, a mantle of praise for the spirit of heaviness, that we might be trees of righteousness, the planting of the Lord, that He might be glorified."

Lord, I thank You for these revelations, and for the truths they have revealed of the reality of Your care and love for me and all Your people.

I need to be perfected a lot more, and I still fail often, but You do not give up on me, and continue to do all the work necessary to get me to what You know I can become. Thank You!

Maggie, this time is a gift. It is a gift from Me to you, for I did indeed call you and I have lifted your burdens. It is a gift from you to Me, because you have chosen to listen and come and have realized and acknowledged My gift. So just stop and enjoy the peace and the love of two gifts – Mine and yours.

Jesus, this is wonderful. No fatigue, no pain, no rush, no frenzy, just Your love and peace and joy. Could You, Jesus, and You, Holy Spirit, take me to the Father, so I could worship in Spirit and Truth?

You want to be grabbed on both sides and fly you to the throne of the Father?

Yes, that's the picture I have in my mind. Jesus on my left, Holy Spirit on my right – no one can come to the Father but by You.

Do you want the direct route or the scenic one?

Direct is probably better right now.

Direct it is. There are a few stops along the way. The stop of washing and dressing is where you drop your spirit of heaviness and put on the garment of praise.

Jesus, I do drop the heaviness. You have loosed its bonds, but I now drop it at Your feet. I realize that I did nothing to get loose, it was simply Your goodness and kindness that has set me free. But I shall not hold on to the dirty rags that have clothed me, but gladly drop them and I gratefully accept the beautiful garment You are giving me instead.

Good. Now you are ready to enter His gates.

With thanksgiving – Father, I thank You for sending Your Son and Your Holy Spirit to free me and bring me to You. Father, I thank You for Your goodness and kindness and gentleness toward me. Thank You for Your peace and joy. Thank You for all those who love me and all those I can love and care for. Thank You for Your great love – through Your creation, through Your people, and through the knowledge of You that I have been given.

Now you are through the gates so enter the courts.

With praise – I enter Your courts. Father, You are holy and mighty and worthy of all praise. You are good and kind and gentle. You love me with an everlasting love. You draw me with Your loving-kindness. You are Husband to the widow and Father to the fatherless. You are my Provider, my Glory and the Lifter of my Head, my Comforter, my Counselor, my Savior, My Redeemer, my God. You are the Trinity – Father, Son and Holy Spirit – Three in One – Mystery – yet Reality – Holy, Holy, Holy – and You are my God – and I am Yours – Your daughter, Your servant, Your grateful friend, Your bride.

This is true. I have redeemed you; I have called you by name, you are Mine. And you are welcome in My Presence. Come and stay and rest a while.

…Father, I thank You. I cannot say any more, but just want to curl up in Your arms and be held by You.

Go ahead. Put down pen and paper, turn out the lights – let your bed and covers be My lap and arms, and come, rest a while. I do give you rest. Enjoy it.

*****

As you are experiencing this warm weather, pause to truly enjoy it. It is My gift to you. Let it remind you of the warmth of My love. Pause and enjoy that as well. Take time to bask in My goodness. Yes, there are troubles and tragedies, and I help you through them, but there are also joys and pleasures that I provide in your life. Reclaim the awe and wonder of a little child at the beauty of My creation. See My artwork in the clouds and budding trees and flowers as they emerge. Today it is springtime.

*****

[Temple of the Holy Spirit]   Lord, I was thinking of Psalm 100, "enter His gates with thanksgiving and His courts with praise." You showed me that Your gates and courts are also within me, for I am Yours – that the temple of the Holy Spirit – which I am – has been and still is under construction – that all the self-denials, devotions, kindnesses and good works, love and care that were and still are a part of my life – not just my own good works but also all that I have received – all have gone into the building of this temple for You. You showed me that I have given much to You and my interior castle – temple – is fit for the King of Kings and Lord of Lords though it has occasionally needed renovations and it still is under construction in places, but that You are delighted to take me directly to the Father's dwelling right there – that the Father considers it a fitting place to dwell. Thank You so much. Now let me be quiet again.

*****

In the Spirit, I see You, Jesus, leading me by the hand and walking with me and, after a particularly difficult stretch of the road where You almost had to pull me along, You stop and turn, still holding my hand, and You embrace me and kiss me and hold me tight. And You don't let go until I am again refreshed and reassured and ready to continue on. And if I should stumble or fall, You will bind up my wounds and caress and heal whatever hurts. Let me continue to walk with You this way until I collapse in Your arms and You carry me home to Your Father and my Father. Hold me tight, dear Jesus. Don't let go of my hand. I know the road ahead is not easy, but with my will I choose to follow You.

*****

Chapter 10

DO THE THINGS

There are two Scriptures that apply in this chapter the first is John 5:19 "Jesus said to them, "Truly, truly, I say to you, the Son can do nothing of his own accord, but only what he sees the Father doing; for whatever he does, that the Son does likewise." *And the other is John 14:1* [12] "Truly, truly, I say to you, he who believes in me will also do the works that I do; and greater works than these will he do, because I go to the Father."

Lord, I couldn't sleep during the night and I came out to pray, I couldn't settle down enough to keep my focus on You. I was worried and troubled about many things. But You invited me to come back during the day and You would meet me. So here I am, Lord, trying desperately to trust in You. I promised a friend that I would fast for him today, and so far, that's going well. But, Lord, I know that it does not depend on me, but on You. You are his Savior, not me. Your will is important, not mine. Yet You listen to my prayers and You act on behalf of those who love You. Lord, I love You and desire that my love for You may grow much.

Lord, it is when I am weak that You can show Yourself strong. Here is a great opportunity for You, Lord; I am very weak and feel totally useless. Yet You have given me faith to believe that regardless of how I feel, You can and will use me. So here I am, Lord, I come to do Your will. Speak clearly to me and let me know how I can serve You best. You give me strength when I have none of my own, You hold me and keep me together when I'm sure I'm falling apart. When I twisted my back a few days ago, You were with me through the pain and You allowed me to unite my pain with Yours for the good of others. "I believe that I shall see the goodness of the Lord in the land of the living" (Ps 27:13). And, Lord, I *have* seen Your goodness.

I need You to speak to me, yet I worry that I might run from You. Help me to be still and listen, for even a rebuke is a sign of Your great love for me.

Maggie, I do not come to rebuke you – I am the One who forgives your sins, not the one who accuses you. Yes, I do hear your prayers and the intensity of your heart's desire. I see your struggles, your pains, your failings, and your attempts to rise again. I am with you. I have not abandoned you. I am still able to save and rescue and help and forgive. You have much confusion right now, but I will guide you through. Fear not! For I have redeemed you, I've called you by name – you are Mine (Is 43:1).

These are difficult times. I have not called you to save the world, but it is good for you to pray for it. I see chaos and turmoil and sickness, and death and injustice. I see it all. I feel it all. Your care and concern are a gift, one I give you, and one you return to Me through your prayers. You do not see My gentle hand upon you. You have not believed that I might be pleased with you despite your failings. You do not doubt My love, yet you continue to act as if there was more you needed to do to earn it. NO!!! My love for you is everlasting, infinite; it cannot be withdrawn. You are Mine. It has nothing to do with your unworthiness or wretchedness. I love you. Dwell on that today.

Continue in your good works. Continue to pray, to work, to be kind, loving, and thoughtful. But let my love come into every particle of your being. Yes, you should repent and make reparation for your sins. But your need for forgiveness should propel you back into My arms, not keep you hiding in corners. Come to Me, you who are burdened and heavy laden, and I will give you rest. You are burdened and heavy laden. Leave all your burdens at My feet. Your back has been hurting because you have been carrying too many burdens that were never meant for you to carry. You cannot handle them; they are Mine. If you take My yoke upon you, the burdens must be put off. All

you are required to carry is My yoke, and walk alongside Me. All you need to do is walk with Me. Do not be concerned with anything else.

Lord, I do take all my cares and leave them at Your feet. I will walk with You and rest in You. And I thank You for Your great love.

*****

Maggie, you were not created out of pity. You were not rescued from your land and brought to this one without a purpose. You have not been trained – and trained carefully – for nothingness. You have not been given the Holy Spirit as a token gift. But as long as you see yourself this way, you are doomed to doubt. I have called you and you have repeatedly answered My call. I continue to call you to even greater things than you can imagine. Banish this fear from your life. Are you not happy when a student is eager to give an answer or do a problem? Am I not as good a teacher as you are? Are you not facing greater challenges now than you ever imagined? Do you presume to think that this was all your doing? Do you think I would allow you to commit to what is impossible? Don't I love you enough to stop you? Didn't you ask for My guidance? Don't you believe I have been providing it and will continue to do so? Fear NOT! For I have redeemed you, I HAVE called you by name. You are MINE!

But I do not only call you to be a servant, but to be friend. As a friend, do not doubt My goodness or friendship. Do not fear losing My friendship – you can't. Yes, just as I called My disciples, I call you. Just as they came and followed Me, so have you. And just as they came to know Me, so do you grow in knowledge and love and service and friendship. A friend does not need to be ordered to do something – but does it often without even being asked. Do you think I would despise you for jumping to do what you think I want? Of course not. I love you and it delights Me to see you anticipate My desires. I have put goodness into your heart. I love to see it at work. Have I not thanked you often for what you do? Yet you are always surprised when I do that. Would your God be impolite? Come, allow Me to be good and kind and gentle with you. Allow Me to love you more than you have ever been loved. Yes, and accepted and wanted, and appreciated and cherished and valued. See Me looking at you

this way. Not finding fault with everything you do, but truly loving and admiring and holding you – My Maggie – in My arms and so happy to have you there.

*****

Good morning, Lord. I'm a bit slow this morning, but it looks like it will be another busy day, so I am making sure I come to You before it starts. You are allowing me to be available to help others again – thank You. Today Mom and Dad hope to retrieve their car after it was stolen and found abandoned. Then I will pick up Anne and Marion and, while Anne and I are at water therapy, Marion can use my car to run errands. Then I tutor this evening. So, the days fill up, and You are providing me with opportunities to be of service.

Maggie, you were worried that, since I wanted your friendship rather than your service, you would not be able to serve at all. But a friend does a lot of the same things that a servant would do – only with a different motive. Since you delighted in serving Me, you already had that motive in place. You have been acting like a friend even when internally feeling like a servant. I had to make you stop seeing yourself as "only" a servant and begin to see the friendship that has already been developing so the intimacy of union would be possible. Humility is truth – not abasement. If I call you friend or bride, then that is how I want you to act. My Mother started out as "handmaid of the Lord" but became Queen of all. She can take charge or wait in the background – she is free and very powerful – motivated only by love. Learn from her.

*****

Lord Jesus, I am in awe of what You spoke to me so many years ago. Did I really learn all You were teaching me? Or did I lose it all by not using it like I have with calculus? Or did it go deep into my soul and do the work it was meant to do? Where have I grown, and where do I still need to grow? Can I make up for lost time? And how? Are You actually directing me through the editing process of my book? There are so many great revelations and ideas and teachings You have given me, and I wonder whether I have failed to use them.

Maggie, I do not want you to sink into recriminations over what you think you have forgotten. How much of your classes in grade school or high school or college or even grad school do you remember or use as it was taught to you? But as you were taught, you progressed, and used what you needed even if you were not aware of it. It is like you teach your students about math. You might not ever use a particular part, but having learned it at the time, your thinking matured, became better ordered, and made you capable of more learning. It is with My teaching in your life. Sometimes there is greater closeness, sometimes there is greater joy in the revelations, sometimes My strength comes through, sometimes it is My provision, sometimes healing, or consolation, but always My love. You cannot keep all I have given you over all these years in the forefront of your thoughts. But as you are now revisiting them, you are again blessed and encouraged to keep looking to Me. You have not lost what I have taught you. It is there. You have matured, progressed, grown. Is there still room for growth – of course there is. I have not finished with you yet. I am still with you. I still love you perfectly. I am not disappointed in you. Rest in My love.

Thank You, Lord, I will indeed rest in Your love now.

*****

At our prayer meeting, we reviewed the corporal and spiritual works of mercy, and You have given me a natural desire and delight in doing them all. It is Your mercy that gives me such a gift, and it is my joy to please You by exercising this gift. Lord, I thank You and I ask that You remind me that I am doing works of mercy as I do them so that I can offer them to You as gifts. You have given me opportunities to feed the hungry, clothe the naked, visit the sick and imprisoned, and You also gave me a nature that delights in doing these things. You even gave me insight once in a while that I was actually ministering to You as I did these things. I long to be holy, to get rid of all the sin in my life so that I can be more useful to You right here on earth. I do not want the blind to stay blind, the lame to stay lame, the sick to stay sick, and the ignorant to stay ignorant. I want You to be able to use me to heal the sick, preach the good news, convert sinners – whatever You want done, I want to be able to do it. Yet if all You want of me is that I should be with You and love You and praise and worship You, then let me do that. If cleaning my house and loving my husband and raising my sons are all You want of me, then I want to do the best possible job of that.

*****

Lord, thank You for the revelation You gave me about ministry. When You spoke to Peter about being young and old and going where you want versus going where others take you (see Jn 21:18), it can also apply to ministry. When we first start out, we choose what we want to do, but as we get older, it is no longer our choice. Our ministry becomes what others need or demand of us. Yet if we learn to trust You rather than insist on our own way, and cooperate with Your grace, it is a much better and greater ministry, for it is Yours.

Maggie, you are indeed useful to Me. And I delight in using you in many ways. You do not notice sometimes when I have you at just the right place to lift someone's spirits, but tonight you did. It is good. Did you hear yourself praising Me? I did. Did you hear how you extolled Me? I did. Did you feel your heart burning within You? I did. This is a time for rejoicing. You are doing exactly what I want of you. How does it feel to be in the center of My will?

Lord, it feels wonderful.

*****

As I was struggling with my thoughts and feelings, I noticed that Jason, age 12, was having pain in his knee. I looked at him and asked if it hurt; he nodded. I scooted my chair closer to him and held his knee with my right hand while lifting up my left hand and praying quietly. The prayer meeting was continuing, and we were not noticed – and it seemed that Your healing power was flowing right through me into that hurting little knee. Jason closed his eyes and worshipped You silently as I prayed, and the heat I sometimes feel on my hands in the center of my palms was very present. I felt like I was having the effect of a heating pad on his knee, if nothing else, and Jason calmed down. I don't know if the pain left or not, but he didn't seem to hurt any more after that. I prayed for several minutes that way – I wondered if I would know how or when to quit. I saw myself as that pitcher in Your hands, but it had a hole near the bottom, so as it was being filled there was a stream coming out from one side. And You showed me that You could use even a leaky pitcher and aim the leak at where Your love and healing was needed.

Lord, I was so overwhelmed that You could use me even in such a pitiful condition that my heart leapt for joy and Your greatness became much more important than all the petty little struggles I had been fighting. I never knew if Jason felt better – he left with his parents before I could ask – but *I* certainly did. Your perfect love cast out my fear and rejection and self-hate and depression. I was able to see these feelings for what they were, demonic attacks. And to see the solution – immersion in Your love, which is what You have given me every time I've attempted prayer recently.

Lord, I could not understand why every time I have come to You lately expecting a scolding, You gave me only love and encouragement and support when I really deserved Your wrath. But You saw past my sins, and knew Your love is what I need. I see that every problem I have can be solved by some aspect of Your character – the fruits of the Spirit: love, joy, peace, patience, goodness, gentleness, kindness, faithfulness, and self-control. The old saying, "Jesus is the answer to all of our problems," took on a new meaning. You are the answer, You are all that I need, and I have You in my life and so all I lack is available to me because You are here. But the application still eludes me: this will take some experimentation.

Lord, here I am, back in Your loving hands, delighted to feel Your arms around me, and needing You desperately. Without You I can do nothing; with You, all is possible.

*****

After the 9-11-2001 disaster"

Lord Jesus, I don't even know where to begin. It seems that my method of mourning is some form of feeling lost and unable to do anything. I can't do anything I want to do so I don't do anything at all. I don't think it is good, but that is what has been happening this week. I don't know whether I need to repent or ask for consolation. You have protected those I know and love and I am not very emotional about the great loss of life throughout the country. But there is the same feeling of loss and helplessness that I have felt when those close to me were gone.

I do not understand it, but I bring it before You as I don't know to whom else I could go. Before it gets worse, I ask You to deal with me and these feelings as You see fit. If it is correction I need, I await Your correction. If it is consolation I need, then please console me. If You are the One Who needs consolation and I can console You – for Your heart must hurt much more than mine – then allow me to console You. It seems that sleep does not come easily during these nights. So, I am at Your service. Lord, I do believe that You are God and still in control. I really do want to be useful to You, but I can't even seem to obey Your simplest requests. I feel useless and full of sin and failure.

Well, child, at least you are not battling pride.

Thank You for that smile – I needed to lighten up a bit.

Maggie, I am not disappointed in you. I do not consider you useless. I am simply training you for a different task than what you have done before – behold, I am doing a new thing. Your role as a disciple, a friend rather than a servant, is different. You have to have the time to get accustomed to it. Your heart is already in the right place – you want to console Me even while you still hurt. But your emotions and actions do not yet follow automatically. This is better than you think. You see, you cannot depend on automatically doing things now; you must will to do anything at all. If you consult Me and unite your will to Mine, then you will see progress. It is not going to be sufficient for you to pray once a day and feel you have discharged that duty. You will have to pray often, perhaps constantly, for I want a more prominent position in your life. Your current difficulties are magnified by the fact that you cannot do too many things at the same time.

*****

I do not want merely to be a spectator in your life. I want to be a participant. I await your invitation daily. I care about all that you care about. I am ready, willing, and able to help you. Ask for My help. You will be surprised by the new possibilities that will emerge. But do not rush off right after asking. Seek My answer, wait for it if it is not immediate. See what I am teaching you during the wait. Knock on the doors and windows of Heaven. Everything you need will be given to you if you ask, seek, and knock.

In the same way, I do not want you merely to be a spectator in My life. I want you to be a participant in My life. Think of what I came to earth to do. I preached, taught, prayed for, fed, healed, and sacrificed for people that they should know, love, and return to My Father. I still do all these things, but I do them with and through you. I invite you to participate in My life by joining Me in doing these things. Be alert to what I am doing and join Me. You can preach by your good actions, teach those I put in your path, pray for those in need and for those in authority, feed the hungry, heal the sick, offer your pains and frustrations as sacrifices for others.

Will all your problems cease if you do these things? No, you will still have needs and I will continue to help you. Will the world become perfect as you cooperate with Me? No, but it will be a bit better. And your relationship with Me will grow stronger and closer and My Father will be glorified.

*****

Lord, last time after I stopped writing, I started saying to the Father that I needed Fathering, as I have done before, but then the thought came – and I'm sure it was of Divine origin – that perhaps I needed to give the Father some "daughtering." So, I asked how I could serve Him better as His daughter. The answer came as a quote from You – "Whatever you do for others, you do unto Me." I was very encouraged that the Father accepts what I do for Mom, did for Mom E., and for many others when I respectfully served them as if I were being a dutiful, loving daughter to Him. I mentioned this to Fr. Sanders, and he echoed it. Lord, Holy Trinity, thank You for making it so easy to serve You by serving others – not only easy, but a true joy.

Maggie, this is one way you have found to focus on My love. Love – and service – is never an isolated event. It is like throwing a pebble into a river. The circles of water keep expanding. It is the same with good actions and bad ones as well.

Lord, I see. It really brings awe and wonder. You teach me so much using water to illustrate. Thank You.

*****

I am aware of every prayer you utter or even think. I respond with joy that you turn to Me. You may not see or know My response but be assured that I do. I see a much bigger picture of things than you can. Fear not! I am still in control.

Look for goodness, beauty, truth, and be sure to take note of such things. Speak encouragement to others. As the world is focused on terrible things, you need to point out the good. Be My ambassador of love and kindness. Especially notice good in the young. They need your encouragement. Just as you are grateful to anyone who gives you a gift, does a kind deed for you, or encourages you, I, your God, am grateful for what you do for others. It is an appreciated service you provide to Me. It is a sign of your love for Me. Keep it up.

*****

Dear Jesus, there are two really neat things this morning. One is a tomato. As I got up, I was thinking that it has been so long since I've had a chance to be of service to anyone, I'm drying up on the vine. I pictured myself as a large green tomato – not yet ripe, but so big that the stem was bent and not allowing enough nourishment in, needing to be staked – a minor adjustment – Confession – so I can become what I can be, fully ripe and beautiful.

The other thing is marriage. Last night Mom E. and I saw a really nice little movie about a meddlesome mother trying to marry off her son, which made me think about one of my sons and his wife. I see each giving and each receiving love. Neither is self-sufficient, but each gives what the other needs. I married Rae because I thought he needed me. I was miserable when I realized that he felt quite self-sufficient. As long as each of us tried to hide or cover up our needs, we were miserable. But when the real needs surfaced and each of us rose to the occasion to meet those needs, true love blossomed and grew and ripened into a really good marriage.

How silly we are to hide our needs. Of course, sometimes we don't even know what they are. Lord, I have great need of You. And I am delighted to do whatever You want me to do – to meet Your desires. If You want someone to go to the grocery store for Anne or anyone else, here I am. If You want me to be a loving and kind teacher, here I am. If You want me to be a listening ear for a family member or friend, here I am. If You want me to be an understanding daughter-in-law, here I am. If You want me to be a good mother, then here I am also.

And You – when I need to be held, You are here. When I need strength, You provide. Without You, I cannot even take a breath. You teach me, understand me, listen to me, encourage me constantly, nourish me with Your own Body and Blood, forgive me and restore me to intimacy when I grow distant. And so quickly. I have needed to spend time with You and I have been running away again. But You caught me this morning with the thought of a tomato, and it is wonderful. It is wonderful to know that this is true love – both on Your part and on mine – that is so marvelous. Perhaps I can be a good nun. Please lead me to the place where You want me and open the right doors so I can be let in – and let me complete the work You have for me here. Show me the right time as well as the right place. Hold me tight, Lord. I really need You.

*****

You are with me, sustaining me, and giving me the opportunity to serve my mother-in-law. And You have given me a heart that loves such service. Lord, what a gift! How many people serve their families grudgingly – miserable for those who need their help – yet with us there is joy and gratefulness and true love. Someone described love as both wanting the good of another person and desiring to live with them. You have given me this love for my mother-in-law. This is indeed a great gift. Thank You, Lord.

*****

Thank You for the marvelous gift of being able to wake up at night quickly, do what is necessary, and be able to get back to sleep. Last night Mom E. woke up with her eye bothering her. I put an eye drop in it, and we both readily got back to sleep. I realized what a great gift this is, which I have had since age 15, to wake up easily, do whatever I need to do, and then sleep soundly again. This is Your provision for me to be able to be useful and Your provision for all those I have cared for and will care for in the future. I feel incredibly gifted and blessed.

*****

Lord, I realize that the care I give to Mom E. is a pro-life activity, in that I am helping to preserve her dignity in her old age. It makes me feel like I have a ministry. By my loving care of her, I am extending Your love to her. Thank You for showing me this.

*****

Lord, I think I know what my priorities should be, but I'm not sure I live according to these.

What should they be?

Well, You first, then my three children and three parents, my job, my friends, and others.

That sounds good enough – but where do you come in?

Lord, I don't know where I would fit. But isn't all this *my* priorities? So, if I put You first, then it is You and me You take care of me while I focus on You. You meet my needs as I spend time with You.

If that is true, then you are built up by the relationship.

Lord, are all relationships supposed to be like that?

The healthy ones are. And I want you healthy.

But what about the ones that drain and wear me out?

Those are the ones you need to leave behind.

But aren't we supposed to serve those who cannot repay us?

Yes, you are. But when you do, it is not a relationship you have with them but with Me. It is My work that you are doing, and your reward comes from Me.

What about my children?

Expect a return. If you cook for them, expect them to do things you ask them. Do not legalize – feel free to be generous – but give them the opportunity to be generous as well.

Lord, my relationship with the parents is already like that.

I know, and that is why it does not wear you out.

And school? Same thing?

Certainly.

I'm not to give and serve until I drop?

No, that is not what I ask of you. For every commandment, there is a reason with your good in mind. Each one frees you from much greater evil. Whatever you give Me, I repay abundantly. My promises are not empty ones. You see how cynical this world can make you. This is not My way. This is where you will find the balance to which you are called. I do not call you to a life of misery and pain. Every pain you bear and give to Me has a reward attached. I am God – I will not be indebted to you or anyone. You cannot out-give Me. This is a strange idea to you, but you have heard it before. Dwell on it a while as you go through the day. My love for you is better than you expected. Receive it – it is freely given.

Thank You, Lord. I do accept – and I will need to mull this over. Wow!

*****

During the time of prayer, I was inspired to give You all of my possessions, including my house. Thank You for affirming Your love for me and inviting me again to spiritual marriage. Lord, You showed me that, as I give my house to You, it becomes totally Yours, and You take me into Your house as Joseph took Mary into his house. I gave You my house. It is Yours. You brought me to Your house. I am Yours. And You are confirming it with Your Presence right now. Thank You.

Maggie, you are indeed Mine. Though you often feel like you are not as close to Me as you or I wish, you are Mine. I delight in having you in My house. This Christmas you are giving Me a great gift. And I give you the gift of taking you into My house. It is a good house. You don't even need to change anything. You are very familiar with it.

Lord, it is wonderful. I am delighted with Your house. I will help You keep it up.

Maggie, there is some humor in all this, but it is also real. You have remembered your illness of 2001 and realize how close you and I were through it. You have also had several other illnesses and surgeries and much pain, and you have come through it all with faith and trust. But now it is a new level of closeness and union you and I both desire. Come away with me, yet not away at all. Right here is where I live. In this house, in this body, in your soul. Experience the union you have sought for so many years.

Lord, how can I begin to thank You? I thought I was slipping away from You. Yet Your love brings me closer than ever before. Please keep a tight hold of me. I do not want to be even slightly separated from You.

Fear not. I have not let you go all these years. I certainly will keep holding you close. Get some rest now. Sleep in My arms tonight.

*****

Lord Jesus, the simplicity of the Gospel and even of life is overwhelming me. Not my will but Thine be done. That is what maturity is about. That is what holiness is about. That is what love is about. Once one sees it, it becomes so obvious, yet until one sees it, it makes no sense at all. It is simple enough that a child could understand it, yet very few people do. As I have been spending more time with little children, I see the immaturity of demanding one's own way, of being so self-absorbed that nothing can penetrate – not logic, not threats, not promises – nothing. Learning to wait, to share, to give up your own desires: these are the great lessons of childhood. If one learns these, love is possible – if not, then there is much trouble both for the individual and those unfortunate enough to have to be around him. Now I understand why we need to see Your body on the Cross, not just the Cross itself. You showed us complete surrender of will. You had no desire to be nailed to that Cross – but it was Your Father's will that all should learn to give up their own desires for His, which is total goodness and total harmony and unity. That is the only way we can survive eternity. Temporal pain or discomfort is trivial compared to learning surrender of will, which is our only way to enter eternal happiness. This is also a key to redemptive suffering.

Lord, You did it again – what I just read in a devotional book had the reading, "not My will but Thine be done." What confirmation! Lord, I need help. I have the theory down, but the practice is more difficult.

Maggie, the reason the practice is so difficult is that you get so overjoyed at understanding the theory that you think you should then be able to do it in your own strength. That may work in math – but not in the Kingdom. You needed Divine inspiration to understand the theory. Now you need Divine intervention and strength and help to actually do what you now understand. You are not meant to do these things alone. Today you were feeling alone. Even when you had others around, you felt like you were alone.

Lord, how am I to handle these times? I have no legitimate escapes, so I use ones I know will be counterproductive.

Escape is not My will for you in these circumstances. Submission, surrender, and supplication are necessary. Submission in that I have a purpose for allowing the uncomfortable situation. Surrender in that all your own solutions are ineffective and only My will can accomplish My purpose. Supplication in that you *must seek My help!* There is no universal solution. Each case must be handled individually – you MUST ASK for My help and guidance. I am faithful to provide it.

You gave me the three S's – submission, surrender, and supplication. This morning You have also given me the ability to follow them. I submit to Your will and plan, which is much better than what I have or can come up with – You know I have tried. I surrender my ways and plans, having found them useless anyway, and I ask (supplication) for Your will and plan.

Maggie, this is good, but not enough. My will is all you have said: for your good and happiness, better than anything you could imagine, involves the present as well as the future. But it is more – it involves a continuous relationship. You cannot ask once, get an answer, and be done with it. It is a continuous asking, receiving, seeking, finding, knocking, opening, and entering. This continuity is what you lack and what holds the key to your happiness and contentment. You have come a long way – some never ask, seek, or knock. You do – occasionally. And you are learning to receive, find, and enter – also occasionally. When you do, you have joy. But now you must learn to keep it up. This is a learning process. There was much to un-learn before you could get to this point. There is no room for self-hatred in this process, nor is there room for self-seeking. My will for you – you must ask for it, seek it out, and when you have received and found it, you still have to knock and enter into it. There are seven steps. Three depend on you: ask, seek, knock. Three more are from Me: receive, find, open. The last one – the Sabbath – the seventh – is to enter into the joy of your Master. This is the union you so desire. It is not necessarily passive, but it is continuous, and it will satisfy you.

*****

I received a new twist of a teaching on the seven parts of ask, receive, seek, find, knock, open, and enter. In the past I always thought that we ask, and You give the answer which we must receive. We seek, You help us to find. We knock, you open the door, and we enter. Tonight, I saw the roles somewhat reversed. You asked us to pray, and You received our prayers. You seek out the lost souls, and You find us. You knock on the doors of our hearts, and if we open them, You enter.

*****

After an extended retreat where I had the freedom to spend much time in the Lord's Presence and He kept reminding me to focus on His love and to be joyful.

Maggie, do you see how your enthusiasm has improved? I am delighted.

Lord, I did not even know how hungry and thirsty I was for all that You have given me in the past ten days. You have filled me to overflowing.

There is more to come. Your joy will continue as you continue to seek Me.

Lord, I see it. My joy was pretty much dried up and You restored it. Thank You.

You are most welcome.

Lord, help me express myself well as I try to tell my friends and counselors all I experienced. And please help me do the things I need to do – medications, computer work, clearing Mom's house, etc.

Maggie, I am with you. You need not fear. Do all you can but continue to make prayer a priority. I reveal Myself to you in prayer. And do not forget My love for you and your love for Me. For the last ten days your main goal was to please Me – and you have been very pleasing to Me. Yes, I know you like pleasing others as well, and that is fine, but it works so much better if you love them through Me. In the not-too-recent past you tried to please people according to your own ideas. Now when you want to love them, ask Me how I want to bless them through you. The actions may end up being the same, but the motive behind the actions will be much better. Most of all, remember My love for you. I desire to please you as well. And it would seem that I have been successful.

Oh, Lord, You have indeed. I don't know how I could be more pleased.

I, too, am greatly pleased with you. Hold on to this as reality. Let nothing steal your joy and come to Me quickly when you feel that there is a threat to take it from you.

*****

Good morning, Lord Jesus. Thank You that the sewing machine was fixed and I was able to do a few things last night. It really felt good, Lord. I still love being of service to others.

Me too.

Lord, You are revealing Yourself to me in just those two little words. I see now that Your life was one of service – not just because it was necessary for You to serve, but because You loved to serve others. And You gave that part of Your character to me – and to many others who also love to serve. That is what You tried to teach the apostles when You washed their feet. And they learned it, too. That is why they are now called saints. Thank You, Lord for this quick little revelation.

*****

I was told about prayer being the key to success. I do pray, but do I pray enough? How much prayer is enough? Can one pray too much?

These questions are not as silly as you think. Yes, you can pray too much, but you are not guilty of that. If your prayers keep you from the duties of your state in life, then they are too much. If your prayers are impersonal when you are capable of deeper prayer, then there is something wrong. There are many forms of prayer. The advice you were given, "Pray as you can, not as you can't," is very good. Do not try to impress Me or anyone else by your prayers. Let them be simple and genuine. There is nothing wrong with formal prayer nor with informal prayer. There is a time and place for every kind of prayer. But it is not wrong to be fully engaged in the present moment, either. When you do your duties and kindnesses you can be concentrating on what you are doing. You often complain that you lose your awareness of My Presence when your daily activities begin. This is a part of your nature. Even great saints did not maintain awareness of Me until late in their lives. This is not yet a way you can pray. But you can come to Me and you can stay with Me more now than you could before. Do not worry about what is enough, but do not give up on improving your relationship with Me. I will guide you, but you have to keep asking, seeking, and knocking.

*****

Even though I have not had much specific prayer, You have stayed with me – guided me, and allowed me to enjoy whatever I am doing.

I feel I have done a good job with the teaching and tutoring and have been serving You to the best of my ability whenever and wherever I see any needs. Jesus, all I can offer You is my service. I haven't done anything out of the ordinary, yet I feel that I am serving You and You are pleased with my service. I hope this is not my pride speaking. Thank You for peace within all the turmoil.

Maggie, relax. You are not required to account for how many minutes you spend in what form of prayer. I ask you the same question I asked Peter, "Do you love Me?" and for you I will continue before you have a chance to answer, "Are you feeding My lambs?" In fact, I will answer it for you. You are feeding my lambs, my sheep and my lambs. The first lambs are your own children. The sheep are the adults – mother-in-law, Anne and Leonard, and others. The second group of lambs is your students. You do feed them all. Remember, I gave only one commandment. Yes, you do love Me because you love others. So do not worry. I don't say that you shouldn't come to Me in prayer, but that there is more to your life in Me than just sitting still. Enjoy the peace and do not worry.

Jesus, You encouraged me tremendously. I am to find You in the people I serve. I usually get caught up in serving them and never think that I am serving You through them. But You encourage me that it is OK, because when You separated the sheep from the goats, the blessed asked when did they see You and do good to You. They did not do it consciously either, yet You accepted their service as unto You. So, my love and care for my students, my children, my friends, and whoever I serve is not wasted; You take it as my gift to You even if I forget to specifically offer it as such.

*****

Shortly after entering the convent and contemplating that I simply needed to do God's will:

Lord Jesus, I spoke to Fr. Sanders about this whole thought of doing things simply because it is Your will. He assured me that right now it seems I am doing Your will and the fact that I enjoy it is actually a confirmation that it *is* Your will. Your will and my desire are not mutually exclusive – on the contrary, Fr. Sanders' definition of Your will is where my desire and the needs of others meet. I like that. I do desire to serve You by serving Your people. You have given me these abilities and I am using them the best I can. You have taught me discernment, and I usually know when I have overstepped my bounds. And then You give me the grace of repentance and re-surrender to Your will.

Maggie, this is the answer to your questions of who you really are as a result of the change in your state in life. You were worried that you could no longer be who you really are but had to fit into a mold. Some changes are necessary, but the gifts and talents I have given and nurtured in you can and should be used. I loved you before you came here. I love you now. The basic person you are has not changed, nor does it need to change. But growth is built in. Your growth is molded by your state in life. But these states in life are not mutually exclusive, either. You need flexibility, humility, a teachable heart, some sacrifice, compassion, and attentiveness to the needs of others in both states of life. Having learned them as a wife and mother makes you a good candidate for religious life. The message you are receiving – to relax and continue to do the best you can and be secure in the fact that this *is* My will for you – is a good message. Take it to heart. Enjoy what you do. Keep doing it well. Fear not. Do include Me in your day as you go along. I am with you, in you, around you, in those you serve, and even in your sisters. Build, unite, gather. Avoid tearing down, dividing, and scattering. I see your efforts. I continue to love, guide, and help you. Rejoice and relax in My love.

*****

A part of the ministry while I was in the convent was St. Joseph's Workshop, a live-in place for men who were trying to restart their lives after addiction to drugs or alcohol. This was my favorite part of the ministry.

Lord, today one of the men who is living at the workshop was arrested. I felt like I was kicked in the gut. I want so much for them to succeed. To see them go through such difficulties makes my heart ache. You feel that way about all of us, Your children, as well. Lord, I want to love Your Father's will, too. None of this should be so difficult. For me, love of people is so much easier. Why is loving You so difficult for me?

This is a transitional period. Transitions are difficult, uncomfortable, uncertain, and even painful – but very necessary. I will help you through it – keep seeking, keep asking, keep knocking. I am indeed working in your life. Bring all these feelings to Me. Yes, My heart hurts as My children are hurt. I will heal the hurts of your heart and, as you allow Me to heal your hurts, you also bring comfort and healing to My heart. The more you love those I want to love, the more you comfort My heart.

Oh, Lord, the thought of bringing comfort to Your heart does give me feelings of love for You.

You see, all you needed was that I need you.

Do You need me, Lord?

If I did not need you, you would cease to exist. Not only do I need you, I want you. I enjoy your company. I desire your love.

Lord, I give You all I have. Yet it is so little.

I have not complained.

I guess I need to be needed. Yet *You* also need to be needed. We try so hard to be self-sufficient and all You want of us is to need You and turn to You.

No, that is not all I want. I also want you to love and need and appreciate each other. I have already given *you* this gift of love – you now see that I am like you in needing to be needed. You have not seen this part of Me before. You see your God as self-sufficient. Yet self-sufficiency is not very attractive – it pushes people away. That is not My nature: I gather, not scatter. Yes, I do have needs and desires – and I do need and desire you. I need and desire you to love My people. You can love them with your smile, your care, your listening, your talking and praying with them, by taking them seriously, even by listening to their jokes. You can love them by sewing, cooking, visiting – sharing your life. You do all these things and you love serving Me, yet you think you don't love Me. I think you love Me. You have given your life, day after day. You do not refuse Me anything. You anticipate the needs of others – thus You anticipate My needs.

I do come to you through others. You have been very good to Me by being good to others. You have not seen apparitions or supernatural things – yet you continue to serve Me in very natural ways. This is the Nazareth spirituality – it is what I have called you to. The ordinary things of life done with great love. Be at peace. You are meeting My needs.

Lord, I thank you so much.

In loving others, you thought that you could not see past them to see My needs and desires. You met their needs and desires readily but did not see that it was your God that you served. See Me and My hurts and needs as you minister to My people. You have marveled at how easy it is to love and care for them. Begin to see that it is My needs you are meeting as you help each of them. I come to you as very needy. And I love you in return through their gratefulness and love as well. Do not distrust your value or love because you are loved back – I am the One who loves you through them. Be at peace. Your love is quite good enough.

*****

Lord, how easily prayer has become a "have to" instead of a "get to." Please keep reminding me that prayer is a gift and a privilege, not a chore.

Maggie, this is a key to any relationship. Spending time with one you love should never be a burden. It is not meant to be. It is a time to talk over the things or people or problems or joys on your mind. The written prayers are meant to focus your mind on things you may not naturally think of. They put in words deeper realities you might not be able to. You may not be as poetic or eloquent, so others have already done it for you.

Lord, that makes sense, but I have trouble with the repetitiveness of it.

That is part of it becoming familiar – like a song. The words and music are the same each time you listen to or sing a song, yet the meaning is there. So it is with formal prayers. When you stop fighting it, it can bring great comfort and meaning.

Like the Mass? Once I came to know You, the Mass became so much more meaningful. That is why after so many years I still try to come daily.

Exactly! All prayer is to become like that. It is time spent with your God. Rejoice!

Thank You, Lord.

Thus, we try to do the things Jesus did, and also greater works, but only within our relationship with Him. We can only do anything He wants us to do with His help. There is always such a great need for prayer.

*****

Chapter 11

KNOW, LOVE, AND SERVE

*F*or most of us, the Christian life is not a straight line aiming upward to heaven. It is more like an uneven wave with hills and valleys and even gaps. We are doing great and reaching new heights, and then we don't even know how we are in the pits again. My search to know, love, and serve God has been like that. But He was always encouraging me and lifting me up from whatever pickle or tragedy I happened to experience.

My child, I see your willingness to do My will. And I bless you. I will make My wishes clear to you so that you might accomplish that which I assign you. You are reluctant to come to Me because you do not know Me very well. Today you are wondering, "Well, what now?" Are you not?

Yes. Lord, I am.

I will tell you. I already know you. But you do not know Me as well. Search the Scriptures about what I am like. Go ahead – start looking and write down what you find.

Isaiah 50: You owe no one anything. You do not divorce Yourself from whom You love. You can redeem. You have power to deliver. Isaiah 51:12: You comfort me – I should not be afraid.

Lord, I've been so distressed by all the world's evil I've seen lately that I have forgotten about Your power to redeem and deliver. I have forgotten that redemption and deliverance are Yours in the first place. That You will gladly do that – it is not a bother to You.

Today you have touched your God. You have a little more understanding now. It is not so hard for you to praise or worship now.

That's true, Lord. Thank You.

*****

I will not allow myself to be robbed by tiredness or by lack of privacy. You are present regardless of my circumstances. Lord, yesterday at Mass, I saw something new about the Living Water spoken by Jesus to the Samaritan woman in John 4; that means a relying on You – daily, constantly – Your availability, Your refreshing revelation. You do refresh my soul. Lord, You are the living water. You provide refreshment any time we turn to You. You are within us. Lord, I'm finally finding You within me. I don't need to go to a place like church or a retreat house to find You, You are here. You are right here within me, a river of living water.

Maggie, you know I've been trying to teach you this for a long time. And doing the will of My Father is food. Fellowship with Me is water. Both are available in abundance. Neither will weigh you down, but refresh and strengthen you. This is why I am the Bread of Life.

Lord, I feel so silly. I've been spiritually starving and parched for years, and both food and water have been right here. But I tried to satisfy my hunger and thirst with physical or mental food and drink, wondered why it didn't work, and why I was getting more and more frustrated. Lord, I need constant reminders to turn to You.

*****

Maggie, I see you are having trouble today. I don't love you because your house is neat and clean. I don't love you because your brain is superior. I don't love you because you serve Me well or because of anything you do or don't do. I love you because I love you. I don't need a reason. I want a relationship. Your problems stem from getting your focus off My love for you and onto your shortcomings. Yes, I want you to improve some here or there, but that is not the basis of our relationship. Stop seeing Me as a taskmaster. Stop feeling

guilty every time you sit down for a rest. I am not nagging you or scolding you. I want you to experience My love for you. That is what will transform you into one whom even you can like. Yes, I have noticed that you don't like yourself much lately. But I still LOVE you. Get out of that rut and begin to feel My love.

*****

Lord, I'm back again to the fact that You do the work, and I benefit. I used to have it backwards. Lord, I feel puny and foolish.

You are, but I love you anyway.

Lord, I couldn't survive without Your love.

I know. I didn't create you for your strength or beauty, or even great works. I created you for My love – to receive it, to enjoy it, and to spread it to others. Do that and you will have strength and beauty and great works. But your focus must be on Me. If you can focus on My love, your life will be much easier.

Rejoice – you are now learning one of the hardest lessons I have to teach My people – it is also one of the most painful. You hear it often enough. Without Me you can do nothing. Here is humility. This is truth. When you find yourself helpless, I can begin to pour My love into you. If I pour it into you while you are full of your own worth (pride) it gets polluted and distorted. But when I see that you are empty of that self-importance, I can fill you with the purity and full strength that I desire you to have.

Lord, I see it. Your undiluted power can only be seen when the vessel started out empty.

I didn't with you. I often start with ones that are so full of junk that there is hardly any room for Me. The sins, hurts, and pride have been baked and caked and stuck on there, and I just have to chip out the junk to get a little room to start with. But I keep pouring in clean water and the vessel keeps pouring out polluted water, until it is totally empty and clean. And even clean things need to be washed after they have been used. You need regular cleaning and washing if you are to be useful.

Lord, thank You for Your persistence. Cleanse me and wash me and scour me if you have to. I want Your pure water or oil or whatever You wish flowing out of me.

*****

Lord, I need You to quiet me and calm me. There is such a battle within me. I want Your will to be done, but I also have such a strong will of my own that I often can't distinguish mine from Yours – especially when mine seems noble and kind. I guess that is why You don't let me see results right away when I pray. Lord, I don't know what You are doing, but I know that You are trustworthy and good and kind.

I have intensely prayed for a new infilling of the fire of Your Holy Spirit. Help, Lord, I don't want to miss Your answer to my prayer or misinterpret it. I know it is by the fruit that all this is known, and fruit takes time to take shape, so I will wait.

Father, I submit to You as best I can. Please teach me to be more completely trusting, yielding, and obedient to You. Jesus, I need more of You. I seem to know much about You, but I don't seem to know You or love You nearly enough. You have called me to be Your bride, and I have said a resounding YES – but just like I felt on my wedding day to Rae, I feel I hardly know You. Yes, I love You. Yes, I know You are good. Yes, I trust You. Yes, I know I did right by saying "Yes." I need Your touch, Your voice, Your constant presence to grow in this relationship to which You have so graciously invited me. I feel totally inadequate and unable to contribute anything except the desire to learn and the need to be taught. If submission is pleasing to You, then I submit the best I know how.

Lord, then why am I so undone? I seem to have lost all the great qualities I thought I had and am only aware of my great need of You. I have no fear, for I know You are able to give me whatever I need to serve You. And right now, serving You is the only thing I really want. Like Peter at the Transfiguration, I want to say, "Lord, it is good to be here, would You like me to build three booths for You?" (The fisherman is offering to do carpentry for the carpenter's Son!) I am content that You have called me and am waiting to be empowered to do that to which I have been called.

*****

Talking to You always does good because it brings me closer to You. When one of my kids wants something, even if I say "No," the conversation is not wasted, it is communication. I seem to have had an incomplete idea of prayer. It's as if it is worthwhile only when I see my desired results. How horrible life would be if we only talked to those we love in order to get results. Yet that's what a lot of us do with You. If You say "No," then we go off pouting that it doesn't do any good to talk to You. Lord, how can You stand us? I repent. Let me keep praying whether I ever see results or not. Let my relationship with You be based on love, not "I want." Let me serve You and listen for Your voice all the time – even if I'm disappointed about something. Lord, I'm in awe about the variety of ways You can speak to me and have taught me to understand. You also told me this morning that the key to not getting discontented and grumbly as I have been lately is "with thanksgiving" to make my requests known ("rejoice always, pray constantly, give thanks in all circumstances"). Lord, Your will for me is good. Thank You.

*****

Lord, this morning I want to take a few minutes with You before Mass. I simply want to come into Your Presence, prepare myself, and then go to Mass and participate in the union You already have given me through the Eucharist. Lord, I seek a total and perfect union with You. But You have already given me many ways to be united with You, and I miss more of them than I catch. The grace I ask for today is that I should be alert and aware enough to see, hear, feel, and respond to the moments where You are offering me any gift, any closeness, or any way of revealing Yourself. Lord, thank You, for this prayer is inspired by You. This is Your desire for me today as well. If I can find You in little ways, then the little ways can join together to form that perfect union I so desire. Just as if I am faithful in little things, You will then be able to trust me with bigger things. Come, Holy Spirit, and open my eyes, my ears, and my heart. Come, Lord Jesus, let me know You more, and take me to our Father that I may serve the Triune God as You desire.

Know, Love, and Serve

*****

Lord, Lent is over, and what have You and I accomplished? I'm still fat, I'm still not a very good housekeeper, we're still in debt, but I know that You love me anyway. And during this Lent, I finally discovered that I kind-of like myself, too. I still don't like being fat or a poor housekeeper, but I am a lot of other things that I do like. I am generally kind, loving, thoughtful, understanding, truthful, unpretentious, capable of handling most situations, cheerful, and an all-around nice girl (OK, woman). I am diligently seeking You, and am finding You more often than I used to. I still love being used by You and delight in serving You. I know I am very much loved by You and that Your love is sufficient to make me holy (though it may take a lot longer than I'm prepared for). I also know that the journey is at least as important as the destination. I also know I am not qualified to evaluate my own progress. I am not to make grandiose plans for self-improvement, I do not have to be perfect immediately, but neither am I to quit altogether or give in to sin. I am healed and forgiven, but always in need of healing and forgiveness. I can relax, in that very little actually depends on me, yet I am to use what energy and talents I have to the greater glory of God.

Lord, You have taught me a great deal this Lent. You have taken me, accepted me as I am, called me by name, chosen me. You have blessed me beyond my fondest dreams – with closeness (though I still want more), with revelations, anointing, loving, inviting, challenging, sustaining, and calming. You have shown me my sins of not trusting You enough, my rebellion, my insisting on my own way even when I know Your way is better, my judgmental nature that can reduce a person to being identified by a sin, my misconceptions of what You want of my life and how You work, my tendency to be a hearer rather than a doer, and my inability to change any of these things on my own. Yet You still love me, despite all my failures and sins. And Your love is permanent. I will always be Yours, and You will always be my God. I, who once was so insecure, am now secure. You have called me to return and rest, to be quiet and trust You. I am doing that the best I can; You will show me how to do it even better. Lord, I thank You and ask that You continue and give me even more.

*****

Jesus before Herod

Lord, Herod looked on You as a performer to amuse and entertain him. How many of us look for signs and wonders simply for our amusement! But You are not a magician. You do not perform on command. Herod got no show, not even a word. Lord, let me look to You not for signs, but for the reality of living in You. If You choose to do miracles, let me participate in Your work; if You choose to work solely through natural means, let me also participate in that. Let me not prefer one way to another, but simply obey You.

*****

The prayer meeting was wonderful. Lord, You are still calling us to repentance. But so gently and lovingly and without condemnation do You call us – You see how our sins confine and imprison us, and You seek to set us free. You want our chains to fall off. You want only what is good for us.

The grace I ask is that my self-image would be Your image of me. Lord, Your self-image was totally healthy. You knew Who You Are. The chief priests wanted clarification and proof. Pilate wanted to know if You were who he thought You were, Herod wanted to see signs – but You did not need to prove anything. You are Your Father's Son and Your purpose on this earth was to reconcile man to Him. Neither Herod, nor Pilate, nor the chief priests could understand that. They turned against You and swayed the people to do the same. But their rejection of You, painful as it was, did not alter Your status or purpose. You are the Son of God regardless. You came to save, redeem, set free, sanctify, restore, heal, and ransom mankind from the power of sin. You chose to do this by demonstrating infinite, unconditional love even to the point of death by horrible torture, all the while having the power to stop at any point but choosing not to use that power.

Such love demands a response. I choose to respond by overwhelmingly accepting all that You offer me. I also respond by giving You my life and begging for Your constant help to keep giving You my life, and resist my tendency to take it back. Lord, I want to give

You more. Show me how. Thank You, Lord, for such love and care and gentleness. You do not push or force, You simply show Your love and wait until we see and respond. Thank You.

*****

You again showed me how Your ways and thoughts are different from mine. I'm still expecting that I will dramatically improve in any or all of the areas I want to change as soon as I discover some magic formula. But You showed me that it is not some momentous occasion or decision, but rather a continual succession of seemingly insignificant occasions and decisions that, with Your constant help and participation, will change my life and grow the fruits of the Spirit that I ardently desire. That is why I must take up my cross *daily* and come follow You. I behave as though I only need to take it up once, and I'll be fine. But I put it down very easily and then "forget" where I left it. Lord, help me to remember to keep taking it up again and again. Thank You for Your patience and mercy that You continue to teach me and guide me. Lord, I want to know, love, and serve You more. Thank You that You are bringing this about.

*****

Lord, my desire for union with You is growing again. This morning I woke up pondering the Eucharist. (I ponder things in my heart like Mary.) I remembered a sermon during Holy Week that we are a Eucharistic people. That Jesus took the bread (accepts us), blessed it (blesses us with so much good), broke it (discipline, sorrow, suffering), and gave it (service), and how at various times in our lives we can see which of the four aspects is happening in our lives.

I continued along those thoughts and realized that once we are given, we are often consumed (take and eat) but we are also transformed into the body of Christ, and as long as we serve others, we become one with those we serve. Then when we are done, the Lord has to start all over and take us again, bless us, break us and give us – but in between perhaps we have to become mere bread again.

Lord, Your loving hands have formed me and continue to mold me into the image and likeness of You, the Living God. I delight in being useful to You and in serving You. Let me be a profitable servant. Keep taking, blessing, breaking, and giving me, and then picking up the pieces and forming me again.

*****

Lord, thank You for the awe and wonder You have filled me with. This morning I woke up praising You and envisioning the Great, Powerful, Mighty Creator of the universe, for whom the whole earth is no more than a golf ball, who stoops down and gathers up a mere speck (me) and holds me in Your mighty hand and loves me and delights in me, and has a perfect plan for me, and provides everything I need so that someday I can be exalted and magnified to truly be a companion to You. You become small that You might make us big. And You do it in such ordinary ways that we miss the point so easily. We look for Your mighty hand – but it is so big that we cannot possibly see it, so You touch us through the everyday ordinary things of life and we don't see or feel Your touch at all because it is so simple and always there. Thank You, Lord, for Your ordinary and constant love and guidance in my life. Let me cooperate with Your plan, Your Most Holy Will, that I might truly become totally united to You.

*****

Lord, I don't love You like I think I should. I don't know You like I think I should. All I know for sure is that I want, sometimes gently desire, sometimes urgently demand, to be totally and completely united to You, permanently bonded; yet I don't even know what that really means. I didn't know what marriage entailed when I got married, and this is the same idea I have: to enter somewhat blindly so that I can both enjoy the good parts and endure the trials and sufferings. And I know there are trials and sufferings to come, but You are there to guide and carry me through.

*****

Thank You that I am secure in Your love, the love of my husband, my parents, my children, and many others. Thank You that You have taught me that I need not strive to earn love, but instead that I can respond to Your love and the love of others by doing the very things I used to do to try to earn love. The motive is different, but the works remain the same. This is a great gift of freedom You have given me, and the beginning of that freedom and union I crave so desperately. The desire came from You, the teaching came from You, the grace to learn came from You, the circumstances through which I learned came from You, and the continued growth and fulfillment of this shall come from You. Thank You so much, Lord.

*****

I seek Your face, Your will, Your teaching, Your direction, Your thoughts, Your ways, and Your kingship over me. I knock at the door of Your Kingdom, which You opened to me before and invited me in, but somehow, I have managed to exit. I knock, and I realize that I am on the wrong side of that door through my own fault.

Maggie, I said ask and you shall receive, seek and you shall find, knock and it shall be opened unto you. So now it is time for you to receive, find, and enter through the open door. So often My children ask, seek, and knock but then leave before they receive, find, or come in through the door I have opened. You have done this many times. Even now you are getting restless and could easily leave to go back to sleep or do anything but what I am calling you to do. But stay, and listen to My voice.

You have asked Me to take back the problems of those to whom I have sent you. I do take these problems and I will care for all those you love or care for. You are learning what it means to be a channel of My love, but you also have to learn My ways and to forego yours. But take heart – you are learning. You asked for My forgiveness – you are forgiven. But confess it next time you have the opportunity.

You seek My Presence – My face. Yet you already have found Me, or you would not be here. Let Me reassure you that I will not leave you or forsake you and I do let My face shine upon you and give you peace.

You knock at My door and seek entrance back into My Kingdom. The door is open – enter, rejoice, and come into My Presence. Know that you are welcome and wanted and useful to your God. It is My love that cleanses you – and in My Presence you will become all I desire for you. Keep coming back to Me when you find that you have run away. I welcome you back. And I will welcome anyone and everyone you bring back with you. My Kingdom is bigger than you think. You have not gone outside of My Kingdom – only outside of My castle. But your home is within the walls of My dwelling place, and you are no longer satisfied outside. This is good. Come in, and hold on to your Master's hand, and rejoice. You are learning, you are growing, and you are loving your God more than ever before. Take hold of all this: I do love you, I do accept you, I do take you, I do bless you, I do break you, and I do give you to others. But then I take you back again. You are Mine. And you will continue to learn, grow, improve, and love more and better. Things that seem impossible to you shall become simple and natural. Yes, even the condition of your body, your house, your children, and those you love will improve. Fear not! For I have redeemed you, I have called you by name, you are Mine.

Lord, I do accept and find and enter. And I do rejoice, for You have dealt wonderfully with me beyond anything I deserve or imagined or thought. I cannot thank You enough. Let these words of Yours penetrate my innermost being, and let *my* soul magnify You, my Lord, and *my* spirit rejoice in You, my Savior.

*****

Lord, I felt You calling me and You seemed almost to be begging me to come to You – it startled me and I could not refuse – not that I would have anyway, but here I am, Lord – You sounded sad and lonely. What would You have me do?

Maggie, I did call you and all I want is for you to be in my Presence. You do not expect your God to be sad and lonely. You do not expect Me to be hurting or hungry or thirsty, yet I AM. Though I AM powerful, I AM as helpless as an infant. Though I own the cattle of a thousand hills, I AM poor and hungry and have no place to lay My head. Though I have created all, I long for your company.

But Lord, I am less than nothing – I am sinful and weak; and You want my company that much?

More than that much.

Lord, can I actually make a difference in Your life?

YES! It is for that reason that I have created you, called you my own, and brought you out of your land of birth. My love for you is so much greater than you can comprehend.

Lord, I can give You joy and alleviate Your sadness?

Does this surprise you?

Completely – yet I don't know why.

After all these years of proclaiming a personal God, you are just beginning to see how personal I really AM.

But, Lord, you really mean that I can make a difference in Your life?

YES! The words I was hungry and you gave me to eat, and following, are not there just to be pretty on the page. My hunger and thirst right now are for your company – for your love.

Lord, I had forgotten what love can be like. I thought I had grown too old to ever feel that way again.

My child, I do not see you as old or fat or weak or useless. I see you the way I have created you. I desire your beauty, even if it is hidden from everyone else, including you. If a million years are like a second to Me, do you not see that so much of what concerns you is irrelevant to Me?

But, Lord, I thought for that very reason, I was also irrelevant, that it was only out of Your infinite goodness and kindness that You continue to tolerate me. I think of myself as an irritation to You – an inconvenience. Yet You did not have to make me. You wanted me, not just for anything I can do and then I am finished, but to be with You forever in perfect love.

My love for you has never been passive. That is not My nature. You have felt longing for love. You have felt loneliness. You have

felt rejection. And you have felt the joy of companionship and acceptance and appreciation. I, too, have felt all these things. And I am truly affected by your companionship and your gratitude and your love. You have been able to enjoy so many things – yet how seldom do those who give you joy realize that they have the ability to give you such joy.

Or pain, either.

That is true. This is the key to forgiveness.

Lord, I am in awe! All You have taught me this morning demands a response from me. My response is that I desire and delight to give You whatever You want of me. I am here only because You have brought me here. I am Yours totally and completely. Lord, wrap Your arms around me and hold me close. I choose to give You whatever pleasure, joy, love, companionship, or anything else – comfort – that You desire.

Maggie, I like your response.

*****

Lately I have been aware of my own questionings as to whether I love You. No major problems – just a stray thought once in a while. The Great Commandment is to love You with my whole heart, soul, mind, and strength – do I really do that? And how can I do it better? Then I get caught up in the other things. I pray, but I'm so involved in life that I don't feel the intimacy with You that I crave. And I wonder whether my love is what it should be, or could be, and then that question comes again – do I love You? I heard a sermon on TV last night that reminded me, "If you love God, you will keep His commandments." It was taken one step farther: if you don't spend time in the Word, you don't know the commandments enough to keep them. Thus, reading Scripture is inquiring of You as to the specifics of living the Christian life and letting You speak to us about what is sin and what we need to do and not to do. If we continue to sin, then there is a lack of love, for if you truly love someone, and give offence, then there is automatically deep remorse and shame. *That* love can keep us from doing wrong, because we can't disappoint the one we love. Lord, lately I've seen my kids disappoint me by refusing to do what they know to be my commandments. It has felt to me like hatred.

Yesterday as I was helping Papa, (my earthly father) I found out how I can love him better, how to show my love for him – this is back to love being action rather than just a feeling. Lately I had wondered how I can show love for him – it seemed the only avenues were birthday and Christmas presents. I never know what to get him, and they usually fall flat. But one day while in a dollar store, I saw a little horseshoe change purse like he always used to have. It reminded me of him and I bought it. I had it in my purse for several weeks and forgot about it, but last week I was at his house, and in searching for something in my purse I found it, gave it to him, and watched his utter joy that I had thought of him when I didn't have to. My heart overflowed with love and delight that I had managed to please him. Yesterday as he and I were working with the word processor he had just bought, there were more of the same feelings; I was actually doing something that was truly helpful to him. It was something he really wanted to learn, and I was teaching him and he appreciated it. Now I have a way of showing him love and care in the next few weeks by going to help him learn more about his machine. It's not something he demands of me, but I know if I make time for it, it will be an opportunity to give love that will benefit both of us.

This brings me back to spending time in the Word. I did not know how to love my father in this particular way until I spent the time with him and the opportunity to be helpful came about. As I spent time with him, I saw the opportunity. I did not know the "commandment" or "need" which I could fill until I spent time with him and saw the need. Then, out of love, I filled the need, even though I have many other things to do. And now, even though my schedule is about to get overwhelming with teaching and other things, I will make time to spend with him and teach him more about the machine. So, Lord, I see some marvelous lessons on love. "If you love Me, keep My commandments and My Father will love You and We will come to you and make our home with you." The intimacy I crave – that union – comes through loving You by keeping Your commandments. And they are not difficult or burdensome. Jacob worked many years for Rachel's hand and it seemed to him like a few days because he was in love with her. (Gen 29:9-30) There is such a difference between doing something because it will bring joy to someone we love and doing the same thing out of duty or because we fear the consequences of not doing it. This lesson has always been in Your Word, yet right now it is clearer and more meaningful than it ever has been to me. I want to find out what I can do to bring You joy. I want to keep Your commandments and thus show You love. I want to experience Your approval and gratitude. I want You to dwell with me – to make Your home with me because You find me welcoming You by doing Your will. "If any man loves Me, he will do My will and My Father will love him and We will come to him and make Our home with him" (Jn 14:23).

Lord, this is what I want.

*****

During the Holy Thursday liturgy, I was asked to lead the procession after Mass to the small chapel and I was the one carrying the Cross. What an honor! And afterwards I felt that now I need not be afraid of loving You because You have allowed me to carry Your Cross, and I was able to do it. Lord, I was afraid to love You because I was afraid that I could not bear the pain of feeling Your hurts. When one is in love, whatever is felt by the beloved is also experienced by the lover. I was afraid of hurting whenever You hurt. I know so much sin is in this world, and I could not bear even a small part of it. So, I was afraid. And the thought that *my* sin causes You pain – how could I bear that if I loved You? But You have taught me love through Rae. You allowed me to love him so much that I could feel his pain and be able to occasionally soothe it. I also felt his joys – love is not just pain. You have given me love for my children, my family, my students, and Your people, wherever I find them. And You have allowed me to do acts of kindness to many people. Slowly, ever so slowly, You have taught me how to love You. You have not asked me, the way You asked Peter, "Do you love Me?" You simply gave me many opportunities to love Your people and You keep telling me, "Whenever you did it to these, the least of My brethren, you did it to Me."

Lord, just like I had to be told by someone else that I loved Rae, perhaps I love You a lot more than I thought I did, and as I carried Your Cross last night, it did not seem impossible any more that I could love You. I dare to say it: I love You. And the greatest awe and wonder of my life is that You accept that and are pleased. You have loved me with an everlasting love from before the world began, and You allow me to love You in return. And You yearn for and delight in my love, puny and halting and tentative as it is. You accept it and rejoice. You accepted the love of Mary Magdalene, and You were pleased with her love. You accept my love in whatever form I am able to give it to You, and You are pleased. Thank You, Lord.

Maggie, I look upon you and I smile. Last night I told you that during My agony in the garden, I was comforted by angels. I told you that your service and, yes, your love, is an angel of comfort to Me. You have heard My voice; you have not rebelled. I accept your love and your service. Do not be afraid that you would show up in My Passion as one of those who yells "crucify Him." See yourself comforting Me. See yourself with the love you feel for Leonard and Anne, the love you have for your mother-in-law, the love with which you accept and care for your children, the love and compassion you have for your students. These are real. They do not require any great effort on your part. They flow naturally through you. And I see each act of kindness as your love for Me. You are My Mary Magdalena, My Veronica, My Simon of Cyrene. You may have thought you were afraid of My pain, but you have borne it for many years. You have been afraid of failing Me. You have not failed Me – I do not look upon you with the sad love I had for the rich young man. I look at you and I rejoice in your love. Now you need to rejoice in My love. I do not ask of you anything that you cannot do. I teach You all that you need to pass the test. You need not be afraid any longer. Enter in to My Passion and death – whatever you feel is sufficient. Fear not, for I have redeemed you. I have called you by name, you are MINE.

Yes, Lord, I am Yours.

*****

I think I need to pay more attention. Lord, my relationship with You requires more from me than a quick attempt at a specific prayer.

No, child, it isn't like that at all. Your relationship with Me is not measured by what prayers you say, how many minutes you manage

to spend in prayer, or even the number of good works you do. **You cannot earn My love; it is already yours.**

Then how will I ever get closer to You? I read about the saints whose love for You was so rich and strong – and I still often doubt if my love for You even exists.

Relax, child. Your love for Me exists. And it is growing even if you don't see the growth. Did you have to strive very hard to love your husband?

No. Lord, not really. It just happened.

And how hard did you have to work to have it grow and deepen?

Not very. It did require choices occasionally.

So is your love for Me. It will grow and mature and deepen without much work, but it does require choices. But not every little choice is earth-shattering. Give yourself some room. It is hard to love when you are bound up in fear or legalistic red tape. Your love for Me will not die because you were sewing curtains all afternoon. Did you not sew those curtains in My Presence? Were you not listening and praying while you were sewing?

Yes, Lord, but I was not actually talking to You – was I?

Is love expressed only in words?

No, actions are better.

What were your actions today?

I suppose most of them were OK.

Consider your personal prayer done.

And tomorrow?

Come to Mass if you can, teach the best way you can. Be patient with yourself. And come to Me however and whenever you want – not just because you should – but because I will draw you closer and hold you and love you and you will be refreshed. If you expect only to have to continually apologize in your time with Me, it's no wonder that you put it off. Come to Me expecting good things. I will not disappoint you.

Thank You, Lord. I will come.

*****

I was instructed to definitely prepare for my time or prayer by reflecting on what I want from that particular prayer (closeness, union, order in my life), what I might want to say to God, what He might want to say to me. I am to approach Him aware that this is serious business – show God that I am serious about wanting closeness with Him and realizing that He is serious about wanting closeness with me. Also, I am to realize that I am in His Presence – that He is watching me – listening to me with His full attention – that He is watching me with full knowledge of everything about me – and with love and care and concern. He reacts to what He sees and is ready to help, enlighten, communicate Himself to me, and draw me to Himself. And as I realize all this, I can respond to Him with reverence and humility and begin to pray. I am also to reflect on what makes a prayerful heart: one that is open, generous, listening, believing, peaceful, longing for the living God. And every aspect of this prayerful heart is focused on Him – open to Him, generous toward Him, listening to Him, believing Him. My *actions* are to flow out of my prayer – because I am open to Him, I shall do … Because I am generous to Him, I shall use that generosity that He gave me to do … for …

Lord, this put a whole new light on living my life for *You*. I have done many things in hopes that You would be pleased, but my focus was not on You alone. This left a void and never quite satisfied me. It made me often think of myself as a man-pleaser rather than a God-pleaser. It's as if the actions came first, and I hoped that the motives would prove at least somewhat noble. But to establish the motive first, and then do the actions to show forth the motive, this seems to be a wonderful and freeing thought. So, Lord, give me the grace I need to begin to pray this way. I am to also end the time of prayer and take my leave from You as with the end of an audience with royalty. Then I am to write a report on how my prayer went. I am not to write during the prayer, but afterward, recalling what went on inside me during the prayer time.

*****

Lord, my prayer time was much better. I began at 9:00 am in the chapel, not in my room, and without books, paper, or pen – it was too dark to read or write. Your Presence was very strong. And when I started having trouble, You took over. As I again called to mind the aspects of the prayerful heart, I recognized each as Your gift to me that I could give back to You. Lord, You told me this morning that when You give me a gift, and I accept and return it to You, it becomes more precious to You than when You originally gave it. It is because You love me so much that the fact that I touched it makes it special to You. Lord, that is love.

*****

Lord Jesus, I did a meditation on Your Nativity this morning, and though I struggled to keep my concentration, I experienced some consolation when I imagined myself holding You as a baby. The helplessness of a baby touched me, and that Your Father chose human beings to care for You, totally and completely, that is amazing. That You, Lord Jesus, would become so helpless both at the beginning and the end of Your life on earth – just as we are – totally dependent on others for all needs.

*****

Lord Jesus, I was struck by the fact that You did not as much come into the world so You could experience our humanity, but much more so *we* could experience *Your* humanity. Not so You could relate to us, but that we could relate to You. And You raised our humanity to reach for Your Divinity by showing us Your Father. That You would do anything and everything to bring us closer – even stripping Yourself of all divine powers and choosing to take on our flesh – to be helpless as a baby, the same way we are when we come into the world. Father, I am impressed by all the angels and people You inspired to help in this endeavor. You not only prepared places but also people. And so, You do for us. Each of us has a place and many people (and I suppose angels as well) to care for us and help us when we are helpless. And thank You, Lord, for also allowing us to be the helpers where others are helpless.

*****

Maggie, you are running on empty, and you think you need to give more when you have nothing left to give. The week that you felt you were doing well you were receiving grace – and appreciating it. These last two weeks, you have been trying to do things for the wrong reason – not a bad reason, just a grace-less reason. Before you were testing the waters – and saw that the grace was really there for prayer, for fasting, for exercise, for even personal things like sewing. Then you moved into doing things out of commitment – not a bad reason – but not out of love or gratitude. You stopped looking for, and finding, the grace. You went on doing the things you found delightful the previous weeks but now there is no joy – you just trudge along. Doing the same task out of love is different from doing it out of duty. When in love, you are energized; when out of duty, you are drained. Right now, you are drained – that is why you fail. So come to Me, you who are burdened and heavy-laden, and let Me give you rest. Do take My yoke upon you. Lay aside the yoke of duty and take on the yoke of love, for My yoke is easy and My burden is light. This goes for your other work also.

Lord Jesus, thank You. I see what I need to do differently. I have been bound up by the many duties and lost track of love. I have been trying so hard to give that I neglected to receive, so I could have enough to give. Please help me today to be open to receive.

*****

Maggie, I, too, am here. I have called you and I am delighted that you have answered My call. Stay a while and be refreshed. Let My love fill every pore and particle of your body. Let it wash and fill every part of your soul and spirit. My love is powerful enough to do that and more. I know all your projects and doings. I also know how exhausted you get in the midst of them. What I want you to learn is how to allow My love to revitalize and strengthen you so, when you are empty, you may return to Me and be filled.

*****

How do I see You? As walking beside me – not yet face to face, but side by side. I suppose that is good; friendship. Yet I long to look into Your eyes. The love I need – right now, I accept and receive it by faith. I do not yet see it. Sometimes I feel it, so I suppose that is also good. But why do I weep as if I am not loved when I really do believe? Touch me again and cure my unbelief. Hold me close and wipe away my tears. Show me how to love You – my ways seem so useless and futile. I need so much more of You in me. Help me to empty myself of my ways and replace them with Your ways. No longer my thoughts, but Yours. This is my prayer of petition. To know You, love You, and no longer just serve You but truly follow You wherever You lead. Let me step back and let You take the lead. Help me to remember to look to You first before I rush into anything else.

*****

A thought just came to me: Holy Spirit, was that You? My rebellion and refusal to do the things I need to do – could it come from a desire, a holy desire, to be fathered? Could the emptiness from missing my husband, the authority in my life, be filled by the authority of the Father? This is the year we are asked by the Holy Father to focus on God the Father. I desperately need to be loved and guided by My Heavenly Father. I need His encouragement and instruction. Yes, and correction also. As my children mature and need less and less of my attention, and I no longer have a husband, I need somehow to feel "special" – loved and cherished and important. I need to see the eyes of the Father approving me, proud of me and rejoicing that He made me. This is what I want – my "felt need." Father, this is what I ask for. Is this what You desire to give me? Please open my eyes and ears and heart.

My child, how starved you are for approval. Yet you have been afraid to look for it or ask for it. You have been hurt in your childhood in this area. I will give you your heart's desire. Do not be afraid to receive My approval. I do not criticize and find fault. You do not have to be perfect yet. Yes, work toward perfection – but you are in process. I love you in all the ways you desire to be loved and more. I see your helplessness and give you My power. Come back to My arms again and again. I will not turn you away. I will welcome

you and rejoice that you are there. You only have to come to make Your Father rejoice.

*****

Many years ago, on one of my first retreats, I thought The Lord repeatedly told me that He loved me. My response was a very weak" That's nice." But He kept repeating it until I could respond better by showing me how every wave coming to shore at the river was His telling me that He loved me. A few years later, at the very same spot by the river, I asked Him how I could also show my love for Him. He then allowed me to notice that after a wave came to the shore, the water returned in small ripples into the river. He told me that these little ripples were my kindnesses to others, which were done as unto Him, and thus an acceptable and cherished response to His love.

You talk as if I had not been teaching you before now. But I have been, and you do have a teachable heart. Remember the ripples in the waves – remember that I accept every little gift as proof of your love. Your care for others – your extra help to your students, all the things you have done for years. But now, I call you to a higher form of love. Not that you have to stop these things, but concentrate on being with Me. No longer just doing loving things, but being loving toward Me. Remember, I wait for you. Come to Me. If it is awkward at first, let it be. But listen for My love. Do not come out of duty, but let Me give you reasons to come. This is how you involve Me in your day. Try again to come often.

*****

Now about my breakfast – You just showed me how I very carefully consumed every crumb. You also showed me that I am not so careful with my spiritual food – Your words to me. Too often You begin to speak to me and I wander off without letting You finish. I don't treasure every morsel. I need to – or You need to – change this completely around.

Maggie, you did not want to see this today. Yet you did, and did not hide from it or deny it. There is a beginning and an end to most

conversations. There is also a continual presence. Do not confuse the two. Your times of prayer should have a beginning and an end. But My Presence to you and your presence to Me should be continual. This does not mean that a look, a phrase, or even the direction of intention cannot be considered prayer – but they are different. As you go about your duties, you pass others and acknowledge them with a greeting, a comment, or just a smile or nod. But when you sit down to meet with someone, it is different. Your prayer time is a meeting with your God.

Lord, it sounds so serious.

It is. You are no longer an infant or toddler that wanders aimlessly and becomes fascinated by any bright object. It is time to get serious and focus on specific topics and themes. How serious are you about My words to you, about holiness, about My will? You cannot just play about your Christian life any more. If you want to be My disciple, you must take it seriously. This does not mean you will not have any fun along the way. I am not opposed to laughter and joy and fun. You saw that last night at the prayer meeting. But My Way leads to the Cross. That is serious. I am giving you an opportunity for serious prayer. Use it. Do not let it slip by. Do not sacrifice the important at the altar of the urgent. Trust Me and do your share. Listen much, speak little. Be prepared for a marvelous period of great growth.

Thank You, Lord. I do feel like I'm in training camp.

You are. This is what you asked for. It will be worth all the pain and trouble in the end. Don't give up. Now go and do what you need to do.

*****

My peace I give to you. Let it settle upon you as the dew settles on the ground. Stay still and let it cover you. Let My peace permeate your very being. It is My gift to you. It will sustain and calm you. Open your eyes and see the beauty I place above, around, and within you. I am healing, transforming, purifying, and sanctifying you. Give Me all your hurts, pains, troubles, sins. Watch Me transform them into comfort, joy, glory, and virtue. See the character of Jesus

forming within you. This is My work. I delight in doing it. Allow Me the joy of doing My job. It is with great love that I transform you. Be assured that I will complete what I have begun. Fear not, for I am gentler than you can imagine.

*****

Lord Jesus, thank You for sustaining me another day. The pain is still severe. My feet are swollen, and it is very difficult to stand up or walk. The pills only help a very little. I have all this to give to You.

Yesterday it was suggested that I pray the Sorrowful Mysteries of the Rosary, or perhaps pray the Stations of the Cross. I prayed all 15 mysteries of the Rosary on the road while I was driving yesterday, and today I want to pray the Stations. I suppose while I am in pain, I can identify with Your pain.

No, Maggie, it is the other way around. As you contemplate My sufferings, you will see that I can identify with your pain. It is not your compassion for Me that I desire, but that you understand and appreciate My compassion for you. It is still difficult for man to comprehend a loving God. Yet that is what I am. Think of your love and care for a sick or hurting child. I put that love and care into your heart. It is but a small portion of what I feel for My children who are hurting. See the goodness in you, and see that I have that same goodness without measure. Rejoice in this! My love for you is greater than your pain and discomfort. Your love for others helps you bear the pain. My love for you helped Me bear the pain of the Cross. Love is much greater than pain. Rejoice in My Love.

*****

During a long and painful illness:

The pain is still severe. The high doses of anti-inflammatory medicine do not give full relief. And when it wears off, the pain comes back full force. At 2:00 AM yesterday morning, as I was about to take my pills (so they would work by morning), I sent a thought Your way: "I don't usually ask why things happen to me, but if You have a reason for all this, I sure would appreciate knowing it." Then I turned on the TV and Mother Angelica was just coming on. She was reading from a book on Fatima about how Your Mother asked that we make sacrifices for poor sinners. Well, I understood that to be Your immediate answer. I thanked You and went to bed with a new attitude of thanksgiving that You provide me with opportunities to make sacrifices.

In the morning my niece Julie called – she wants to look into homeschooling and is pregnant with her fifth child. I congratulated and encouraged her. My oldest son came by so I could go grocery shopping and to church, and he cooked a marvelous dinner for us while I was at Mass. After dinner, I was even able to pay bills. At 11:00 PM a friend called needing a tow truck on the beltway. I finally found him one, and went to bed. The nights are difficult. I think I will ask the pharmacist if I can take some other painkiller as well. Then I will talk to the doctor on Tuesday.

This is the current story. You are still in charge and Your love is very evident. Today I will need Your help to make some progress in sorting and filing papers so I can get all the tax papers ready for the accountant. I also have schoolwork to do, but tomorrow is a holiday. Now, Lord, I really need to hear from You. I need a good long hug and You to tell me it will all be OK. Lord, I believe; help my unbelief.

Maggie, it is OK to cry. Remember that it is for those tears I died. I know your heart and your will. You have chosen to accept this struggle even though you keep looking for an end to it. That is healthy. Continue on. I know your fears and yet I will take you through this valley. I know it is dark and cold and you cannot yet see where this road leads. But it is not the road that leads you; I lead you. This is training for you to lean on Me and follow Me and hold on tightly. I will not tell you how long it will take. I will not tell you what will end it. But if you learn to rely on Me through this, the results will be glorious. This is a time of growth. You could call these growing pains. You will have the strength to do whatever you must do – and everything else is a gift. As you can see, I have provided all that you need and I am closer to you than you can imagine.

Thank You Lord. I do accept. I will do my best to follow You and hold on to You. But I still would like that hug.

My hugs and kisses come to you daily. Learn to recognize them. Right now, you already feel better – don't you?

Yes, I do. Just being reassured that You are in this helps.

I am. Remember the saying Steven's godfather, Bushey Baker, used to love: "God fixes a fix to fix you. If you fix the fix before you're fixed, God has to fix another fix to fix you." You are in a fix being fixed. You are being strengthened and made ready for battle. Not too long ago you lamented your unpreparedness for war. This is boot camp. The really good news is that while you are being trained, you are already fighting the war and having great success. Every sacrifice saves a soul. Every effort, every pain is acceptable. You are buying the freedom of the slaves all the while you are learning and becoming strong. I am building a great army – and you have a place in it already. You are where I want you to be.

Thank You, Lord. Now I do feel Your hug. It is so good to be in Your service.

*****

Lord, I have offered You all my pain, and You are drawing me closer to You through it. I confessed the pride and self-seeking I see in my reactions. You assured me of cleansing. Thank You for Your great mercy. Help me to cooperate with your grace and Your continually drawing me nearer to You. Let me rely on Your strength and direction. Give me clear discernment as to what I must do and what I should not do. Cause me to pray more. Let me return to daily Mass, daily Rosary, daily contemplative prayer, and daily offering my pain and sacrifices. Keep me in moderation in all things except love. Let my love for You grow by leaps and bounds. Let my awareness of Your love grow exceedingly.

Right now, I willingly take this cross at Your hand, for I see it as a gift with the Giver attached. You comfort me and it feels sooo good. Thank You for Your comfort and compassion. Thank You for the grace of being able to feel it. If You should take away the feelings, please remind me that it is there whether I feel it or not. I trust You to bring me through all this for Your greater glory.

Maggie, I would speak to you now. Listen carefully. I see your surrender and willingness to follow Me regardless of where I will lead you. Your prayers are good. Your offering is good and acceptable. I see some fear, yet I also see willingness to trust. I will remove the imperfections. I am in charge now. As you are seeing some progress in one area of your life, so will you see the other flaws in your character go. Your only job now is to stay close to Me. This is passion - passive. You asked for total union with Me. You were serious. This is the Way - walk in it. At one time you were overwhelmed by having to make too many decisions. Now there are few decisions to be made. Only stay close to Me. I will lead. I will light up every step. Do not worry about the emotions as they come and go. Now is the time to let faith lead the way. Fear, frustration, pride, pain, restlessness, fatigue will come and go, but I will stay by your side and continually love and uphold you. I will wash your wounds, caress your aching body, kiss away your tears, lift you up and build you up and present you to My Father as my beautiful, worthy bride. This is My promise to you. Do not even try to gauge how you are doing. Only look to Me and be encouraged and radiant. In time, even you will see the transformation. Others may see it sooner. You will be busy enough going through it. I do not promise a short time or a long time. But I will complete the work I am beginning. Your transformation is not a trivial matter to Me. I have prepared you a long time for it. You thought it would never happen. It is happening. Rejoice and be glad and fear not.

Wow! There is nothing I can say to thank You enough. I accept, of course - with great gratitude. I await Your direction. Let me spend a few more minutes in Your Presence.

*****

Most of all, thank You that You are in control and that even in all this pain, it is Your great love that is coming through. Help me learn the lessons You are teaching me quickly. Thank You for assuring me that it will all turn out well. Thank You for the faith and trust You are developing within me.

Maggie, I am with you. Yes, many things are going wrong. You are going through a difficult time. But even a dishwasher malfunctioning is bringing you closer to Me. The longing you have in your heart for your sons to be there and care for and about you is the same longing I have for My family. You are My family. The possibility that your sons do not consider you as important as their pleasure or friends is very painful. Yet that is the way My people treat Me.

Lord, I too have treated You this way, through prayerlessness and being distracted by so many things. I am so sorry. Please show me how to always put You first.

I am not telling you this to condemn you. I do forgive, just as you must also forgive. But in intimacy, the pain is shared as well as the joy. In your desire for union with Me, there is great joy. I will teach you and am now teaching you how to put Me first. I am pleased that you are not usually giving in to fear. Your trust is growing. It is not just words. There is virtue coming through. Even when your mind does not work because of the medication, you can rest in Me and know that I am holding you. This is a gift from Me. I am the One in charge. I do not require anything of you except what you are doing – relying on Me.

*****

Lord Jesus, last night I was feeling depressed. I was tired of the pain, tired of being confined to the house, tired of being tired. I wanted someone to pray with me just for a little while. I called a couple of people and it did not happen. In fact, I got yelled at instead by someone. This morning the pains seemed worse. There were cramps in my legs during the night and my arms and hips are more tender today.

But this morning's Mass readings were incredible. The psalm readings were from Psalm 103. Forget not all Your benefits. You heal all my diseases, forgive all my iniquities, and remove my transgressions. Thank You. Then the Epistle told me not to grumble. I repent. Then the Gospel reading about the fig tree that produces no fruit told me that You give me another chance. My illness is the manure that will help me produce good fruit. Yes, I am listening. And You are teaching and speaking to me in many ways.

At the retreat house:

I need deeper faith and trust in You and Your power to heal my body. I seem to trust You when the pain is not too severe or constant, but I waiver when it is. I need You to show me any areas of unforgiveness in my life that might block the healing You intend to give me. I also need to be faithful to a regular time for prayer whether or not I feel good about it. Even with my life as it is now, I cannot seem to commit to a particular time, but perhaps I can be more attentive and obedient to Your call. So please call me to prayer daily, and give me the grace of obedience to come. And some of my devotional prayers, Lord, bring me back to them as well. These are my needs. I thank You for both Confession and the Eucharist which You allowed me to receive today. I also thank You for allowing me to come here and for the exquisite beauty of this place at this time. I also thank You for reminding me through the books I am reading how present You are in the Eucharist. Let me now adore You and listen to You.

Lord, I'm in the car with the windows open by these beautiful cherry trees. I wanted to walk down to the statue of Your Mother, but my right ankle is not cooperating so this will have to do. I was told I should make this afternoon count and to do some of my praying outdoors. I have one hour left and I am sort-of outdoors. I tried to listen to You in the chapel, but I kept dozing off. I hope to do better here.

Maggie, I love you. I love it when you come here to seek Me.

And I always find You here. Can You increase my faith enough to find You at home, too?

I can and I will.

And the other things I asked for? The wisdom and clarity?

I will provide. The decisions do not need to be made now. When the time comes, you will know what I want.

Thank You. And my trust?

It is an ongoing growth. Do not worry. If you did not feel the need for more, then you would not grow. The very desire for more shows growth. Be patient – you are on the right track.

And the intensity of my likes and dislikes? Do I still have unforgiveness, bitterness, or resentment within me? At the healing Mass I attended at the end of March, I got a copy of a Forgiveness Prayer, ("Forgiveness and Inner Healing" by Betty Tapscott and Fr. Robert DeGrandis, SSJ) and I wonder if I should use it regularly.

Remember the Baobabs. [*This is a reference to Antoine de Sainte Exupery's The Little Prince*]. **The large trees and growths are indeed gone. Even most of the roots have been dug up. But vigilance is necessary. Every seedling must be removed immediately to keep the roots from re-infecting the soil. Go ahead and rewrite the Forgiveness Prayer to fit your life. I will bless it and use it. Skip the parts that don't apply. Add any you learn that may be needed. Begin your prayer time with it every day for a while. See what I will do.**

Lord, I'm willing, but I'm so afraid of failing again.

I know. But you have asked for the grace of obedience. I provide it, but you must accept and use it. Do not become legalistic. Do what you can, not what you can't. Pray as you can, not as you can't. I also want you to pray in the Spirit more. You want to build up your faith and trust. You have been frustrated that the doctors don't tell you what to do and what not to do. See Me as your Great Physician. If you do these things, I will tell you more and you will see that they help you. Try now: the Forgiveness Prayer here, and then in the Spirit on the way home.

I think I can do that.

I know you can. I empower you.

*****

Lord Jesus, You gave me so many graces yesterday, and I thank You for them all. Today I don't want to let any opportunities to slip away. I need to spend time with You before the day takes off. So here I am at Your service. I think I learned some things yesterday.

What did you learn?

I saw that the way I have usually served You for the past 25 years has been with my hands and feet. I have been a servant that does things or goes places. I run errands, transport people, make things, or carry things; and I thought it was good.

And it was good. You did many good things with your arms and legs and hands and feet.

But through this illness, I can no longer do those things. For a few moments I was going to blame Satan, but then I realized that You are really in control and it is You who chose to take away the use of my arms and legs. Not because You desired to deprive me of them or that You wanted me to have pain, but to teach me a higher way of relating to You. It is not what You want of me to remain a servant – a handmaid – a foot-soldier. You desire a friend, a bride. I was content to stay a servant because it gave me great pleasure to serve You. I could see the good I was doing. But now, You want to lead me to something much better. So yesterday all You asked of me was to pray in a different way than I was accustomed to. When I did, I felt no great joy or consolation. No great revelations or inspirations, but I had asked for the grace of obedience and I obeyed. It was not difficult and did not require great sacrifice, but it was good. For once, I did what You wanted, not what I wanted to do to perhaps please You. I became aware of how for the past 25 years I have been trying too hard to do things for You that You never wanted, but I neglected the things You really did want. Not always; occasionally through Your grace I did manage to obey, but most of the time I did things and then hoped that it was good enough to call it serving You.

Maggie, it is good. But do not be too hard on yourself. I am the one who gave you the nature that delights to serve others. I nurtured and directed it all your life. I gave you the delight in it. You will be able to use it again, but in balance. But you are right. I am calling you to a higher level of relationship. And the change is difficult and painful – literally. In My life there were times of serious change. Some involved great pain. The transition is very difficult. But you cannot progress without the change.

Now, I have given you a topic for meditation and contemplation. Look at the stages in My life and the transitions. They were not easy

for Me either. When I thought I was ready at 12, it was not yet right. When I was not really ready at Cana, My Mother pushed Me, and out of obedience, I moved into a whole new level. Then finally, when I knew the time had come, it was very difficult and painful to choose to do My Father's will. For the past 25 years, your service has been a training ground. When you thought you were ready, it was not yet time. Now you are being pushed through this illness, and through obedience you may find a much higher level of life and relationship with Me. I invite you. Yes, I have pushed you, but the choice is up to you. Will you obey, and serve Me by your prayers more than your actions for now? I am not saying that the actions are wrong or unnecessary, but for now, I am more interested in your prayer life and your knowledge of Me than in anything you may do with your hands. Will you come away with Me to get to know Me – not physically come away, but through prayer? Join Me in the times I call you. Today you realized I was calling you. Build on this victory. Continue to obey by praying the Forgiveness Prayer, praying in the Spirit, and praying other devotional prayers at night. This works so much better when you have been aware of Me throughout the day. That is why it has been so difficult in the past. It will be easier now.

Lord, You have given me so much this morning – I can hardly take it all in. Thank You.

You are welcome. I have desired to bless you abundantly, but I have to wait until you can receive. Enjoy this day. I will stay with you.

*****

Last night I was reminded how I often wished in my childhood that I had been adopted. In my immature way of thinking, that would have meant that someone actually wanted me. But I *am* adopted by my Father in Heaven. I *am* wanted. Thank You. I have the best of both worlds – my natural family, who loved me the best they knew how, and my adoptive family in Heaven, that loves me perfectly with everlasting love. And the Creator of all things is Your Father and my Father. What more could I want?

Father, You have given me so much and have been so good to me. Thank You. Help me to give all back to You – precious to You because

You love me so much that if I touched it, it means more to You. Also, let me look upon all Your gifts to me as precious because You have touched them.

Maggie, I your Father love you that way and many more wonderful ways. You are wanted, accepted, and cherished by your heavenly family. And that family grows as each mortal becomes immortal. As they are transformed from earthly life to heavenly life, their love becomes conformed to My love – perfect agape – and you are loved even more. Dwell on this. It heals all the rejection you formerly felt. This is the truth. It is light that dispels darkness. It is the perfect love that casts out all fear. This is the love you are invited to live in. Live on in My love.

*****

After listing all that was happening in my life one day:

Help me to have things in order here. So that is pretty much all in my life – how about Yours?

My life is good. I live in Heaven. I am with My Father. My friends from all the centuries are with Me and yet I can also be with My friends who are still on the earth – like you.

Lord, I cannot dwell on Your sufferings or sorrows or wounds or such things. But Your joys are wonderfully exciting to me.

I have not asked you to dwell on or contemplate those things. I do want you to see the good things in My life. People today need to see a God that does delight in them, and enjoys them. I am love. These are not just words, but few have considered how that love actually looks and is to be experienced. Yes, there is suffering. I have experienced plenty, but that is not where I stayed. The cross is a pathway to your salvation. It is not to be forgotten or devalued. But go beyond and see the glory of My Resurrection, My Ascension, and the descent of My Holy Spirit. This is what I call you to right now. Stay with the fruits of My Spirit – a good place for you right now. Just as you were when you had your first child about motherhood, so you are now about Christianity. You had heard of and knew about all the problems and

difficulties – waking in the middle of the night, dirty diapers, crying, sicknesses, and the like. But no one told you of the inexpressible joy of being able to calm a fussy baby by simply picking him up, or that first smile, or the giggles or warmth of nursing, or seeing the world through the eyes of a child. So now, you have heard and know of troubles, temptations, crosses, persecutions, and suffering – but there are many more good things you have overlooked. They have always been there, but are not often mentioned. No wonder so many leave. Be an apostle of joy. Explore and teach others about the "good stuff." See, change is not always difficult, but this is a radical change in your thinking. Learn it well, and then teach others – your teaching days are not over. But now your teaching will change. In the past you taught math and slipped in teachings of life and Christianity. Now it will have a new focus. I am not calling you to be a Pollyanna. I do not want a caricature. Learn balance – do not despise teachings on the cross and suffering, but do not stay there, either. You have said God is good – now show Me to an unbelieving world.

*****

Lord, this is what You have been telling me throughout my illness – no longer a servant, but a friend. "But a friend" because You have revealed to me all that the Father has told You. I need to pay attention to all You have told me about the Father. I have been more preoccupied with what *I* was saying, than with listening to You. Forgive me for that. Forgive my self-absorption. I want to be absorbed in You. When Rae and I were dating, and he used to drive me to and from work, the others at work kidded me that, every time they saw us in the car, my head was totally turned to Rae and I was absorbed in him. That is what I want to be seen in me with regard to You. Let me listen to You talk about Your Father so much that I can truly see Him in You. Then there is that whole "love one another" thing. Don't I already do that? One of my greatest fears in my Christian life has been to be in the position of the rich young man. Is there something You want of me that I am not willing to give? Search me and know my heart and see if there is any wicked way in me. I was glad to take Your encouragement, but now I am reluctant to let You speak and answer the question I just asked. How double-minded I am! I want to know what needs to be cleansed in me, but what I really want to hear is that I'm fine the way I am and nothing more needs to be done. I seriously doubt that. So, let me grit my teeth and listen to Your answer.

Maggie, are you afraid that My love for you is diminished by your imperfections? Are you still trying to let Me see only your good side? Do you forget Who I am? That I see the whole truth of your being – good and bad, imperfect as you are, and still love you? But I am also merciful. You are going through many changes now and they are for good. Keep at them. The rest will wait. I will tell you only what you need to know. I know how easily you get discouraged. But remember that even in reproof there is no condemnation from Me. You need not be afraid. I will empower you to do whatever I ask of you. Keep listening to My voice. I will continue to guide you gently.

*****

Lord, once again You tell us to ask the Father for anything in Your Name, that our joy may be full. My arrogance of a few days ago has quieted down. I am beginning to see that healing physical problems is not necessary to make our joy full. Yet You did heal people. So, it is OK to ask for healing, as long as we are prepared to receive the answer to our prayers in other forms than the physical healing that we seek. You see a much bigger picture. My own illness is curing several more-important problems in my life. Would I like to be free of pain and disability? Yes, most definitely! But I will gladly keep them if they bring me into union with You. I will continue to look for You in all things, and I will try to seek You and Your will before I jump. But I also know I will fail, so I ask for Your forgiveness.

*****

What is it about God the Father that we didn't know before You, Jesus? His Fatherhood, His love, His tenderness, His gentleness, faithfulness, patience, care, provision, forgiveness, healing – a whole lot. All these qualities had always been there, but our eyes were not open to them until You, Jesus, showed them through becoming flesh. You did what You saw the Father doing and You did a lot. Lord, this brings me back to the why – why I do things and why You did things. I know my reasons need to change. I need to act instead of react. You acted. You did things with a basic purpose of showing us the goodness of Your Father. Please put that motive within me so that when I do something good, it is the goodness of my Father that shows. I'm still not sure I understand glory, but grace and truth are easier to see.

Maggie, grace and truth are sufficient for now. It is good that you begin to see My Father's work. You will yet see glory as well. Stay alert.

*****

You have given me so many gifts, yet You have clipped my wings and are not permitting me to use them right now. What is it You are trying to teach me? What am I missing?

The relationship. It cannot be rushed. It is said that I comfort the afflicted and afflict the comfortable. I am doing both to you. You are more comfortable doing than being – but doing only what *you* want to do. For a while I am not letting you do much of anything. I want you to learn to wait on Me. If a soldier fires a shot before his commander gives the signal, he puts his entire group in jeopardy. I am your commander. You must wait for My signal. But you must know the signal and be alert to it. Right now, you do not know My signals.

So how can I learn them?

By finding Me first in each situation, and watching Me to see what I am doing.

But I have such a hard time finding You in any situation – in fact, there are so few situations in my life now that – well, it seems like there is nothing happening in my life right now.

Your discontent is blinding you to all that is going on within and around you.

So, I am back to contentment?

Yes, but much more than that. You really have to find Me in all situations – and now you even have to identify the situations. So

today, concentrate on defining the situations you find in your life as it is now, and where I am in them.

*****

After a long soliloquy:

So, Lord, I've gone on and on without giving You a chance to speak.

That's OK. At least you were not upset over having nothing to say.

Funny how the least little thing can be upsetting. How do You stand us?

Love makes many things possible.

Oh yes, You told me that love needs no explanations or reasons. While I could not think to write anything, You made me aware of my two cats and how they would not be anything really special compared with all the cats in the world. But they are mine, and I enjoy them and care for them and love them simply because they are mine. I am Yours. And it seems You enjoy my company and care for me and love me even though I am not really special compared with all the people in the world. But love needs no reasons or explanations. When love is there, however, some lovely attributes can be discovered – like I really like the friendliness, softness, and affection of my cats. I would love them even without these attributes, but they make my love for them *seem* more reasonable. But my commitment to care for them came before I discovered these attributes.

Perhaps this is why commitment is more important in relationships than feelings of love. Once the commitment is made, the feelings and reasonableness can naturally emerge. Perhaps this is why we say that true love is an act of the will. I choose to act loving and I thus become loving. The feelings help, but do not need to control the situation. How is it that I'm almost 55 years old and just discovering this?

You really are a slow learner?

You got me there.

No, that's not it. But few people really take the time to contemplate love. They leave such thoughts to poets and mystics. It is also why

they make so many mistakes in their relationships. There are so many people suffering today because of misconceptions about love and because they mistake feelings for reality. Even such a basic feeling as hunger can be false – you checked your blood sugar and found you did not need to eat right now. The feeling of hunger is not the only measure or even the most reliable one.

Lord, our civilization is so screwed up. We have lost sight of these truths.

I know. But I can reveal these truths to anyone who will take the time to listen. Their hearts cry out for truth but they have so many distractions. I had to take away almost everything from you before you were able to listen. It isn't even a matter of time. It isn't that there isn't enough time, it's that too many unhelpful things rush in to take up time. This is why discernment – of what is helpful and what is not – is so important. Use what is helpful – get rid of what is not.

St. Ignatius really had something there.

Where do you think he got it?

From being sick and spending time with You.

I had to debilitate him, too. You are in good company.

Thank You. I hadn't thought of it that way. Lord, daylight is now coming. Thank You for a marvelous time.

One more thing – this commitment theory works in prayer, too. First you committed yourself to spending an hour a day in prayer. At times it seems like an hour is impossible and what seems really long has only been five minutes. At other times, like now, an hour and a half has passed and it was no problem at all. But without the commitment, the difficult times would discourage you from even trying again and thus the better times would never have a chance to happen. So, keep to your commitments. They produce the possibilities for much good. But discernment before making commitments is very important.

Thank You, Lord.

*****

Lord Jesus, today I am to consider Your love within the Trinity. That never struck me before as any of my business. Yet therein is how You reveal the perfection of Your love. The love within the Trinity is the perfect model of love that we humans might work toward even though never attain. I don't think I have ever considered Your Trinitarian love as something beautiful and perfect and wonderful in itself. It's sort-of like a sunset or sunrise – beautiful, magnificent, glorious, uplifting – yet having nothing to do with me but at the same time doing wonders within me in the enjoyment and wonder and awe it inspires. I have often heard it said, and believe it completely, that one of the best way parents can love their children is by loving each other and letting their children live in the security of that love. Our world is very aware of the untold misery when that love is missing.

"You shall love the Lord Your God with all your heart, soul, mind, and strength" is not just a commandment that you thought you could never fulfill – it is also My promise to you that you *can*. You SHALL love. I know you desire to love Me totally – My commandment is also My promise to you that I will truly make it possible. Look again at My commandments as promises that I will empower you to live by them. This is My great love for you. I do not ever ask the impossible of you. With each command I give the grace and promise that this shall be possible in your life. Look again at the virtue you seem to lack and look to Me and My promise that holiness IS My desire for you and I will provide all you need to grow in holiness and every virtue.

*****

Lord Jesus, today's readings helped. I read that Dorothy Day said that we must learn the rules of love. Then St. John of the Cross is quoted as saying that loving is wanting the good of another or for another. Lord, it never occurred to me to desire *Your* good. It never seemed possible that I could, by desiring, or even doing, anything, have any effect on what is or is not good for You. You have me in a strange but perfect place to see this. As I have been watching little children these days, I see their almost total self-absorption: "I want," "It's mine!" Civilizing the strong self-will is what takes up the time and energy of parents. At the other end is caring for the needs and wants of the aged, not so strongly expressed by Mom E., though there are some who are much more demanding. I need to love both the young and the old by wanting and doing what is for their good. That seems simple enough though it may take all the time and energy I have. But the concept of loving You seems so different. Lord, what good could I possibly wish for You? What good could I do for You?

You told the rich young man to keep the commandments. He replied that he had done this since his childhood. You told him that he lacked one thing, the same one thing that Mary chose and Martha didn't: The love that can get one to sell all one has and give to the poor; the love that sits at Your feet and listens to You; the love like Your Mother's that accepts God's will, painful or sweet, understanding that Your will is nothing more than Your love. That You are not a slave driver of Egypt, that You also want our good, that even difficulties are meant to produce good in our lives, that You and I do not oppose one another but work together, that Your commandments are also promises of possibility and help to achieve them. Yet in all this, what possible good can I be to You, do to You, or even wish for You? The question, "What do You want of me?" takes on a different, more gentle and loving tone. I have asked it in the past in a frustrated, exasperated way, as if You would want the impossible. I have also asked it in an exhausted, complaining way when others had already drained all my energy and resources and You seemed to be at the end of the line of those taking all I had to give. But now, it is more of a combination of, "Speak Lord, Your servant is listening," and, "Here I am, send me or use me – ready to do Your will." You have rested me, strengthened me, and made me ready. Perhaps I am not yet completely ready – You know that better than I. You are preparing me for good works; I'm just not sure what they are. It seems it is better that I don't know – I don't have as much chance to mess it up. So, I am back to, "Not my will but Thine be done." To be equally content to be on the shelf as to be used.

*****

John 15:12-17

"This is My commandment, that you love one another as I have loved you." The grace I ask is to love as You love – totally, completely, without measure – laying down my life, my will, my strong feelings.

Lord, how can I love as You love? You are infinite, I am finite. You are God and I am not. You see all and know all – I hardly see at all and I know so little. You are great and I'm so puny. Yet You command me to love as You love, and You never ask of us what is impossible, so the only way I can love as You love is to invite You in – to love through me. I cannot do it, but You, in me, can. So come, Lord Jesus, love through me and let me be so filled with Your love that I disappear entirely and only You can be seen – loving totally, completely, without measure, and thus I become Your friend, for I will have kept Your commandment.

Lord Jesus, I may not understand, comprehend, or even visualize what it means to have You in me, but I see that that this is the only way I can possibly love at all. So, I choose without understanding to believe that You are there already – in me, and I am in You. And I thank You for this gift of faith.

*****

One of the things I'm repenting of is not listening to You anymore – so now I would like to give You a chance to speak.

And what if I don't want to speak?

Then I'll go back to bed.

Not so fast.

Lord, I don't think You have ever refused to speak to me.

Nor would I now.

Thank You.

Let Me start by affirming My love for you. Neither your discontent, nor your resentments, nor your willfulness diminish My love. They simply amplify your need of My love.

I can see that.

Let My love cleanse you.

Lord, You are so amazing! I come to You deserving Your wrath, and find instead Your loving arms eager to embrace me.

This is your God of love.

Thank You. I don't deserve it, but I do accept it.

Good – accepting My love is the first step. Accepting My will – realizing that it is motivated by My love for you – is next.

Lord, I do accept it now, but how do I keep accepting it, and not let the resentments back in?

Ask, keep on asking, and receive the grace I so freely give. Seek Me, keep on seeking Me, and find My love that is calling to you from everywhere, "Here I am." Knock and keep on knocking until you find the door is open and you cannot or need not knock any longer, and then enter into My embrace. See Me waiting for you, ready to shower you with My love and grace and help.

But Lord, it is so one-sided. How can I love You back?

The same way – seek for ways; I will provide them. Ask Me, I will answer. Knock and enter. Your receiving and gratitude are great evidence of your love for Me. Your surrender to My will – your obedience – even your desire are acceptable gifts of love. And then the love you show to others – that also is a two-way gift of love – to them and to Me.

So, I don't need to look for great sacrifices to perform to prove my love for You?

Not at all; that only fuels your discontent. I have given you all you need. Now just enjoy My love and let Me enjoy yours.

I can do that. Thank You so much.

*****

Lord Jesus, thank You for a new beginning in my prayer life. This is now the third day I am coming to You as You asked – to receive Your love and grace, and I have the desire to give You my love as well. It seems I had it backwards – I thought I needed to give You (offer You) everything I could, and then You would bless me. Now I see that Your blessings come long before, and regardless of what I could or would give You. But the gratitude You have put into me requires that I should give back to You for the marvelous graces You have already given me. So here I am, Lord, ready to receive again.

*****

Lord Jesus, once again You have surprised me. This morning the response to the intercessions is, "Come and reward Your people's hope." There is a reward for hope? As I thought about it, the second question answered the first: "Why shouldn't there be? Isn't the fulfillment of hope like a reward?"

Lord, Your goodness and kindness and tender love still continue to amaze me. Little by little I am beginning to see not just Your greatness but also how Your character has all the qualities I long for and value. The beauty of Your gentleness, Your tender loving care, Your inexhaustible giving both of Yourself and Your gifts of provision, Your unlimited patience, Your constant availability, Your delight in dealing with me, Your humility, Your attention to the smallest, most insignificant aspects of my life while also taking charge of the big issues. Lord, all these years I worried that I didn't love You, yet You *are* everything I really love and care about. How is it that only now can I see this?

*****

While recuperating from ankle surgery:

Loving You or being aware of Your love, that seems difficult again. Help, Lord, I need You.

Maggie, I am here. And I am delighted to see your continued attempts. Trust Me that nothing is wasted. You cannot see growth, but it is ongoing. You have not given up and you even encourage others to keep going. I am not complaining. I will help you. Be patient. I am. Just as you do not know how well or badly your ankle is healing, you cannot know how your love is growing. But you do

know what to do and you are doing it. Come to Me – keep coming to Me whether it is easy or difficult. It will bear fruit. Your priorities are mostly in order. Your desire to love Me more is very pleasing to My Father. Neither death to self nor growth in virtue are easy. Both entail a struggle. You are now aware of both the need and the opportunities I provide in the death to self. But you have not seen the flip side in that each death to self is also a growth in virtue. Try to identify the virtues more than concentrating on the deaths. It will not eliminate the struggle, but it will put a more positive spin on it. This is necessary for growth. Several of your muscles ache now from having to use the scooter instead of walking. Yet you also see that some muscles are getting stronger. Progress, however painful, is being made. I see and am with you through each pain and struggle. On a brighter note, you are enjoying learning more about Me. That is very good. I am not teaching you in the same ways as in the past, but I am teaching you and I am delighted that you still have a teachable heart. Delight in the truth you are learning, and come to Me – the Truth – to discuss it. I will be here waiting.**

Lord, I have needed to hear Your voice, but I was afraid that You had stopped talking to me.

No, child, I am still talking, just in different ways. You may think you are not responding, but you are – and very often responding very well. Do not be discouraged. All is going well.

*****

Lord, You value my companionship much more than I do.

This is true. I see you from the inside as well as the outside. Neither you nor any other person has such a perspective. I also see in a timeless fashion. Who you were, who you are, who you will yet be are all in My view? Even those who know you best cannot see all that.

Lord, that is awesome. Thank You.

You see, being known feels like being loved. Just the thought of My knowing you that well has already lifted your drooping spirit.

You see me inside and out, past, present, and future, and it's OK?

Better than OK. Lovable, desirable, yes, precious in My sight. So much so that I will keep others away from you so I can have you all to Myself.

I'm afraid I have not responded well to that.

Sometimes you have, and now that you see it, you can respond better. My love for you is a fact. It cannot be lost, diminished, or forgotten.

*****

Lord Jesus, thank You ever so much for yesterday. You answered my prayer through a talk at the Eucharistic Congress. It was a few words that really struck me, though the speaker's entire message was wonderful. He said that You did not want to leave us and You don't want us to leave You. You stayed with us with Your gift of the Eucharist. That touched my heart and brought me to tears, it still does. That Your love and care for me is so tender that You *want* to be with me – not just tolerate me, or have to put up with me, or that I need You so much, or it is Your job or duty to stay with me and help me. Lord, I need You to carve that into my being – it raises me to a new dignity. It makes it possible for me to love You in a much better way.

In the talk by another priest, Lord, I also heard that once You come into that bread and transform it, You do not leave. It does not revert back to simple bread again after Mass. I knew that, but did not realize its significance. It's a part of Your *wanting* to stay with us, no matter what we do. Lord, help me to stay with You more now. You have always been here, but I leave so easily. Draw me more and more into this marvelous love You have for me, and let me respond with similar love and desire to stay with You. Never let me come because I must or should, but only because I want to.

Lord, I see another aspect right now – You are opening my understanding. I see two different levels of desire – the wanting *to do* something and wishing I *could do* something. They are both desires, but wanting is immediate and seems stronger and positive while wishing is more distant and involves the possibility that it may never happen. I think my desires to love You was like the wishing desire until now.

Suddenly, with just a few words that touched my heart, the desire became a *want* within me, and with it came the ability to *do* it.

*****

Maggie, do you love Me?

Yes, Lord, I love You.

No, I'm not going to ask you three times. But I want you to be sure before you go home. You are espoused to Me by your consecration. You have given Me your life – and I have accepted and received you. You are indeed Mine. And I am indeed yours. My love for you is more than you can comprehend, but you need to continually contemplate it. My love will make your love grow.

Lord, I want my love for You to grow.

Keep coming and it will.

Wow, Lord, You really are expanding me. Thank You.

Hang on, it's going to be a wild ride.

Lord, my prayer that is in my notebooks is still my prayer. I ask that You do all those things not just for me, but all those I pray for. Let Your will be done. Just hold me real close.

Don't worry.

Lord, I desire to be so much a part of You that I could not be scraped off of You.

Union?

Yes, total union.

Nothing is impossible.

*****

Maggie, come focus on love.

Lord, You need to help me.

OK, try the Night prayer.

It says, "It is the Lord who grants favors to those whom He loves." Lord, You have granted me favors – many favors this week. Now I see that You do this because You love me. Thanksgiving suddenly becomes different. My thanks are now connected to a deep realization that whatever I am thanking You for, You did it because You love me. It is no longer a polite little "thank You" but a deep gratitude for Your love and care and attentiveness to me personally.

You see, My love for you *is* personal.

As is Your teaching of me. Thank You ever so much.

*****

Lord, I thank You for meeting me here every morning. And for caring about my little struggles. You, the God of the universe, spending time with such little things.

So now you are a little thing? What happened to "precious in My eyes and I love you?"

I guess I am precious – You are awesome!

Maggie, don't be afraid of My love. Don't belittle it. Don't think it will pass away. It grows – as you are learning more of My love for you, you are learning of Me. I reveal Myself to you through My love. St. John wrote, "God is love." You don't quite know how to receive this love yet. But joy is one way. Rejoice in My love. It has nothing to do with your worthiness. I simply love you. All I ask in return is that you enjoy it and pass it on to others. You are doing that. It is good.

Thank You, Lord. I do rejoice. It is an awesome thing to be loved by You. Please work that into my innermost being while You hold me the rest of this night.

I will be right with you. I am working in, holding on, and loving you. Go ahead and sleep a bit now.

*****

Lord, You showed me that not only do You want me to focus on Your love, You gave me a quick demonstration of it. Just as I stopped what I was doing to help Mom, and spent that little time (12 minutes) with her so she did not have to eat alone, so in the Incarnation, You also stopped whatever You did as a member of the Trinity and came to be with us – and stay with us by means of the Eucharist and Your indwelling Holy Spirit so that we do not have to be alone. And every time we pray, You are not too busy, but stop and listen and spend time with us. Lord, thank You for the joy of spending these times with my mother, and thank You for all these times You spend with me.

Maggie, My love for you makes Me delighted to be with you just as your love for your mother makes you delighted to be with her. I came to make the Father known – the love within the Trinity is what I want you, and everyone, to experience. That takes eternity but it begins here in time. Now you get glimpses. Heaven is unending love.

Lord, I sense the strength and urgency of Your desire that we should know this great love of Yours. It cannot be put into words.

But it can be felt. So come, feel My love, feel the Spirit's love, feel the Father's love.

*****

Lord, it is raining pretty hard right now. We really need the rain, but I am looking more at how we will transport Mom. You know my needs – I trust in You.

Maggie, just as the rain washes the earth and the air, so I wash you. My love not only comforts you it also cleanses you. It was out of love that I became Man. It was out of love that I redeemed mankind from sin. It is out of love that I remain with you and come to you in many ways. You can find Me in the Eucharist, in My Word, in prayer, in others. Sometimes you find Me in beauty or truth. Right now, find Me in the rain as well as here in prayer.

Lord, I am so grateful that I can find You. Thank You that You come to Me daily. And, yes, thank You for the rain and for washing me clean.

*****

Maggie, my love for you is as great as my love for each of those you think are holier than you. You need to bathe in that love. It is not reserved only for great saints. It is available to all – to you. Do not think you are only worthwhile because of your service to Me and to others. I know you enjoy being of service, but I see much more than just your service. I see true love – a desire to please. And this is very pleasing to the Trinity. And even if you could not serve, or if you could do nothing to please anyone, My love would still be as great for you.

Lord, the more I learn about Your love, the more I realize that I know so little. But I guess that is the same about knowing You. The more we know, the more we see that we hardly know anything at all. So please keep teaching me.

Maggie, I am teaching you. And the more you learn, the less you concentrate on yourself. As I increase, you – like John the Baptist – will decrease. Mathematically, it is like inverse variation.

Lord, thank You for bringing the smile back to my face. Thank You also for the philosophy of mathematics.

Now that we have even brought your profession into prayer, go back to sleep in your Father's arms.

*****

Maggie, Fr. Sanders said something last night that you tried to brush off.

Yes, Lord, he told me what a great labor of love it is that I care for Mom. Lord, I feel like the unprofitable servant – I do no more than I am required to do.

But yet your God appreciates it.

Thank You, Lord. He also said that I'm trying too hard with contemplative prayer, that I need to let You lead.

Maggie, I have been leading you, and I will continue to do so. As he said, do not judge the progress. Join Me in patience.

Lord, that sounds funny, but I do understand. Thank You for Your patience and that You think I can join You in it.

This is why I send you back to bed early at times. I see that you are trying too hard and need to rest. I am with you whether you are awake or asleep. I want you to feel My love throughout the day and night. Even your sleeping is a part of your relationship with Me, as long as I direct you to sleep. You have been grateful for the sleep you get – this is also pleasing to the Father. Sleep is a gift, though like all gifts it can be misused. I do give you rest. You do not have to be exhausted. I know your needs.

Lord, thank You that Mom respects my time of prayer during the night. She just came to get more water, but went back to bed without a word. Thank You for what You are saying and doing about rest and meeting my needs. I see that You do indeed meet all my needs.

And you know how it gives you joy when you know you are meeting someone's needs – you get that from Me. I get great joy from meeting your needs. Do you see that it is a part of your inheritance as a child of God? To be in the image and likeness of God means you inherit certain traits. Begin to see and cherish these – let My joy be full as I meet your needs and let your joy be full as you meet your mother's needs and the needs of others. Now go and rest in My love and My Father's arms.

*****

Lord, last night I think I received a little revelation about the love and the joy of the Trinity. I was going to share it at the prayer meeting, but since there was none, I am writing it down as I may forget it all by next week. I was impressed by what You have been telling me, that I can and do bring joy to Your heart. I began to ponder how my puny little actions can add to the perfect love and joy within the Trinity. How can I really affect that? So I was shown a circle of flame. The circle was perfect, the fire was totally fire, heat was produced by it, light was produced by it – it was complete in itself. But even a little fuel added to it would increase its intensity. The flame would get hotter and brighter. What was full and perfect to start with could still increase in intensity. Thank You for that revelation. Thank You also for a new insight into Psalm 1, it was about meditating on Your law day and night. I saw that it is exactly what You are teaching me to do when You have me focus on Your love. After all, Your law is the law of love. Your two great commandments sum up the whole law – love God, love neighbor. And Your new commandment – love one another as You have loved us – so as You have me learn about and ponder Your great love, and send me back to bed to soak in the Father's love, You are teaching me to meditate on Your law day and night. Thank You so much, Lord.

*****

I have questions about what I have heard: that the world, good as it is, cannot satisfy – only You can. I have come to believe this is right – I cannot be satisfied by all the stuff the world offers, but how do I get to the place where You satisfy? How do I get to where You are my all-in-all? I've been at this quest for 35 years, and I seem to be terribly far away from that.

Getting impatient again?

Yes, and also doing what You repeatedly told me not to do – evaluating my progress, or lack of it.

No bells or whistles? No floating through the air? No voices or fancy visions? Yet you come to Me daily and receive Me whenever you can – and you know that I receive you as well. You know I provide for all your needs – you thank Me daily. You are growing in your trust of Me. You come to Me so much quicker when you fail, you know My forgiveness, you are at peace. You have a vibrant relationship with your God. You are not yet perfect. I am not disappointed.

Lord, I do thank You for all of these things. So many people would give all they have for what I already possess. Actually, I tried to give You all I had, but here I am with so much more.

Maggie, I accepted your gift of yourself each time you approached Me. But when you give something to Me, you are not necessarily deprived of what you give. Many things I return to you, but it is not because I did not accept or appreciate them, but because I have a use for them that involves your participation. Your willingness to serve Me is a great gift. You have and continue to serve Me in many

ways. But I, too, am a servant and I choose to serve you at times. I also delight in serving. We are similar in this. See, you are made in the image and likeness of God.

Lord, once again, thank You! It is hard for me to realize that not being a nun is still serving You. I know it on one hand, yet the desire is still there.

Be patient, child. Desires can be fulfilled in many ways. I do not disappoint you. And I am not disappointed in you. Remember that.

*****

Lord Jesus, I blew it again in so many ways. I seem to do OK in the morning, but in the afternoon all my self-control seems to disappear. So now I feel terrible both spiritually and physically, and I don't know what to say to You.

Maggie, I know what to say to you. Are you listening?

I'm trying to.

OK, here goes: I love you. Did you hear that?

Yes, Lord, and I am grateful.

Listen again – I love you. Got it?

I think so.

OK. One more time – I love you. Remember that time at the river?

Yes, Lord, every wave gave me the message that You love me.

And your response?

I love You, too, Lord. Though I don't show it well.

So how can you show it better? Not how you *think* you should show it better, but how *can* you – what can you do now to show you love Me?

I don't know, Lord. I'm open to suggestions. It's the middle of the night. What would You like me to do?

Well, imagine Me coming into the room.

I would be embarrassed. The room is a mess.

Wrong answer. Try again – I don't notice the mess.

Lord, Your disciples had that happen, and they did it wrong, too.

So, you are in good company. Try again.

Well, I would like to welcome You with great joy that You would come to Me.

Would you smile? You know your smile pleases Me.

Sure, Lord, I would be glad to do anything that pleases You.

Would you do that now – even if you don't see Me coming to your room?

OK Lord, I'm smiling.

You see, it is not so hard. Before, you could believe that I love you, but until you respond, you cannot feel it. You focus so much on your own failures that you cannot get past them until you can feel My love. Your own failures are just as much problems in your life as sickness, or poverty, or relationships could be. You need to get past them and focus on Me, not the problems or failures. You cannot overcome or solve problems by being consumed by them. You have to be able to look past them and see and respond to My love instead.

So, I need to smile at You?

It is a start. You have to know I am with you. That I care about you. That I know your struggles. That you desire to please Me. That you *can* please me. Even if you have just failed, I am not hard to please. Run to My arms, not away from Me – dreading to face Me. I promise I will not turn you away.

Lord, thank You.

*****

Maggie, it does take time and practice. Even when you *feel* nothing, by faith you must know that I am with you, loving you, caring for you, cherishing you. I will not leave you. In fact, when you desire My Presence but do not feel it, I am even closer. You are my beloved. You will find Me in various ways. In faith, in nature,

in kindness, in My Word, in each sacrament, in little things, in big things – never give up seeking Me. You will find Me more and more.

*****

Maggie, My love for you will keep you going. The sweetness of My love is greater than anything you may desire. Exchange your desires for My love. This is a marvelous time of year to see the evidences of My love in nature. The singing of the birds, the frolicking of the squirrels, the trees in bloom, the flowers growing everywhere, the sunshine, the gentle breezes – even the rain. Take moments to enjoy these. See My hand in all of them extending My love for you. And the kindness of others also comes from Me, and the kindness you show others originates in Me. I am everywhere around you – loving you, caring for you, protecting you, and guiding you.

*****

Maggie, I love you. You need to burrow into My love – lose yourself in it, surround yourself with it. Feel it, drink it, eat it, breathe it. Come unto Me – into Me – seek Me, find Me, ask Me, receive Me, knock and let Me answer and invite you in – and come.

Here I am, Lord. I have no other words except thank You.

*****

Lord Jesus, thank You for the Mass and the Bible study. I feel like a soldier who has not yet been assigned but knows he is going into war – still waiting for where and when and what his duties will be. I'm trying to prepare as best I can, but feel like I need a drill sergeant. I am ready and willing to do what is necessary – but wanting to rush those orders.

Maggie, remember how I said I have come to set a fire on the earth and how I wished it was already blazing? This is how *you* feel. Yet you are right. You still need more training. You are not yet out of boot camp. You are correct that you need a drill sergeant. But what I have provided you with until now are gentle and kind teachers. Until

you are firmly grounded in love, you cannot endure the toughening you desire. Remember when I thought I was ready for My mission at age 12? I needed more grounding in the love of family. Then at Cana, I did not think I was ready, but that *was* the time. Let Me decide when you are ready. I promised long ago that I would teach you. I have already taught you much. But I am in charge of the curriculum as well as the instruction, and I will give you your orders again as I have in the past. I have given you great missions in the past and you fulfilled them well. Even now you are serving in several capacities. But there are other missions for which you need special training. I can and will handle it all.

*****

Maggie, today I speak. Despite all the serious things happening – funeral, world events, changes – you must remember My love for you. You came here because you felt My call. You came to chapel early to spend private time with Me. You came with your breviary to help a friend. I notice and appreciate your love. But you must again work on joy. Yes, everyone is aware of your smile – but joy needs to be deeper. And it comes from knowing how much you are loved. Not just that all your physical or even emotional needs are met, but that you are valued and worthwhile – yes, even though you are nothing. The contrast is great. True humility recognizes both the worth which is eternal and the worthlessness which is obvious. You cannot help but smile at this. This is how I work. The whole universe is My creation, yet even the sub-atomic particles are important to Me. There is no comparing. Nothing is too great or too small. But My love is always perfect and beyond measure. And My love is for you. You need not understand or comprehend it – but you need to know it, feel it, accept it, and respond to it. There is no right or perfect way to respond. Your response – feeble, halting, and imperfect though it may be – is what I desire. You have given Me your life. I have accepted it. You are Mine. I cherish that. But I also am yours. No – not to use as if you had great powers beyond others, but to relate to. Enjoy and cherish My companionship as well as the companionship of those I put in your life. Fear *not*. I have not been displeased with you. I appreciate your continual attempts to grow closer to Me. They are not

failed attempts. But You need to believe that you have come closer and are in union with Me. Are you completely there yet? Of course not. But be happy with the progress rather than lamenting how far you still need to go. It is all a matter of perspective. Be delighted. Let's be delighted together. My love for you – you personally – is to be your focus today. And the joy will be unspeakable.

*****

The Gospel (Mt 22:35-40) is about the greatest commandment. Loving You is much more difficult for me than loving my neighbor. It is Your invisibility that has always been a problem for me. But You do not command the impossible, so You have helped me in many ways. What I really appreciate is that You accept as love my desire to love You more. And I still want and need to grow in my knowledge of You. How is it that after so many years of trying to follow You, I feel like I hardly know You? Lord, I need You to reveal Yourself to me more, and teach me Your ways.

Maggie, I reveal and teach you much more than you realize. My help in your life reveals My love for you daily. My love is Who I am. The more you know, receive, accept, and appreciate My love, the more you know, love, and serve Me. This is why I so often want you to contemplate My love. John said it well: "God is love." As you comprehend My love more, neither loving Me nor loving your neighbor is difficult.

*****

Lord, I love being under Your authority. Yes, You have authority over unclean spirits, and the wind and the waves obey You, but You also have marvelous authority over Your servants. I am Your servant, and I want to be a better servant, Lord.

Maggie, I accept your service, but I don't want just your service. I no longer call you "servant," but friend. I have given you great friendships. They are to lead you into a deeper friendship with Me. Yes, I have authority over you, but I prefer the love of friends to the

command of a Master to a servant. Invitations are more My style. Right now, I invite you to rest in My arms.

Lord, I gladly accept Your invitation.

*****

Maggie, there are so many things you *do* that are out of love – yes, love for Me – that you do not consider anything special. But I cherish them and notice them all. Learn to rest in My love – in My arms – in the communion of the Trinity. That is what I want of you now. Each moment you spend in this endeavor will be your greatest possible gift to Me. And as you do this, I will guide you into greater holiness. We both desire this. Continue to trust Me and continue to wait and see what I do. My love for you has neither changed nor grown distant. The more you come to Me, the sweeter you will experience My love. Let My love for you sustain you through this night.

*****

Lord, it is so marvelous how You have dealt with me over the years. Yet I feel like I have been more unfaithful than faithful, despite all Your kindness and patience with me. I have come so close, and then wandered so far. You brought me back again and again. Thank You that I am again on the return, rather than the running away. I truly am the Father's child. He never gives up on me no matter how often or how far I wander. Thank You.

Maggie, it is My desire that you come closer than you have ever been before. Every time you start coming to Me daily, I bring you a little farther along. Sometimes it is more difficult for you to come. I understand that more than you do. That is why it takes you so long to return sometimes. You don't understand why you strayed, but I see much more than you do. And My love for you is so much greater than you can even imagine. Begin to bask in that love. Begin again to just be enveloped in the Trinity. You do not realize how much you need to "feel" My love. But even your family cannot love you the way you need to be loved. Only I can love you that way. I alone can heal, fill, and restore you. And I want to go even beyond restoring you to

raise you to new and more marvelous heights. Yes, it is possible. My desire for you is so great and wonderful that you could not possibly imagine it. Fear not. Though you have failed before, I will never give up on you. The best is yet to come.

Lord, thank You so much. I feel so unworthy of such great love, but I gladly accept it. I want so much to become all that You want me to become. And I thank You for all You have done to make me what I am now, even though I still am weak and sinful.

*****

Chapter 12

LIVE

*T*each me adoration and worship. You have already given me wonder and awe and thanksgiving, but now I really want to begin true worship and adoration. I seek a deeper relationship with You than I have ever experienced before. I seek it with all my heart.

*****

I was contemplating how much I desire that perfect union with You and how You are the One who put that desire within me, and how Your desire for the same union is even greater than mine, and I remembered the old teaching that there is a God-sized hole in each of our lives that makes us feel empty and incomplete until You come (or are invited) in to fill it, and whether this was a part of the old teaching or not, there is a Maggie-sized hole in *Your* heart that longs for me to be put into the perfect union You desire.

The chapel is mostly made of wood, tabernacle and all, and as I was sitting there gazing at the wood and thinking (praying?) these thoughts, the realization (revelation?) came to me that I am a piece (of wood) taken from the heart of God – and as I give myself to Him (submission, self-abandonment, contemplation?) He takes me and fits me right into that hole in His heart where I belong – how I have yearned to belong there over the years! The God-sized hole in my heart is really the emptiness all around me when I am not "in" my place in His heart.

Live

So now I am a puzzle piece. Karl gave me "the world's most difficult jigsaw puzzle" for Christmas. On New Year's Day Steven and I began to put it together. Rae, Karl, and I stayed up until 4:15 AM to finish it. I didn't know why I insisted on spending 12 continuous hours (with a short break for dinner) working on it, and staying up so late when I knew I had to serve the next morning as Eucharistic Minister, but I was driven to complete that puzzle. It was indeed difficult – all the pieces have the same general shape, and the same picture is on front and back, except turned 90 degrees. But the thought tonight that I am a puzzle piece was so immediate because I had just been immersed in putting together a jigsaw puzzle.

The thought has many applications. The Church: many pieces fitting together, all are needed. Marriage: the right pieces completing each other. At this point I realized that in marriage and in the Church, we are living and growing pieces that have the capacity to grow in time to fit together perfectly even if at first there are gaps or imperfect joints.

But in my relationship with God, I am a piece of wood, incapable of jumping into the hole from which I was taken and having to wait for His loving hands to take me and gently place me there Himself. It was His loving hands that took me and made me, formed me and breathed life into me. And He is Life; it is a piece of Himself within me that is my life and He alone has the right and ability to put me in all the places He desires (His most perfect Will). All I have to do is enjoy every fit – in my marriage, in my family, in my church community, in my teaching, in my neighborhood – wherever and whenever He chooses to put me. This is self-abandonment. When He chooses to put me where I truly belong – in His heart – then I am completed and the emptiness around me is completely filled. This must be the contemplative life I seek and want. And perhaps this is Heaven.

*****

Lord, I'm back to the state of coming to You with nothing to say. My mind and emotions are blank. I want to pray, to be in Your Presence, but have no capacity to do anything about it. I don't know if this is what experts refer to as spiritual dryness, or if this is that stage of contemplative prayer where there seems to be a great nothingness. I suspect it is the latter. When this happened before, my response was to quit trying to pray. That led me to guilt for not spending time with You. But now, with Your grace, I want to embrace this state of my prayer life as a gift from You. Let me look upon this emptiness as a peace. Certainly, I can use Your peace in my hectic and frantic life. Lord, rather than being afraid of it, let me draw strength from this peace to keep me going through the difficulties of the day.

Lord, You are now confirming these – thoughts, actions, attitudes? – with a powerfully strong feeling of Your Presence. You are also showing me my natural reaction to something new and my progress. Perhaps this is generally true of most people, a first reaction to something new is questions: What is happening? Why is this happening? Did I do something wrong? A second reaction: I can't handle this – I don't like this – I don't understand this. A third reaction: resisting by trying to go to a previous stage, or – my reaction – stop everything and slide back to a previous stage. A fourth reaction: Lord, with Your grace this is where I am today, stepping out on a limb – just maybe – could this be – perhaps a marvelous gift that You are offering to me? Perhaps it is not even a limb, but more of a ledge on the edge of a cliff. It seems I have been here many times – a threshold I could never quite cross – knowing the door was open, yet I have always backed away. Now I see why I never could cross it: there is nothing that I can see on the other side but a huge drop. Yet You have led me here time after time and every time I backed away, lovingly assuring me that You are with me, showing me how great Your love for me really is, prodding me to trust You more, and continually helping me to fight my great fear. This is what You have done for the last twenty years of my life. And all the while, You nurtured within me this great desire for union with You, even to the point of boldly demanding it but at other times almost despairing of its possibility. You have brought me back to this limb, this ledge, this threshold. I must either back away again, yet I am tired of that reaction. I've been here and done that so many times before! I have to take a deep breath and take a step or a jump, trusting that You are there to catch me. Lord,

*****

Live

Lord, the things You showed me yesterday were so exciting that Your Presence and my joy overcame the emptiness and replaced it with such exhilaration that I could not continue with embracing the emptiness – it was no longer there. Sort of like humility – once you know you have it, you've lost it. So, I wondered how to proceed now that I have this revelation. This morning, I'm back at the edge of the cliff.

Lord, how do I take up cliff-diving? My mind and emotions are blank. I choose to thank You for the emptiness and knowing Your love and care and gentleness and strength, I jump into and embrace the unknown ahead of me, hoping and trusting that You are there to catch me. Thank You for Your peace and Your Presence.

*****

One time I was left in the chapel alone and I could come up close and kneel before the tabernacle. I told You I wished I could become small enough to get right in the tabernacle with You and be even closer to You – and You instantly showed me, before the thought was fully formed in my mind, that it is the other way around – You have already become so small in the Host and the Precious Blood to come into me, for You desire that closeness even more than I do. Wow!!!

*****

Lord, it seems that my cliff-diving is much simpler than I expected. You seem to want nothing more from me than that I should approach You in prayer daily, do basic prayers and live my life one day at a time – enjoying it, rejoicing in Your goodness, marveling at Your wondrous works, and being in Your company. Your commandments are *not* burdensome (I Jn 5:3). You have truly met me and touched me and blessed me today. Thank You, Lord, for such a marvelous day.

*****

Lord, I don't feel very holy, but I choose to be holy. I may mess up continually, but You will triumph in the end, and You will accomplish what You have begun. You have chosen me for Yourself, and I have accepted Your call. I belong to You and You will sanctify me. I present myself to You now, and offer You my prayers, works, joys, and sufferings of this day. Lord, take and receive all I am and all I do. You are worthy of my trust, my praise, my desire, and my love. I ask You to cleanse me of my disorder, my mediocrity, my rebellion, my laziness, my fears, my unfaithfulness, and my lack of self-control. Thank You that, no matter how wretchedly I have failed, You are still able to lift me up and reassure me that there is nothing good that is impossible with You.

Lord, I thank You also that You have somehow pulled me up out of the pit I started in this morning, and now I am ready to take on this day. You are in control and can move me even when I can't move myself. Be with me and guide me through this day.

*****

I was again reminded of how great a grace You have given me in my self-knowledge and that I have a clear direction of where I am and a goal of holiness toward which You are leading me. I was told to pray for the grace of wisdom as to Your will as it regards religious life. So, Lord, I do ask for Your will, Your guidance, and Your wisdom as well as Your timing for that. Let me neither rush, nor miss it if it is to be. I leave it in Your hands, and will delight in seeing and touching it whenever You allow me to. (Like a precious gift to a child that must be handled with great care.)

Maggie, I love you. Your God loves you. I am leading you on new paths. New to you – I have walked them before with countless others. But just as you teach the same math over and over, it is always new and exciting because your students are different and you see it through their understanding. So it is for Me. For 25 years I have led you and you have traveled far. Your childhood has passed. Though you will always be a child of your Father, you have reached a certain maturity. It is good. Right now, you are in a good place. There is relative peace and positive action in your life. You are squarely in *My* will – not trying to escape anything. I will take hold of your prayer life and lead and guide you along this path. Fear not! Find Me in all the joys and in all the sorrows. Look for Me in the ordinary and in the extraordinary. Watch Me, learn from Me, and hold on to

Me. I will not bore you or disappoint you. I will stretch you, mature you, love you, care for you, and form you into the perfection I have designed for you. Rejoice in the plans I have for you. They are so good! Though you cannot see them all now, you can believe Me. It will be more than wonderful. Rejoice!

*****

Maggie, do you like to pray?

That's a hard question. I'm trying to find categories to liken prayer to, and they are not very nice – do I like going to the doctor? Do I like cleaning house? Do I like going to a class?

Prayer is at best functional – a means to an end?

Sort of – at least I have not yet gotten past the concept of "it is something I should or need to do." It never occurred to me to either like it or dislike it.

Let's explore what you really do like to do.

I really liked sitting around the table and talking with family last Wednesday night. I like teaching – the interaction with the kids. I like tutoring. I like serving others – meeting their needs. I like cooking and baking, especially if there are several people to feed. This sounds so terribly selfish – but I like anything that makes me feel appreciated.

Maggie, this is not something to be ashamed of – I also like these things. It is a legitimate aspect of love. Do you also return this appreciation to others?

I think I do. Of course, I'm sure I can do it more or better, if I should work at that.

No, this is not an instruction on what more you have to do. It is a balancing – like to be loved you need to love, to be appreciated you also need to appreciate others. I am not finding fault with you.

I see. I think I'm OK in that department.

I think so too. Do you ever look to Me for appreciation?

Not usually. You have often thanked me for things I have done, but it feels strange and unexpected every time that happens.

Do you know why?

I suppose it is because my parents very seldom showed any appreciation for anything I did – and they always found fault with things I did. I always felt that nothing was good enough.

These are the obstacles I have to overcome in My relationship with you.

Oh, Lord, I never thought You had to overcome obstacles! I thought I was the one who had to overcome everything. I never thought of it as Your relationship with me, but always as my relationship with You. I thought I had to do all the work – all the changing, all the overcoming. You are already perfect – I'm the one who has to change.

But you cannot change by yourself. I have to change you. In any healthy relationship both parties have to participate and work at it. You want a relationship with Me. But I'm the One who called you to that relationship. I want one with you! That is why you were created – not as a slave or a machine – not just functional to do something, but to love and be loved by Me. And you have chosen to pursue and continue in this relationship. But it is not a one-way street. Many people expect Me to do it all and do not bother to carry their share. You are on the other side of the fence. You do not expect Me to carry My share. You think My share was done 2000 years ago. No, I am still living and active. Wherever I am inviting you to change, I plan the work. So how did you like this time of prayer?

I really did like it. I'm also overwhelmed. I want to change and see the work You are doing in me. I was always looking for what I am doing – and was usually disappointed.

I know. I want much better for you.

*****

You have traveled far. I have been with you through many situations. I am with you now. I hold you close and lead you on the path you need to go. Be assured that I will not leave or forsake you

regardless of the circumstances. You will look back on the worst of times seeing how closely I held you. The unity you seek is being accomplished. Rejoice, for you are being sanctified – yes, you are My special people – and nothing, no one, can pluck you out of My hand.

*****

A long time ago, I decided to follow You. I learned a lot and made many mistakes, but You kept encouraging me in many ways through many people and circumstances. You worked powerfully yet gently in my life until I truly knew that You are Who You say You are. My faith grew and I came to Loyola to make retreats.

On one of them, I realized that You were calling me to be more than just Your servant. I was happy enough to be a servant – I enjoyed serving You – but You called me to be Your bride. I said "Yes," but had no clue how or when this was to be. I continued to struggle with the same sins and weaknesses, despite Your call. You brought me through many joys, trials, challenges, growth spurts, and more retreats. At some point, I realized that union with You was what I really wanted, but again had no clue what that meant or how it could be accomplished. Then You carried me through the death of my husband, each child leaving home, and the care of my mother-in-law. Through all this, I learned that, no matter what happens, You will stay with me and love me through. But this year You allowed this illness into my life, and convinced me to give up my job and start putting my life in order. That is how I came to this retreat. Through it You showed me so much about union – between You and Your Father, and how I can begin to enter into that union with the Trinity.

Now I seem to hear You calling me again, as You did Peter, to follow You. By this time Peter understood much more what it meant to follow You. I think I understand more now, too. And, just as Peter did, so do I desire to follow You. I have come to value the will of Your Father, and to understand that I need to seek that. I know I need to work on finding You in all things, people, and circumstances. Before this past week, I struggled to include You in my life. Now I will be looking to see where You are already in my life and what You are doing, so I can participate more fully in Your life – the life of the Trinity. You have taught me much this week. Help me to learn it well. As to Your call, I believe You are repeating Your call to me to become Your bride – to come to union with You. My answer again is a resounding "Yes." The time and place are up to You. Until that time, I shall work on the homework You have given me – to find You in all things, to look to You before I jump into any action, and to open up and allow You to transform my strong will so it is united to Yours. You have truly blessed me with many graces this week. Thank You, Lord.

Maggie, I have blessed you and will continue to bless you. I delight in blessing you. That is one of the perks of love – it makes doing good things for the beloved very enjoyable. My love for you does this. Your acceptance and response heighten that joy. Before you came to this retreat, conversations often focused on joy. The union I want for you and that you also desire is full of joy. And just like the Kingdom of Heaven, it can begin right here and now. Yes, I am calling you to follow Me in a new way. I am also repeating my invitation to you to become My bride. But let Me prepare the time and place. When you see it, you will recognize it as Home. In the meanwhile, find Me and be at Home in Me.

*****

Lord, I've been trying to focus on and contemplate Your love and my response. I feel like St. Augustine when he was contemplating the Trinity by the beach. I can't get the ocean into the hole in the sand.

That is true – you can't. But you can marvel at its beauty and vastness and even find the waves and ripples fascinating. You do not have to understand or contain things to appreciate and enjoy them. You don't even have to own them – pleasant weather, the beauty of the flowers, does it matter where you find these things? They are there for all to enjoy.

Lord, You are expanding my perspective. In my confinement, I have grown to see only the immediate small circle of things directly around me. It seemed like the world closed in on me. Suddenly I'm becoming aware of bigger pictures, more possibilities, and perhaps even a bright future.

This does have reason to it. For some time, you did not even know if you had a future on this earth. When you are in pain and all you care about is slipping away from you, your focus naturally narrows. It is the cocoon phase of metamorphosis. The caterpillar is quite content to inch its way and munch its way through life. But suddenly it is confined and starving and cannot see anything but the walls of its confinement. It has never flown or known anything about being a butterfly. But when the process has run its course, and it emerges with wings, there is a grand and beautiful world to explore in ways that were totally impossible at its earlier stages of life. So, it is for you. This is a time of exploration that will open up vast new possibilities. This is a time of resurrection. It is not to be understood but to be experienced. Awe and wonder are the proper response.

Wow, Lord, I never thought of myself as a butterfly. But I can certainly see the analogy. Is that similar to death and Heaven? Dying is like the cocoon stage and then we burst forth into eternal life?

Sort of. But there it is a much greater difference.

Lord, thank You. You got through my tentativeness and inadequacy and managed to teach and touch me.

You see, prayer can be marvelous even if it starts out uncomfortable.

*****

Lord Jesus, I have much to thank You for today. First of all, I had a dream that I hope is not presumptuous. I dreamed that I died and it seemed like I had gone through a door into a hallway – like a hospital hallway. I followed it and came to a reception desk and felt I needed to tell the receptionist that I was there. I said, "I'm Maggie Edmonson," and she opened a binder and found my name and showed me what I understood to be all the good in my life – it was like a videotape playing right in the notebook. But what I saw was a beautiful city with large buildings – fancy ones with lots of lights and flowers on the grounds – lots of lilies – and the lights and buildings and flowers represented my good works and virtues and services to God, and it was beautiful. I wondered where the bad stuff was, but I didn't ask. But I knew that You did not keep a record of the sins, mistakes, and faults, only the good. Thank You.

*****

Lord, You turned the tables on me again. I thought I would reach union with You by entering into Your pain and feeling with You – having compassion on You – but it is the other way around. I am lonely, I am scared, I am confined. I have tried to overcome these things by making light of them, or denying them, or talking myself out of them. But it is in admitting them and my helplessness over them that I find You having compassion on me and assuring me that You know how I feel, for You have also felt these things: "I felt every teardrop as in darkness you cried, and I strove to remind you, that for those tears I died."

All this and being aware of how insignificant and small my pain and discomfort are compared to what You went through – yet it seems so clear that You chose to go through it all just so You can save and comfort an insignificant soul such as mine. I could never deserve even the sharing of one moment with You, yet You choose to share eternity with me. There is no gratitude sufficient to express the awe and wonder of this. But You are gracious enough to accept our puny little attempts as if they were great and wonderful. Thank You ever so much.

*****

Lord, I suppose I am no longer to lament my weaknesses, hardships, calamities, frustrations, insecurities, pains, or any other problems, for they are opportunities for You to show Your strength and grace. I guess that is a sure cure for my all-too-often complaining. Perhaps I should begin by thanking You for my brokenness and my weaknesses:

1. Thank You that, though I was unwanted by my family when I came into the world, You wanted me to be born, for You had chosen me as Your own.
2. Thank You that though we left all we knew or loved in Hungary, You made it possible for us to come here to a land of freedom and prosperity.

3. Thank You for all the times I felt like an alien – not belonging anywhere, for through that I can understand that here we do not have a lasting city, that only in Your kingdom will I truly be at home, and that I can have great compassion for others who feel alienated or out of place.
4. Thank You for giving me a desire to be Yours alone at an early age and then redirecting that vision – instead of entering a convent, You allowed me to enter marriage.
5. Thank You for all the strife in my family life and the confusion in losing my faith after marriage, for it pushed me to seek and find You through the Charismatic Renewal.
6. Thank You for the destruction of my childhood faith and dreams, for it left room for a more mature faith and goals.
7. Thank You for all the pains and joys of motherhood.
8. Thank You for all the pains and joys of teaching.
9. Thank You for a teachable heart and an openness to correction.
10. Thank You for the grace of knowing my faults and sins and sinfulness, for with Your rebuke comes the grace of repentance and the power to change.
11. Thank You for giving me all that the world considers important, and then stripping me of most of them: husband, career, health, my very identity – but then giving me what You consider important: love, joy peace, patience, kindness, goodness, gentleness, faithfulness, and self-control.
12. Thank You for the ailments of bad eyes, a painful foot, diabetes, arthritis, and aging – for they keep me dependent and humble and, through them, You have taught me to ask for help, to accept the love and graciousness of others, and, thereby You have increased my capacity to receive love from others but ultimately from You – for all love comes from You.
13. Thank You for my clumsiness, for I can have compassion on others who are not well coordinated.
14. Thank You for the strong maternal tendencies that used to be an asset but now need to be quieted – for I see that my role has changed.
15. Thank You for my weight problem – for through it I am learning a measure of self-control.

16. Thank You for my loudness, my earthy language, my talking too much – for they drive me back to You in repentance and make me grateful for Your forgiveness.
17. Thank You for the inability to solve all the problems of our clients – for though it saddens me and frustrates me, it makes me realize that I am not the savior of the world; You are.
18. Thank You for all the struggles in prayer and in loving You, for it keeps me yearning for more of You.

Maggie, My love for you is the reason I became man. My love for you is the reason I stay in the form of bread and wine. My love for you is the reason I want you with Me throughout eternity. Just as you delight in anyone seeing your decorations or enjoying your food, so I delight in your noticing My love in all the many little and big ways I shower it upon you. You delight your God's heart by noticing the love you receive. Focus on love, and it will be the best Christmas ever.

*****

It is My love I want you to see and feel and experience and cherish. It joins you to so many others in both earthly and heavenly realms. The sounds you hear, and those not within your range of hearing, produce a symphony of praise to My ears. Your willingness and attempt at service also rises up to Me. This is union with Me that you are ready, willing, and able to jump into service whenever called. See, you are much more ready for combat than you thought.

And You even put a song in my mind from Morning prayer: "Lord Whose Love in Humble Service."

And it is exactly what you do.

Thank You, Lord. I am so surprised when I actually do something good and right. I am so used to needing to apologize for leaping before I look.

But even your repentance is precious to Me.

It is? It usually seems so futile.

Not to Me. You felt that when you came to Me for Evening prayer and then you heard Me call you to continue with Night prayer.

Yes, I do feel Your love and approval. And the closeness I felt with You was marvelous.

Like now?

Yes, Lord, once again I feel it. Thank You so much.

Look for it again at Mass today. This is true reality. *This* is the union we both seek. Delight in it. Revel in it. Dance and sing in your heart. When you come into My heavenly kingdom, we shall dance and sing together – you will dance and sing beautifully, not off-key, no limp – and I will clothe you with the most wonderful gown of praise.

Lord, I can almost see it. Thank You.

It will be even lovelier than you can imagine. Now go back to sleep and dream of these things. My love for you is so great. And your love for Me comes through even when you do not notice it. *I* notice it.

*****

Lord, You brought my mind to consider how wonderful it would be to have total freedom of movement in air, on land, and in water. This may be an aspect of Heaven – I can only imagine. But to sink into Your Presence, to be completely enveloped in You – it is a great thought.

Maggie, not just a thought, but your destiny. It is that total union you have desired for so long. It is what I created you for. But not yet.

Lord, I'm grateful for that. Both that it waits for me and that I still have time here. Thank You that I am happier now than I ever remember being in my life. Not that there are no pains or troubles, but I am deeply content. Please give Fr. Brady, my first retreat director, a hug for me. It was he who first asked if I was content. It took 25 years, but I think I am there.

And yet it is still just the beginning. I have so much more in store for you. You cannot imagine that yet, but it is good.

*****

Let Your glory come upon me. I want to truly worship You in Spirit and in Truth. Jesus, You are the Truth. Father, I come to You carried by Your Spirit and Your Truth. I want – need – to worship You.

Maggie, when you come to Me this way, you are encountering the Trinity. There is a place for you in the Trinity – a place to abide. It is not a room – it is the three Persons surrounding you, protecting you, holding you, allowing you to stay enclosed in glory. In order to abide here, you first need to be still and allow your God to surround you. In due time, you will learn to move as you are led without stepping out of this place. But it will no longer be your own will that moves you. For now, your assignment is to be still and get to know how it feels to be surrounded by your God in all Three Persons. It takes faith and, for now, some imagination. As you practice, it will become effortless. But practice you must, in order to learn to stay in the center of this love and glory. This is not yet to be shared. It is not a secret you can never tell, but for now a private intimacy with your God. Will you enter in?

Yes, Lord. I do will it. And thank You for Your invitation.

Put down pen and notebook, return to rest and let's begin.

Thank You so much, Lord.

Maggie, you are most welcome. This week you are immersed in My Passion and death, but remember that afterwards there is My Resurrection. You dread the thoughts of My pain and suffering, but that is not the end. Neither is pain and suffering your end. I raise you up. I know you expect more pain and suffering with the upcoming surgery, but just as today you had a glimpse of well-being and strength, you will again have that and will be able to do things that seem impossible right now. I am with you. I love you and will continue to uphold and strengthen you.

Lord, I believe this and receive it, and thank You for Your graciousness. You are so good to me. Words are not enough to say what's in my heart so I can only thank You with the feeble and inadequate words I have. Lord, I want to worship You and adore You and give You all the glory

You deserve. But it is way beyond my ability to do that, so I will do what little I can.

My child, that little becomes much in My sight. Rejoice that your God is pleased with you. Rejoice that you are so loved. Rejoice that I lead you to greater and greater holiness. Look to Me and follow Me. Do not fret over what has gone before. There is a new day, and a new heaven and a new earth are coming. Until then, I will continue to sustain you and help you. Fear not! I am still in control. My plans will be fulfilled. And they are good.

Yes, Lord, I believe that as well. What is there left for me to do? What can I do to please You today? How can I love You more now?

Continue to do the ordinary things as if they were extraordinary. Combine work with praise to God. Your praise brings Me closer than you have yet seen or felt. Not that I am not with you otherwise, but your awareness of My nearness is enhanced with your praise. Sing songs of praise. Pray in the Spirit as you work. Feel My touch throughout the day. Take moments of recognition of My love and favor upon you. Do not waste time or strength lamenting what you have not done or what you cannot yet do. Let Me guide you according to what is important to Me, not what you think is important. I have taught you much already. Some of My ways are now second nature to you. But there is still more. Are you ready to return to My school of holiness?

Yes, Lord, I believe that I am. I am delighted that You are asking me to come once again. I had been afraid that I blew my chances long ago. I have not been faithful in attending to Your teaching me.

Ah, but I have taught you regardless of your awareness or faithfulness. You have learned much, and you are teaching others even when you do not realize it. But as I said, there is more yet to learn and do. Be prepared to continue learning. I will use many ways to teach you. Remember, I am a good teacher.

Lord, I wish I could hug You right now. You have made me smile, and I hope I make You smile. What a glorious day it will be when I can finally see You and touch You and be enfolded in Your arms. But right now, thank You for enabling me to envision it through the gifts of imagination and the power of Your Holy Spirit.

We will yet dance in My kingdom. First there are dark clouds, but we will get through them as well.

*****

Tell my precious people that My love for each one continues to blossom. Do not be dismayed by your physical weaknesses or diminishments as time goes by. Remember that it is in weakness that I can show Myself strong. Notice that despite and through these, your relationship with Me has become stronger as you need to rely on Me for more and more. I still provide. I still protect and defend you. Your strength may shrink, but My power through your prayers and struggles grows. This is a time of great grace. Do not miss it by focusing on what you can no longer do, but focus on who you are – Whose you are. You are Mine. No one can snatch you out of My loving hands. I am with you through every care, concern, pain, distress, and weakness. And I am also there in every joy, delight, beauty, and peace you experience. I am not finished with you yet. There is still much you can do, and even more I can do through you. Hold on tightly to My hand and let Me guide you through this stage in your life. My love for you is everlasting. Your love for Me has grown and will continue growing. Rejoice!

*****

As my aunt was nearing the end of her life, she did not like living alone. Even when someone came to visit her, before they were ready to leave, she would get very sad and even cry because she would soon be alone again. That bone-crushing loneliness was something I experienced during my long illness, and it took me a long time of prayer and reflection to finally overcome it.

One morning, just before the alarm clock rang, I had a dream of an elderly person in a sickbed being cared for by a doctor. As the doctor was almost finished, she cried out, "Please stay with me, I don't want to be alone again." I recognized her feeling as that same despicable loneliness I felt many years ago. But then the answer to that loneliness also came to me.

Lord, You gave me the realization of the fact that we all have that longing that only You can fill. Only You can truly say "I will never leave you or forsake you." It has taken me so many many years to realize that You are always there, always loving, always providing, always gentle, caring, compassionate, and meeting all the deepest desires of our hearts.

The rest of that revelation came to me at Mass. It is that just as You will never leave or forsake us, Your desire is that we should never leave or forsake You in return. Your love is so strong for us that You want that close and constant love and tenderness to be a reciprocal relationship. This is why You created us. To know You, love You, and serve You in this life and to be eternally happy with You in heaven.

Another thing that impressed me was from the Beatitude of "Blessed are they that hunger and thirst for righteousness, for they shall be satisfied." I always knew the first part, but that it is possible to be satisfied struck me as brand new. I never expected to be satisfied. It was always a constant yearning and wanting more that has motivated my life. Not just for righteousness, but for many things. The great beauty of yesterday's revelation was that I saw that Your perfect love and constant companionship is the satisfaction of our hearts. In You, we can be totally secure and content. We only get glimpses of that security and contentment in this life, but eternal life is to know You in such a marvelous way.

You also showed me that we can provide some of these glimpses for each other. Whenever our needs and desires are met and we have that security and contentment even for a short while, it is You who have provided it even if it comes to us through other people. We can be doubly grateful; both to You and to the person through whom You gave us such blessings. To realize this, we can live in continual grace and gratitude.

*****

CPSIA information can be obtained
at www.ICGtesting.com
Printed in the USA
JSHW050825260123
36777JS00003B/10